Rorke's Drift By Those Who Were There

'Well, I must not cry for that which cannot be undone, but my heart is sore for my children, who have all been killed in the wars and disturbances. One was killed at the battle of Isandhlwana; his brother brought him home, but I could not get the bullet out, and he died. My heart was too sore at the time to mind his death much for I was crying for my two eldest boys, both of whom had fallen at the fight at Rorke's Drift. I know not where their bones are laid. Shall I ever see my children again?'

'Job' Telezi, *The Gospel Missionary for 1891*

Rorke's Drift By Those Who Were There

VOLUME 1

Lee Stevenson, Ian Knight
and
Alan Baynham Jones

Greenhill Books

Rorke's Drift By Those Who Were There: Volume 1

Greenhill Books

First published by Greenhill Books, 2022
Greenhill Books, c/o Pen & Sword Books Ltd,
47 Church Street, Barnsley, S. Yorkshire, S70 2AS
For more information on our books, please visit
www.greenhillbooks.com, email contact@greenhillbooks.com
or write to us at the above address.

PUBLISHING HISTORY
Rorke's Drift By Those Who Were There was first published in 2003 by Lee Stevenson Publishing. This is volume 1 of an expanded edition, with new illustrations, maps and expanded and revised text.

CIP data records for this title are available from the British Library

ISBN 978-1-78438-831-7

Typeset by JCS Publishing Services Ltd
Typeset in 11.5/15pt Baskerville
Printed and bound in Great Britain by
CPI Group (UK) Ltd, Croydon, CRO 4YY

Contents

Introduction

It is almost 144 years since the last shots were fired at Rorke's Drift, yet fascination with this battle remains as strong as ever. Many may only remember the name thanks to the 1964 film *Zulu*, nonetheless, it is intriguing that the story of Rorke's Drift continues to enthral, when other, more historically significant, battles of the period fade from public memory.

But beyond a famous film, what of the real battle fought on 22–23 January 1879 and the experiences of the men – both British and Zulu – who fought there?

It is predominantly through the words of the men who successfully defended Rorke's Drift that the story of the battle can be told. Their first-hand accounts – many written just days after the battle as official military reports or private letters home – were readily reproduced by the newspapers of the day, all eager to retell the story. As the years rolled by, interest in the Anglo-Zulu War was in its turn replaced by news of other conflicts, yet the story of Rorke's Drift prevailed, never losing its appeal in the popular press or the many books that have been written on the subject since.

However, it is clear that whilst interest in the battle has continued, myths and misconceptions have evolved, many of them cemented in the popular imagination by the film, so that the real story of the battle, from the perspective of those who were present, is in danger of being lost or diluted. By drawing together all of the first-hand accounts into one reference work, we hope to preserve a truly comprehensive record of the battle – using only the words of the men who were actually there, exactly as they were first reproduced, without any correction or alteration. First published in 2003 and co-authored by the late Alan Baynham-Jones, this new work, fully updated and spread over two volumes, includes many newly discovered accounts – each in turn adding significant elements to the fascinating history of the battle.

In many respects the defenders of Rorke's Drift were the popular heroes of their time, generously rewarded for their gallantry, heralded through the streets and the subject of media interest that, for some, persisted throughout their lives, as evidenced by the many press accounts in this book. It is through their accounts – whilst sometimes incomplete, clouded by memory or embellished – that we gain the most vivid insight into the experience of those who fought at Rorke's Drift. Their words – sometimes jingoistic, often brutally honest, written in quite simple matter-of-fact language – share a common theme, one of extraordinary courage against overwhelming odds, determination in the face of extreme fear and desperation. Yet throughout it remains difficult to contemplate the horror of hours of prolonged close-quarter fighting that left so many survivors with post-traumatic stress disorder in an age when emotional wounds went entirely untreated.

In fact the experience of battle, and the willingness to share their stories, was different for each defender. Many completed their army service, returned to civilian life and relative obscurity, their experiences left unrecorded. Others appear to have relished the fame that came with being a 'Rorke's Drift Man'. For some, however, the limelight proved difficult and they struggled to share their feelings. Indeed John Chard, VC, the officer in command, would often shy away from questions, saying merely that he 'would rather not say anything more about the business'. Years after the battle, one commentator was advised not to ask the cloakroom attendant at the British Museum about Rorke's Drift as the poor chap was loath to keep talking about it. The attendant in question was Henry Hook, VC.

Yet for those, like Hook, who did allow their recollections to be recorded, it must be noted that over the course of time there are often differences between impressions recorded. The effect of trauma on the memory frequently manifests itself initially in a series of jagged, often disturbing images; over time the mind rearranges memories in an effort to impose a sense of order which events did not always seem to have in the immediate aftermath. This becomes more obvious with the recollections of participants who were required to talk about their experiences many times; not only were they subconsciously adjusting their memories to make them more manageable, but they were learning how to tell the story – what their audience wanted to hear and, often more significantly, what they wanted them to leave out. Hook's initial recollections are fractured and full of traumatic, brutal images; later in life he learned to tell the story in a more fluid form, with less emphasis on the visceral nature of close-quarter killing.

We might assume that these 'heroes' of Rorke's Drift were extraordinary men with exceptional fighting skills, hand-picked to defend a strategically important outpost against a formidable enemy. Nothing could be further from the truth. There were no great generals or illustrious commanders at Rorke's Drift – on the British side, at least, the most senior officer was no more than a lieutenant. Indeed it was pot luck that B Company, 2nd Battalion, 24th (2nd Warwickshire) Regiment, who made up the bulk of the defenders, was selected for routine duties at the post. Rather than the tough, battle-scarred veterans you might expect, most were young, short-service soldiers who had been given their baptism of fire only a few months before on the Eastern Cape Frontier. Of the remainder, roughly a quarter were sick and injured, in a makeshift military hospital occupying the home of Swedish missionary Otto Witt, whilst others were there by pure chance – either on escort duties or in transit to other garrisons along the Natal/Zulu border.

Prior to the remarkable events of January 1879, Rorke's Drift was not considered a particularly important spot: it was merely one of a number of garrisons and supply depots along the lines of communication of the British columns invading Zululand. Nor was the battle at Rorke's Drift of great strategic consequence. Despite a widespread belief at the time that its defence prevented a large-scale Zulu invasion of the colony of Natal, this was never in fact likely. The Zulu forces who attacked Rorke's Drift under the command of Prince Dabulamanzi kaMpande formed the reserve during the decisive Zulu victory at iSandlwana just a few hours before. They were not equipped to mount anything other than a limited border raid and evidence suggests their only objective in crossing the river into Natal was to raid nearby homesteads and mop up the remaining British forces in the area. The Zulus, however, unlike their British counterparts, were seasoned fighters, for the most part men in their forties and highly regarded by their peers. They were well aware of the presence of British troops at Rorke's Drift and, following the triumph at iSandlwana, might have expected a swift victory over the few troops left guarding the remote mission station.

Sadly there are far fewer accounts from the Zulu sources that evidence how events unfolded from their side or document the tenacious bravery they displayed. For them, their defeat was an embarrassing footnote to the much greater victory at iSandlwana earlier in the day, one which earned them the disdain of the Zulu people and did not encourage them to leave detailed impressions of their actions. Yet in its way, it took as much courage repeatedly to attack the British barricades and be met by a hail of bullets and curtain of bayonets that could deliver horrific wounds, as it did to defend them. All this with no possibility of immediate medical care and the only hope of survival the chance of a friend dragging you clear of combat; the extraordinary casualty rate – perhaps as high as one man in three killed or wounded – remains a testament to this. Nonetheless, we have gathered numerous insights into the way this battle – so celebrated among the British – was regarded by the Zulu. Whilst looking at the sources, it became clear that one particular side of the battle emerges which contrasts the heroic view of the defence, one that warrants closer inspection: the treatment of wounded Zulus and prisoners. Using previously unseen information and primary sources we have been able to piece together a far clearer picture of what actually occurred in the hours after the battle ended.

What makes Rorke's Drift so remarkable, after more than a century, when the causes of the Anglo-Zulu War and the uncomfortable implications for the Zulu people are largely forgotten and bloodier, more decisive engagements remembered by only a few?

It is the story of a random cross-section of the Victorian army, trapped by chance in a momentous and terrifying event outside their control.

It is the story of very ordinary soldiers – attackers and defenders, British and Zulu – caught up in a horrendous battle, displaying quite extraordinary tenacity and bravery.

These then are the words, thoughts and memories of Rorke's Drift – by those who were there.

Lee Stevenson and Ian Knight
June 2022

Acknowledgements

This updated version of our original book represents over forty years of research into the defence of Rorke's Drift. So many people have helped and offered assistance over the years, and we are indebted to them for their time and generosity. In particular we would like to thank the following for their material assistance with the production of this work.

Major Martin Everett, former curator of the Royal Welsh Regimental Museum, Brecon, for granting us permission to reproduce numerous records from the vast regimental archives at Brecon, also a special thank you to Celia Green, for her kindness and assistance with our research; Lt. Col. Ian Bennett for his assistance with W.A. Dunne's account of the battle and for his help in tracing the letters of Francis Attwood; Pamela Clark, and the staff, past and present, at the Royal Archives. Helen Griffiths, from the Newport Reference Library, for successfully undertaking the long and seemingly impossible search through the *South Wales Argus* looking for a copy of the Bourne roll of defenders. Ron Sheeley, for the free use of his photographs.

In South Africa, remembering the help and friendship of the late Ron Lock; Mrs Pam Barnes for the excellent job of collating information from the numerous sources at her disposal in KwaZulu-Natal and elsewhere; the staffs of: the Killie Campbell Africana Library; the Brenthurst Library, Johannesburg; the Pietermaritzburg Archives Repository, Pietermaritzburg; the Natal Museum, Pietermaritzburg; and the South African Library, Cape Town.

In Sweden, Alfhild Oenema and Nils Högman, archivists of the Church of Sweden in Uppsala, for their considerable assistance, and patience, whilst locating and photographing numerous documents pertaining to Pastor Otto Witt. Our special thanks must also go to Hans Rosenberg for all his kindness and willingness to translate so many of those original documents on our behalf.

Finally a special thank you to the descendants of the garrison of Rorke's Drift, who have been most courteous in allowing us to delve into their family histories over the years. Without their contributions and support many of these stories would be lost: Mrs Cecilia Cheetham, Mrs Kathleen Mysberg, Mrs Elizabeth Sutcliffe, Mrs Rose Morgan, Mrs Rena Mills, Nick Kennedy, Major James Lloyd, Roger Lane, Bill Jones, Edwin Ewart, the Prothero family and many, many more.

‘The most brilliant feat of arms of our day’: Rorke’s Drift and the Anglo-Zulu War

In 1882, the traveller Bertram Mitford visited Zululand ‘with the object of making the round of the battlefields in succession – which, till then, had not been done by anybody’. Mitford was, indeed, one of the first of the thousands of battlefield tourists who have since been over the battlegrounds of the British invasion of Zululand, and certainly one of the most adventurous since for him ‘making the round’ consisted of months of difficult travel in a wagon, living in a country which had only recently been conquered and which showed signs of political unrest. Mitford took the trouble to talk to as many Zulus who had fought in the war as he could. He encountered no hostility and saw the country while the ruin of war was still on the ground, the battlefields still scattered with debris and human remains. Mitford was fascinated by the melancholy atmosphere of oNdini (Ulundi), where the British had finally destroyed the Zulu army and razed the Zulu king’s royal homestead, where the floors of thousands of huts burnt by the British could still be seen, and human skulls still lay in the long grass. He climbed to the top of the Hlobane mountain, where British troops had once been chased ignominiously off, and he wandered about the field of iSandlwana, still strewn with fragments of the wrecked British camp. At one site, however, he was disappointed to find ‘no traces of the old fortifications, but a large house was in the course of construction, the residence of Mr Otto Witt, the Swedish missionary, whose name, it may be remembered, was before the public at the beginning of the war’. Mitford reflected that perhaps the most famous engagement of the war was already, within three years of the last shots being fired, irrevocably changed, and that, ‘save for the little cemetery, where are lying the few who fell of that handful of gallant defenders, it would be difficult to realise that one stood upon the site of the most brilliant feat of arms of our day'.

In an age when British troops were almost constantly in action around the globe, 'the most brilliant feat of arms' was no small claim; and yet, over 140 years later, the name of that obscure mission station on the far-flung borders of the long-gone British Empire is still widely remembered for the dramatic events that took place there across one single brutal night: Rorke's Drift.

The road which had brought the British Empire to war in Zululand had begun, ultimately, with the rivalry of great powers in far-away Europe. Until the first Portuguese explorers rounded the southern tip of Africa and tentatively pioneered the maritime routes to the profitable markets of the Indies, Europe was entirely unaware of the affairs of indigenous Africans who lived there. In 1642 the Dutch established a small way-station in the shadow of Table Mountain to service and revictual their ships, and the outpost achieved a wider strategic significance as the wealth extracted from the Indies fuelled the rise of rival European empires. When the turmoil of the Revolutionary Wars and rise of Napoleon overturned the established order in Europe, Britain came to see possession of the Cape as key to the survival of its Indian possessions, and when Napoleon displaced the Dutch monarchy and replaced it with a pro-French republic, Britain became concerned that Dutch control of the Cape might undermine its mastery of the great maritime highways to the east. In 1806 the British launched an amphibious expedition and defeated the Dutch garrison of the Cape. Britain became the new European power in southern Africa. Like the Dutch administration before them, however, the British looked out at the world from the foot of Table Mountain, not inwards to the interior, and it was only by a process which might be characterised today as 'mission creep' that they found themselves sucked, often violently, into the affairs of the independent African groups beyond.

In 1824 a group of predominantly British traders and adventurers crossed the dangerous sandbar at the mouth of Natal's only potentially viable port and established a small, ramshackle settlement which they called Port Natal. Their intention was to trade with the Zulu kingdom, which had recently emerged under King Shaka; the traders were entirely dependent upon King

Shaka's patronage for the continued survival and safety of the settlement and in return they abused his hospitality, interfered in Zulu politics, took Zulu wives, quarrelled among themselves and contrived to blacken Shaka's name to posterity. It was from this unlikely beginning that all British interests in the region stemmed and in 1845, long after King Shaka's death, Britain officially annexed the country inland from the port, naming it Natal Colony. The boundaries of the Zulu kingdom were fixed further north, along the lines of the Mzinyathi (Buffalo) and Thukela rivers.

For the next thirty years, as Natal slowly developed a settler economy, the relationship between the neighbouring states was largely friendly. By the 1870s, however, Britain was beginning to adopt a more aggressive regional policy in southern Africa, stimulated by the discovery of diamonds in the northern Cape in 1868, which had prompted imperial strategists to consider the advantage of extending unified control and economic infrastructure across a much wider area. In 1877 an experienced imperial proconsul, Sir Henry Bartle Frere, was sent to southern Africa with a view to bringing disparate Boer – the descendants of the Dutch settlers at the Cape – and African groups more fully under British control. Frere almost immediately came to the conclusion that the quickest way to do this was to provoke a war with the Zulu kingdom.

The Zulus were, by that point, the most militarily robust and economically self-sufficient independent African group left in southern Africa. They had resisted the migrant labour economy which was developing outside their borders, had attempted to check Boer encroachment and still maintained a strong part-time citizen militia army. In 1877 Britain annexed some of those Boer territories – the Transvaal Republic – and inherited a long-standing border dispute. Encouraged by settler sentiment in Natal, Frere concluded that the military defeat of the Zulus would both strengthen his influence among the Boers and reduce the wider ability of African peoples in southern Africa to resist British plans. Seizing on a minor border incident, and acting without the support of the government in London, he presented an ultimatum to the Zulu king, Cetshwayo kaMpande, on 11 December 1878. A month later the British invaded.

The task of conquering the Zulu fell to the senior British commander on the spot, Lt. Gen. Lord Chelmsford. Chelmsford was an experienced commander but, as often happened with British colonial campaigns, both under-estimated his enemy and lacked sufficient resources for the job. He had just a handful of regular infantry battalions and artillery batteries to invade a large, rugged country with only a few traders' tracks, and he was forced to mobilise small cavalry units from among the settler population and, at the last minute, to raise an auxiliary force, the Natal Native Contingent (NNC), from among Natal's African population, many of whom were historically antagonistic towards the Zulu kings. His initial plan was to invade at five separate points along the borders and converge on a cluster of royal homesteads at oNdini which constituted the Zulu capital, but this plan required a large logistical commitment with supply depots dotted all along the border. His main thrust was his Central Column (No. 3), which Chelmsford accompanied himself. This he assembled on the central border, where an old traders' track ran past Rorke's Drift – originally the farm of an Irish trader named James Rorke, but recently purchased by the Swedish Missionary Society – on the Mzinyathi and on towards oNdini. At the last minute, an arrangement was made to hire the mission buildings to serve as a supply depot and makeshift hospital at the base of his advance.

The Centre Column crossed the river in a dense mist on 11 January unopposed. In fact, King Cetshwayo waited to see the British strategy develop before committing his own troops; he had perhaps 30,000 warriors available to defend the country, and he ordered some 5,000 to harass the British flanking columns and directed the rest, his main response, to drive out the Centre Column.

Early on 22 January a Zulu force attacked Col. Pearson's Right Flank (No. 1) Column on the Nyezane river but was brushed aside, and Pearson continued his advance to occupy a deserted mission at Eshowe. The prevailing opinion in the British ranks – that the war would be a walk-over – seemed to be confirmed.

On the central front, however, things went very differently. On 20 January Chelmsford camped at the foot of a distinctive rocky outcrop known as iSandlwana, and the following day a reconnaissance party encountered Zulus twelve miles to his front. Chelmsford decided to divide his forces, taking half out to attack the Zulus before dawn on the 22nd, leaving some 1,700 men to guard his camp. Unfortunately, he had misinterpreted the

The invasion of Zululand, 1879

Zulu movements. The main Zulu force had already slipped past his flank and was much closer to iSandlwana than he anticipated, and while he was away it attacked the camp. The garrison's initial defensive line was over-extended and outflanked, and a determined Zulu charge drove them back among the tents and broke up their formations. The camp was overrun and more than 1,300 of the defenders were killed; most of the survivors were African auxiliaries.

During the battle the Zulu reserve, consisting of four regiments of middle-aged men (the uThulwana, the iNdlondlo, the iNdluyengwe and the uDloko) was deployed to cut between iSandlwana camp and Rorke's Drift. Although King Cetshwayo had specifically ordered his men not to cross into British territory, the reserve reached the border without having seen significant action and, led by the king's younger brother, Prince Dabulamanzi kaMpande, they decided to cross the Mzinyathi to take advantage of the exposed state of the border. They crossed below Rorke's Drift, and while some peeled off to loot abandoned homesteads, about 3,000 men, led by Dabulamanzi himself, moved towards the post at Rorke's Drift.

The depot at Rorke's Drift was considered to be on the safe side of the border – in British territory. No attempt had been made to entrench it. It comprised two low thatched buildings guarded by a garrison of one company of infantry – B Company, 2/24th, under Lt. Gonville Bromhead – a company of the NNC and small detachments of medical and commissariat staff. There were over thirty patients in the hospital building, mostly suffering from fevers, dysentery or from injuries on the line of march, and there were thirty wagonloads of supplies – sacks of mealies and boxes of army biscuit – waiting to go forward to iSandlwana. Further off, by the river, a Lt. John Chard of the Royal Engineers had been supervising the repair of the pont. The sound of fighting at iSandlwana had been heard at the post and at about 3.30 p.m. the first exhausted and demoralised stragglers rode past, telling of the disaster there. A hastily scribbled note from one of the survivors, Captain Alan Gardner, urged the garrison to hold their ground, and in fact any attempt at flight would have been potentially suicidal as the Zulus would have overtaken them on the road. Instead, Chard – who turned out to be the senior officer – and Bromhead, with the guidance of James Langley Dalton, one of the commissary officers, decided to fortify the post with the supplies available, and a line of barricades was hastily thrown up around the buildings. Shortly after 4 p.m. a party of mounted auxiliaries, who had escaped from iSandlwana, arrived, and Chard asked them to deploy in the direction of the Zulu advance; they had not long done so, however, when, after a spatter of shots, they broke and fled. Seeing them go, the NNC also scattered, leaving perhaps 150 men at most behind the barricades. Chard just had time to construct a line of biscuit-box barricade bisecting the yard when lookouts announced that the Zulus were coming.

They advanced with the iNdluyengwe in the van, sweeping round the shoulder of a hill overlooking the post (known to the Zulus as Shiyane and the Swedes as Oscarsberg) and rushing straight at the nearest barricade. They were met with a series of volleys which checked them, and they veered off to occupy an orchard and patch of bush in front of the post. Here they were reinforced by the uThulwana, iNdlondlo and uDloko coming up behind. Now the battle began in earnest, with the Zulus launching a series of attacks which drove the defenders back from the hospital veranda and forced an entry into the building. Inside, a handful of able-bodied defenders fought a desperately claustrophobic withdrawal from room to room, carrying the patients with them. By about 6 p.m., as it was growing dark, it was becoming difficult to hold the yard between the two buildings, and Chard ordered a withdrawal to the biscuit-box line and the area in front of the storehouse. This left those men inside the hospital effectively isolated, and with the roof now on fire. While some simply fled to try and hide in the darkness, most were forced to run the gauntlet of the abandoned ground to the storehouse.

The Zulu attacks continued throughout the night, capturing a cattle-kraal at the other end of the position and reducing the area occupied by the British to the storehouse and a few square yards in front of it. Here two large piles of mealie bags were hastily turned into a redoubt which gave the defenders another commanding line of fire. In the early hours of the 23rd, the Zulu attacks began to dwindle, and the rest of night passed in fitful firefights. The majority of the Zulus withdrew before dawn, exhausted by ten hours of intense fighting, and by the extraordinary casualties they had endured. Some 600 dead were left on the field, and an unknown number wounded – as many as one man in three had been killed or injured. As the survivors made their way back into Zululand, they passed Lord Chelmsford's men coming in the opposite direction. After failing to encounter the Zulus beyond iSandlwana, Chelmsford had returned to spend a night in his devastated camp before returning to the border.

The battle of Rorke's Drift had proved an epic struggle of courage and endurance on both sides, and British casualties were remarkably light – just seventeen men killed. Although it was immediately hailed a great victory, and eleven of the defenders were subsequently awarded Britain's highest award for gallantry, the Victoria Cross, this could not, however, obscure the fact that the day had been a disastrous one for Lord Chelmsford. The main thrust of his invasion had been bloodily repulsed, and he had little option but to shore up Natal's defences against the possibility of a Zulu counter-attack, and await reinforcements. Although the government in London had not sanctioned the war, it could not allow British troops to be humiliated in the field, and from the middle of March a steady stream of reinforcements arrived in Natal. No Zulu counter-attack had materialised; partly because iSandlwana had proved a costly victory and King Cetshwayo needed time to allow his troops to recover, and partly because his strategy was in any case a defensive one. By mid-March, however, both sides were ready to resume the conflict. Chelmsford's intention was to consolidate his position by extricating Col. Pearson's column which had been cut off at Eshowe. King Cetshwayo, on the other hand, was increasingly concerned about the British Left Flank (No. 4) Column, under Col. Henry Wood, which had been actively harassing Zulus in the north of the country.

The result was a phase of intense new fighting which took place over a matter of days at opposite ends of the country. On 28 March Col. Wood attacked a local stronghold on Hlobane mountain, but the attack was badly planned and poorly executed, and the coincidental arrival of the king's regiments at the height of the battle turned it into a British rout. Wood retired to his base at Khambula hill, which the Zulus attacked the following morning. Learning the lessons of iSandlwana and Rorke's Drift, Wood had secured his camp with an earthwork redoubt and a chain of wagon-laagers; the Zulus attacked it courageously for several hours, almost penetrating the British defences on a number of occasions, only to be driven off with heavy losses.

In the coastal sector, meanwhile, Chelmsford had led an expedition to relieve Eshowe. On the morning of 2 April, it was camped in an entrenched laager at a place called kwaGingindlovu when Zulu troops from the cordon around Eshowe – including Prince Dabulamanzi, who had commanded at Rorke's Drift, and who lived locally – attacked it. But the Zulus had no more success in penetrating the laager than they did at Khambula and they, too, were driven off; the following day Chelmsford relieved Eshowe.

The victories at Khambula and Gingindlovu had checked the Zulu ascendency which had prevailed since iSandlwana. Chelmsford now regrouped and planned a fresh offensive, striking at oNdini. King Cetshwayo's strategic options, on the other hand, were limited as his losses mounted, and he resolved to save his men for one final effort of national defence.

The second invasion of Zululand began on 1 June, and immediately the British suffered a fresh disaster. Louis Napoleon Bonaparte, the exiled Prince Imperial of France, who had been allowed to observe the campaign as an honorary ADC, was with a British patrol scouting ahead of the advancing columns when he was ambushed and killed. His death was not sufficient to slow Chelmsford's meticulous progress and, brushing aside King Cetshwayo's attempts to open diplomatic negotiations, he reached the vicinity of oNdini by the end of the month. On 4 July he crossed the last geographical obstacle, the White Mfolozi river, and deployed on an open plain near the royal homesteads. Under his command were over 5,000 British and auxiliary troops, four artillery batteries – one consisting of two Gatling guns – a regular cavalry regiment (the 17th Lancers) and several irregular mounted units – the largest force yet assembled by British troops in southern Africa. Chelmsford drew up his forces in a large rectangle, and the Zulus attacked on all sides, only to be cut down by concentrated artillery and rifle fire, and, when they began to retreat, ridden down by the 17th Lancers.

The battle of Ulundi – as the British called it – finally broke the ability of the Zulus to resist the invasion. King Cetshwayo withdrew into remote country – he was not captured until 28 August – and Chelmsford, having retrieved his honour from the iSandlwana debacle, resigned his command. His successor, Sir Garnet Wolseley, was left to pacify the country and impose a post-war settlement.

The disaster at iSandlwana had effectively destroyed the policies of Sir Bartle Frere which had provoked the war. With its honour regained, the British government had no desire to annex Zululand; it simply divided the country among thirteen pro-British chiefs, and walked away from the chaos it had created. The war had cost the lives of seventy-six officers and over 1,000 British troops in action, together with at least 600 African auxiliaries. Nearly 300 officers, men and auxiliaries had been wounded, and a further seventeen officers and 330 men died of disease. Ninety-nine officers and nearly 1,300 men were invalided from the war, mostly through sickness. The total number of Zulus killed may have numbered as many as 10,000 men, with unknown thousands wounded.

CHAPTER 1

'We've got bags of mealies and biscuits. We can build barricades and we'll hold this place': The Defenders of Rorke's Drift – Part 1: Adendorff to Jobbins

1. Lieutenant Gert Wilhelm Adendorff, 1st/3rd Natal Native Contingent

1a. *Natal Witness* (South Africa), 18 February 1879 [this account, although anonymous, is believed by many to be from Lt. Adendorff]

A Brave Fugitive.
The following letter has been forwarded to us, we presume, for publication. The utter poltroonery of the writer is only equalled by his inability to see it:–

Rorke's Drift, 29th Jan. 1879.

I promised to give you a better description of that frightful massacre at Isandhlwana, Zululand. I can assure you it makes my hair stand on end to relate it, but promises must be fulfilled. On the 22nd January, at about seven o'clock, a report came from Capt. Barry, who was on out-picquet, that large armies of Kafirs were advancing towards our camp. I was sent by Colonel Pulleine to inquire into the matter, and see how far they were extended. My report was to Col. Pulleine that a dense mass of Kafirs was gradually advancing, and extending about five miles in beautiful open order. By the time I arrived in camp Col. Durnford had arrived with about

300 Basutos, all mounted, and shortly afterwards these men were put in action to support Capt. Barry, and to try and keep the left flank back. However, they were driven back by degrees. Shortly afterwards dense masses of Zulus made their appearance on the ridges, so the guns were at once drawn into action and fired in between the enemy, which made an opening in their column, though it closed again within ten seconds after the explosion. The rocket battery was stationed about three miles from camp, and only fired a couple of shots when it was taken and every one cut up. The Carbineers were attacking the enemy on the right flank, but were driven back by degrees. They retired gradually towards camp. By that time the 24th Regiment had opened fire on the Zulus at 700 yards range, pouring volley after volley into the brutes. I can assure you it was more like the roar of thunder than firing, but to no avail. They seemed not to care a bit for it, although many thousands were killed. It was one mad rush towards camp and our noble warriors, and when the savages came within about fifty yards of the gun it retreated, and soon all that were in camp ran for their brave lives. Then the massacre commenced. It is something awful to relate the sad event. The brutes did not spare one man or living object that came in their way. The poor man is hardly dead when his stomach is ripped open. They pursued to the Buffalo River, a distance of about four or five miles, stabbing every one they came across, or, rather, butchering them. You can imagine that out of over 900 Europeans only twenty to twenty-five to the very utmost escaped. The real statement cannot be found out because some might probably have hidden themselves in rocks and holes.

About my escaping I will give you a short account. When the Kafirs drove the 24th Regiment back I stood firing at them as fast as I could load. The last shot before I mounted my horse was about thirty yards from them. I then mounted and gave my horse the reins. I did not go more than 300 yards when my horse was shot under me. As luck would have it some of Col. Durnford's men came past on horseback. I caught at the bridle, and luckily I got a firm hold of the reins, it checked the horse, and sent the rider to the ground; the poor devil was too frightened to look to the horse, but ran for it. I made one jump into the saddle and started again; we had to pass over a kind of neck or hollow, and a little lower down I found my way through the brutes, how I got through that part I am not able to relate, and after passing through them all safe, my horse was shot again. Fortunately one of the same lot I got the first horse from had a led horse, which he gave me. I can assure you it did not take me long in mounting; I proceeded further on my way but did not go very far when the other one was shot through the front leg, so I made a run for it, and after running for about a couple of hundred yards some more men came past me, and some led horses. So I levelled my gun at one and told him if he didn't give me a horse I would blow out his brains, so I got mounted again, and rode in company with about 150 of Col. Durnford's men towards Rorke's Drift, when my horse was knocked up and one of the same party kindly gave me another, so I arrived at this place in time to give them warning. I can assure you that it was hard work for a couple of hours to rough up some kind of wall, which was made of mealies, oats and biscuits boxes; we made some kind of wall, and made several loopholes in the two houses, when the savages came down on us, but we mowed them down. About dark they set light to one of the houses which we made into a hospital and killed several of the sick, and a few of the men that were here. In all we numbered eighty men available. Our losses amounting the next day to thirteen killed and a couple wounded; and on the enemy's side were 475, which were buried.

I must inform you that mostly all our men, or rather that the General and all the remainder of the 24th Regiment was out some distance from camp, and nearly all our N.N. Contingent, with the exception of which 89 officers and non-commissioned officers, of which 83 were killed, as well as 21 officers of the 24th Regiment, two colonels, and all the band and non-commissioned officers with the exception of one bandsman, who escaped. The most disgusting thing is that not a single one of our noble warriors is buried; they are all lying on the butcher's field for the wild beasts and birds of prey, and here we are within twelve miles from the place and no trouble is made to bury the poor fellows.

I am placed in a fine state. I have no horse and only one suit of clothes, that I have on; so if it gets dirty I must undress and wash it, and remain there until it is dry before I can go back to camp. If they do not let us go from here soon I shall have to go with a gunny bag as my dress; I believe that they intend to keep us here. I really do not know how I shall stand it, for I have nothing to cook in; if I want to make a cup of tea or coffee I have to run about to try and borrow something to cook it in. I can assure you that I am in a delapidated state now, and as soon as the war is over I will never volunteer again.

1b. Extract from the recollections of the battle of iSandlwana, by Walter H. Stafford, late Captain in the NNC, c. 1939 [Killie Campbell Africana Library, Durban, KwaZulu-Natal]

... Reverting to Rorke's Drift, a friend of mine, Lieut. Odendorff, and another man, as both could not swim, hugged the bed of the river up to the punt and were ferried across the river. It was them who gave the alarm to Rorke's Drift. Lieut. Odendorff escaped again but I think his friend was amongst the 18 that were killed. I met Odendorff in 1883 and he told me that Rorke's Drift was saved through two Godsends. The first was that the Zulu retired in the middle of the night, apparently to hold a consultation and that gave the garrison time to strengthen the weak parts of the little fort, and the Martini Henry carbines to cool off. The other was the Zulus setting fire to the thatch building which gave a bright light round the little fort and when the Zulus came volley after volley was poured into them.

He also told me that Rev. W. Smith was a great help. You will always find that in a tight corner there is a hard case and there was one at Rorke's Drift. This man was cussing all the time. The Rev. Smith went to him and said. 'Please, my good man, stop that cussing. We may shortly have to answer for our sins.' The reply he got was, 'All right Mister, you do the praying and I will send the black B's to Hell as fast as I can.'

Odendorff told me that there were 460 Zulus killed at Rorke's Drift. Although it was a case of do or die it was one of the most noble and glorious defences put up by 114 men against approximately 2000. I often wondered why there was no Rorke's Drift Day!

1c. Extract from the private diary of Lieutenant Pogge, Kaffrarian Rifles [courtesy Ron Lock]

… Lieut. Adendorff left us in PMB as he had been offered a post in local regiment, later in the defence of Rorke's Drift he excelled himself but I have not seen him since …

1d. Extract from *A Lost Legionary in South Africa*, by Colonel George Hamilton-Browne, London, 1879

… I went with Lonsdale round the laager to have a look at the debris of the fight. He told me that three of our officers had escaped and got into Rourke's Drift. Two of them, however, he was sorry to say, had ridden on, the other, a Dutchman, named Ardendorph, had remained, had fought bravely and was well spoken of …

1e. Extract from *Reminiscences of the Zulu War*, by John Maxwell, Cape Town, 1979 [referring to the escape from iSandlwana of Lieutenant Higginson of the NNC]

On his arrival in Maritzburg, he and the only two others of the 3rd N.N.C. who got out of the fight, Lieutenants Vane and Adendorff, were placed under arrest and ordered back to Rorke's Drift. In the case of Adendorff, his escape must have been most miraculous, according to his own account, but considering he managed to get along the road to Rorke's Drift, it was the opinion of most of us that he left the field rather early. Lieutenant Vane came out by the Refugees' Drift and gave his horse credit for his escape …

2. 2-24/1240 Corporal William Wilson Allan, 'B' Company, 2/24th Foot

2a. *Brecon County Times,* 29 March 1879

Helpmakaar, 4th Feb., 1879.

My dear wife,

I am able to write this myself, so you will see that I am getting the better of my wound, more rapidly than could be expected. We got here (that is the sick and wounded) on the 26th of January, and have been waiting an ambulance to convey us down the country, which is expected every day. My arm is mending quickly, though I am sorry I cannot say the same for the other wounded men, who appear to be making no progress towards recovery.

We are in a strongly entrenched fort here, with two companies of the 1st 24th, three of the 2nd 24th, detachment of the 13th, part of a company of the Royal Engineers, and a battery of Artillery. Smith is still at Rorke's Drift, where the whole of the regiment and part of the 1st 24th are assembled. Everything is quiet, and we don't expect any fighting till the arrival of troops from home.

My dear wife I trust you will feel too thankful to God for having preserved my life, to fret over what might have been a great deal worse. I feel very thankful to God for leaving me in the land of the living. Give my respects to your relatives and love to yourself and the children, from your loving husband,

W. Allon.

Corpl. W. Allon, P.M. 2nd 24th Regt., Natal, South Africa

2b. *Alnwick Mercury,* 31 January 1880

A local Hero of Rorke's Drift.

During the past week Sergeant Wm. Allen, V.C., a hero of Rorke's Drift, has been on a visit to our townsmen, Mr. Jas. Burn (late corporal in the gallant

24th Regiment). Mr Marshall, photographer, who, it will be remembered, lost a son at Isandula, has obtained an excellent photo of Sergt. Allen. We are glad to learn the gallant sergeant, who lived for many years in this district, has recovered from the dangerous wounds he received at that memorable defence, where he gained for himself the honourable distinction of the "Victoria Cross."

2c. *Monmouthshire Beacon – South Wales Advertiser,* 15 March 1890

Death of Sergeant Instructor Allan, V.C.

Much regret was felt in the Town on Wednesday, and especially amongst the Volunteers when it became known that Sergeant Instructor W.W. Allan had succumbed to a complicated attack supervening on influenza. Three years and a half ago he succeeded Sergt. Prendergast as Instructor to the local C. Co., 4th Volunteer Batt, S.W.B. He came here with a good reputation as one who had won the much-coveted Victoria Cross at the famous engagement of Rorke's Drift, and he has always been popular amongst the Volunteers and respected by the townspeople generally. The influenza epidemic, which attacked so many people last month, was the originating cause of Sergeant Allan's illness. He was laid up first six weeks ago, partially recovered from the influenza, and then suffered a relapse, a complication of disorders setting in, and although having the advantage of the Co. Surgeon. Mr. T.G. Prosser and his assistant, Mr. Groves, the patient gradually got weaker and died early on Wednesday morning, aged 46. He leaves a widow and seven young children, for whom much sympathy is felt, they being almost wholly unprovided for.

Deceased joined the Army when young and served with the 2nd Batt. of the 24th Regiment for about 25 years. He was in India for 13 years of the early part of his military service, and in February, 1878, sailed with his Regiment on board the *Himalaya*, which took out reinforcements for the Cape of Good Hope, where the campaign against the Kaffirs had taken a serious turn. Everyone recollects the terrible disaster which overtook the 1st and 2nd Battalions of the gallant 24th Regiment at Isandhlwana mountain on the 20th of January, 1879, and the memorable defence of Rorke's Drift which followed. The latter stands out as one of the grandest achievements in the annals of the British Army. It was for his brave conduct on this occasion that Sergeant (then Corporal) Allan obtained the V.C., in historical records of the 2nd Batt. 24th Regiment, a vivid account is given of the defence of the hospital and other buildings at Rorke's Drift, and referring to the part played by Corporal W. Allan and Pte. J. Hitch, the author says;– "It was chiefly due to the courageous conduct of these men that communications with the hospital was kept up at all, holding together, at all costs, a most dangerous post, raked in reverse by the enemy's fire from the hill, they were both severely wounded, but their determined conduct enabled the patients to be withdrawn from the hospital. When incapacitated by their wounds from fighting, they continued as soon as their wounds had been dressed, to serve out ammunition to their comrades during the night."

Private Hook, a Monmouth man, was associated with those who helped hold the enemy at bay, and subsequently received the Victoria Cross, while still at the Drift, from Sir Garnet Wolseley, who had taken over from Lord Chelmsford. Sergt. Allan received his Cross from the hands of the Queen herself, while lying in Netley Hospital.

The remains of the late Sergeant Instructor will be interred at the cemetery on Monday with full military honours. The cortege will leave the Volunteer Drill Hall at 2.30pm.

2d. *Monmouthshire Beacon – South Wales Advertiser,* 19 April 1890

The Late Sergt. Instructor W.W. Allan, V.C.,

In the list of subscriptions for the benefit of the widow and family of the late Sergt. Instructor W.W. Allan, V.C., last week, was an item of 10s. from the Whittington Board School, Highgate hill. We have since been shown the following letters, which accompanied the subscriptions, written by two of the scholars, aged eight:–

The "Whittington" School, Highgate Hill,
March 19th, 1890,

My dear Madam, – I am sorry to hear your husband is dead. There are a number of little girls who have been saving up their half-pennys because they would like to help you. We have learnt some poetry about some British soldiers, and how the soldiers got wounded. We have a photograph of him (Sergt. Allan) now. We are all very sorry for you and your children, and I dare say you all will miss him very much. Our teacher told us that our Queen gave him a Victoria Cross because he did such brave things.

I remain, Your affectionate little friend,

Gertrude Bamford

My dear Friends,

I am very sorry to hear that your father is dead. He suffered much pain. Do you no that we have leart some poetry of the Defenc of Rorks Drift, and we have got his photograph in our class. He was a very strong and plucky and brave man we no. When he was fighting he would not stop he helped the other soldiers to fill their guns and put powder in them, – I remain,

Your offectionate little friend,

M. Crane.

3. C/2469 2nd Corporal Francis Attwood, Army Service Corps

3a. Extract from two of a series of letters written by Corporal Attwood to his aunt and uncle during his stay in South Africa [Brenthurst Library, Johannesburg, F. Attwood Papers, MS. 455]

Dear Uncle & Aunt,

I have to thank God for being now alive, as I told you in my last letter I was stationed at a place called Helpmakaar, 12 miles from Zululand. I was sent from there to a place called Rorkes Drift on the Border of the River Buffalo that divides Zululand from Natal. I arrived all safe and was so until the 22nd January when news came to us that our Camp was taken and about 800 men of ours killed. I should have said that I belong to Col Glyns Column consisting of the 1st/24th and 2/24th Regts some Mounted

Infantry, Police, and Native Contingent and a few others, I was with a Company of the 2/24th Regt about 90 men, in charge of Commissariat Stores &c, the news was too true, and 4 Regiments of zulus attacked us with the idea of taking the stores, we immediately looped holed the house and put up a kind of fortification of sacks of oats &c all at once they came down upon us and fired, we returned it and it lasted from 4 in the afternoon till 6 the next morning

Thank God I escaped unhurt but we lost 13 men killed and 10 wounded.

Shortly after it commenced they set fire to the Hospital and I am sorry to say that some of the poor fellows were burned to death, we killed 390 we found them on the ground the next morning after they retired we came out to look round well such a sight met our eyes, all the white men that were killed were cut open and their entrails protruding, the stench of the Burning bodies was something awful, we all made up our minds for the worst, such a night, and the next, although we were not attacked we had to be up watching. I should have said that we were relieved by the remainder of the Column and got some more ammunition we have no tents or any camp equipage we have plenty of food for the present. I should have said that the zulus fight with spears (called assegai.) and all kinds of guns from the oldest pattern to the latest, they do not seem to have much fear, they are very daring, coming right up to the guns, such horrid looking brutes, quite naked except a string of something about their loins, we do not know the moment we may be attacked. I do not know how we may fare but their abilities as fighting men have been sadly under estimated, and we have a very big debt to wipe out. I cannot write any more I am too tired no sleep at night and working issuing rations all day, Love to all – up to now thank God I am quite well and remain

Yours affectionately
F Attwood
Rorkes Drift
<u>25.1.79</u>

I have not heard from you since I have been out here. F A.

3b. Extract from a second letter dated 'Rorkes Drift 14 April 1879'

… such a horrible night, I never shall forget. I am specially recommended for promotion, and I was the only one of my Corps, at the attack on the Commissariat under Lieuts Bromhead & Chard. I must tell you that I made an awful mess of one fellow, he was running towards the house in a slightly stooping position, when I let fly at him and struck him in the Crown of the head the effect of which was to blow the entire side of his face away. I must tell you that I was at an upper window the only one in the Barn I call it. Mr Witt the Swedish Missionary calls it a store house that he used as a church, he is looking after the 'rhino;' in compensation for loss …

3c. *Tralee Chronicle* (Ireland), 15 July 1879

One Lucky Bullet Saves Hundreds of Lives.

In the middle of the fight at Rorke's Drift, when the Zulus had fired the hospital, a rush was made by the band of the enemy to fire the storehouse, the other building which outlasted the defence. As fast as these Zulus came on with the firebrands they were shot down, but one managed to escape the fire, and got close to the wall of the storehouse. The defenders, with their rifles through the loopholes, could not slope their weapons to kill him, and it seemed as if his purpose of firing the thatch on the roof house would succeed. Fortunately, a young corporal of the Army Service Corps, named Atwood, bethought himself of a plan to rid the camp of the Zulu. As luck would have it, there was a small square hole in the wall which had been used as a window, and the Zulu happened to get below this. Atwood, with his carbine, made his way to this hole, and pushing out his carbine, let it hang, pointing to the ground. It was impossible to take aim in this awkward position, so he trusted to fate. The Zulu had by this time stuck a firebrand on the end of his assegai, and was in the act of rising up to set fire to the thatch, when Atwood, not seeing the Zulu at all, but knowing about his position, fired the carbine with his thumb. The shot, probably, in fact saved Natal from an invasion of the Zulus. The Zulu, at daylight, was found on the spot with his skull smashed in and the assegai, with the firebrand stuck on the end of it held tightly in his dead hand.

4. 25B/918 Private William Bennett, 'B' Company, 2/24th Foot

4a. *Preston Pilot,* 26 March 1879

Another letter from Zululand.
Last week we published a letter from Thomas Taylor, of Wrea Green, now serving in the forces in Zululand. He referred to a friend of – William Bennett – a Fylde man, who was in the heroic defence at Rorke's Drift on the 22nd January. – Bennett also came through the fight unhurt; and his mother, Mrs Bennett, who lives at Wesham (Kirkham), has this week received the following letter from her son –

"Rorke's Drift, January 29th, 1879.

I send a few lines to you hoping to find you well, as I am at present. I hope you received my last letter; I have not received one from you since I wrote to you last. We have commenced to fight the Zulus, but I need not tell you particulars of our engagement with the Zulus at Rorke's Drift, because you will have seen it or heard it read in the newspapers. My company was left in charge of some stores, and the remainder of the regiment went into Cetewayo's country and on the 22nd January the Zulus attacked the camp and killed about 800 of our men, and at night they came and attacked us, but we managed to defeat them, and in the morning they went away after we had killed about 500 of them. We lost about 13 of our men, but, thank God, I am safe yet. It was an awful sight to see about 2,000 to 3,000 Zulus about to attack us. We have had very hard times of it here. I was very glad the following morning to see a portion of our regiment coming towards us, but at first sight I and my fellow-soldiers thought it was the enemy returning, but was glad to find it was a portion of our regiment, and I was also glad to find my friend Thomas Taylor amongst them in good health and strength. I hope you will write to me soon, for I want to know how you and my brothers and sister, and all relations and friends are getting on. With kind love and best wishes to all."

5. 25B/1287 Private William Bessell, 'B' Company, 2/24th Foot

5a. *London Evening Telegraph*, 22 July 1903

Escaped Rorke's Drift – But died at Bethnal Green.

Yesterday Dr. Wynn Westcott held an inquest at Bethnal Green respecting the death of William Bessell, a potman, late 27 Sonning Buildings, Mount Street, E.

The widow deposed that her husband was formerly a soldier in the gallant 24th Regiment, which was almost annihilated in the Zulu War. He was one of the few who escaped from Rorke's Drift with his life, and, strange to say, unhurt. Of late he had been employed as a potman at the Kings Arms, High Street, Shoreditch.

Dr. P.M. Turnbull, of Bethnal Green Infirmary, stated that the man was suffering from delirium tremens on admission, and imagined he could see things crawling about. Death was due to delirium tremens and pneumonia.

A verdict to that effect was returned.

6. 2-24/2459 Colour Sergeant Frank Bourne, 'B' Company, 2/24th Foot

6a. Extract from a letter written by Colour Sergeant Frank Bourne to the parents of Private James Wood, 2/24th, who was killed at iSandlwana [Suffolk Archives, Ipswich, SROBU HA513/12/190 (pt)]

Rorke's Drift, Natal, South Africa
21st February 1879

My dear Mr & Mrs Wood …

… I daresay you have not forgotten Frank Bourne, youngest son of James Bourne, who used to live at the Brook. I belong to the 2nd Battalion & on the fatal 22nd, my Company was encamped on the Natal side of the Buffalo River, protecting a large store of supplies & the Hospital which had 35 sick. About 2.30 p.m. a man who had escaped from the other camp at Isandhlwana brought us the startling intelligence that the camp had been taken & that the enemy was in full force on this place, we at once set to work & barricaded this place with sacks of oats & mealies & loopholed both buildings. Our total number here was 139, sick included. We had hardly completed our little shelter when about 500 of the enemy appeared & opened fire on us, but their numbers very soon increased & I should roughly estimate their numbers as being between 3,000 & 4,000, we returned their fire in right good earnest & for about two hours the fight wavered & once or twice I thought the Black Devils would overwhelm us, but our steady & cool firing & our little shelter was too much for them, but about 7.15 p.m. when it began to get dusk they succeeded in taking the Hospital, which they set on fire but our poor fellows escaped with the exception of two who were delirious with fever, & who were killed in the Hospital, the fire from the Hospital gave us a good view of any moving figures so that helped us. It was a most horrible night of suspense & we didn't know at what minute we might get cut up, but thank God when the morning dawned the enemy had retired taking their wounded with them. Our loss here was 17 killed & 10 wounded, the loss of the enemy was about 500 (About four times our number in killed, so that roughly estimating it I should say it was 30 to 1.) Thank God I escaped with only a slight scratch by a spent bullet rendering my arm useless for a time …

6b. *Epsom District Times*, 29 July 1932

Defence of Rorke's Drift.
The Story Of An Epic Fight Told At Dorking.

The epic story of the fight at Rorke's Drift was told to Dorking Rotarians on Tuesday by one of the defenders, Col. Bourne, who lives in South-street, Dorking. Rorke's Drift was the scene, on January 22nd, 1879, of the most heroic event of the Zulu war. A party of 140 British soldiers, 25 of whom were hospital patients, were attacked by three to four thousand Zulus. At the end of the terrific fight, the little British force had lost 17 killed and nine wounded. And the British soldiers went out the next morning and buried 351 Zulus who had been killed in the fight. Ten Victoria Crosses were awarded among the brave men who defended Rorke's Drift. Only four survivors of the fight are now living.

Col. Bourne was a young Colour-Sergeant – he was nicknamed "The Kid" – in those days. Before Rorke's Drift, he had spent, as he told the Rotarians, some months in "chivvying" the Kaffirs in Cape Colony. And then came the Zulu war. Col. Bourne explained graphically the nature of the operations in that war. He told the story of the main British force leaving camp under Lord Chelmsford, and forcing their way through the centre of the horseshoe formation of the Zulu force, but the strong flanks of the horseshoe closed in on the British camp. The Zulus killed all the soldiers and all the animals in that camp at Isandhlwana, the British loss that day being 21 officers and 655 men killed. Then the Zulus attacked the party who had been left in charge of the hospital and commissariat stores at Rorke's Drift.

Rapidly Prepared Defences.

There were 25 men in hospital, and with one civilian, the total of the British at Rorke's Drift was 140, under the command of Lieuts. Chard and Bromhead. When news came of the impending attack, rapid efforts were made to prepare defences with the only materials available – biscuit boxes and sacks of mealie. With these defences, the buildings – principally an old farm house and the hospital, a building of the bungalow type – were connected together. Also a waggon was brought inside the compound. "About 500 of the enemy appeared first," said Col. Bourne, "and by 5 o'clock we were completely surrounded. They made rush after rush, but we kept them at bay. Still they carried on. There was no question of quarter. They asked for none and they gave none. About 7 o'clock, they set fire to the thatched roof of the hospital. That was an advantage to us, because it lit up the countryside. We got most of the patients out of the hospital. I think there was only one Zulu who got into our inner line of defences. He was killed instantly. The Zulus kept us going the whole night. Rush after rush came, but we kept them down. And when daylight broke the next morning they had disappeared."

The Defenders Saved.

In that simple language, Col. Bourne described the epic fight which holds an honoured place in the pages of British military history. He went on to tell of the work done quickly to repair the rough defences, and then, he said, they saw a column approaching. "Many of us thought we were in the pincers again," he remarked, but the approaching troops were British, not Zulus. The little garrison at Rorke's Drift was saved. It was possible then to review their position.

"At the beginning of the fight," said Col. Bourne, "each man had 70 rounds of Martini henry ammunition, and I had 34 boxes of Martini ammunition in reserve. The next morning, when the column joined up, I had only six boxes left. We lost 17 killed and nine wounded. Several men were killed in the hospital. We could not get them out before the fire occurred. Our strength was 140 all hands, but of that number there were only about a hundred fighting men. The Zulu strength, as estimated by Lieut. Chard, was 3,000. Others estimated their strength at 4,000, but I think Chard's estimate was nearer correct. Their loss was 351 killed." The number of the wounded was unknown.

Cockney Humour.

Col. Bourne explained that, during the morning after the fight, the men went out to bury the dead Zulus, and the bodies were counted as they were put into the grave. Only one wounded Zulu was found. In connection with that burial of the dead, Col. Bourne told a story typical of the queer humour of the British Tommy – although in those days, the soldier was a "Redcoat"; he did not become "Tommy Atkins" until the South African War.

There were, he said, two Cockneys among the men engaged in burying the Zulus. One said to the other, "George, when I started work I sold newspapers in the Strand. My mother didn't think I had a very good job there. Then I started cleaning boots. Mother didn't like that much better. But she thought I had done well when I got a job as 'Buttons.' Then I joined the Army. Mother liked that, but she never expected me to become sexton to a lot of Christie minstrels."

"The men at Rorke's Drift behaved splendidly," Col. Bourne said. He described Lieuts. Chard and Bromhead as two single-minded, good-hearted soldiers, and he related that, on the day succeeding the fight, Bromhead wrote a despatch which he (Col. Bourne), had to copy. Not a man's name was mentioned in that despatch. Later, however, it was discovered that Chard was senior, and another despatch was written in which the names were mentioned. Those two officers were so free from selfishness that they did not trouble to discover who of the two was senior …

6c. *Daily Mail,* 24 August 1932

Rorke's Drift Survivors

Sir, – The death is reported of "the sole British survivor" of Rorke's Drift, the famous engagement of the Zulu War of 1879.

Will you kindly allow me to point out that there are at least *five* survivors of the Rorke's Drift defence – viz., Sergeant Saxty, Privates Buckley, Cooper and Williams V.C.; and myself.

F. Bourne, Lieut.-Col., Late Colour-Sergeant, B Company 2/24th Regt., which defended the Drift.

Stoneroof, Dorking, Surrey.

6d. *Northern Mail,* 17 May 1934

Zulu War Epic
Broadcast By Veteran Survivor

A graphic account of the historic defence of Rorke's Drift during the Zulu War of 1879, one of the finest episodes in British military history, is to be broadcast to-morrow night by Lieut.-Colonel Frank Bourne, a veteran survivor.

Special interest will be given to the talk by reason of the fact that at the Northern Command Tattoo, to be staged from July 7 to 14 in the grounds of Ravensworth Castle, Gateshead, the 2nd Battalion the South Wales Borderers will re-enact this famous battle, in which that unit actually took part 55 years ago.

6e. Transcript of Bourne's first radio broadcast given in 1934, just prior to the Northern Command Military Tattoo [author's collection]

I am Lieut Colonel Bourne and I have been asked to speak on the 'Defence of Rorke's Drift' which took place on the 22nd–23rd of January 1879 during the Zulu War of that year.

I was Colour Sergeant of B. Company 2/24th Regiment which defended the 'Drift', the strength of the company being one officer and 91 N.C. officers and men, the total strength of this small post was 7 officers and 141 other ranks including one civilian, of this total there were really only about 100 fighting men.

During 1878 Cetewayo – the Zulu King – had been frequently warned by the Government to cease raiding the Natal Border and also that he must disband his army of warriors in the case of the latter he showed not the slightest intention of doing so that it became certain that he could only be brought to heel by the invasion of his country and the defeat of his army, therefore in January three columns under the command of General Thesiger – later Lord Chelmsford – crossed the Natal Border into Zululand, the third Column, which Genl. Thesiger accompanied, under Colonel Glyn of the 1st Btn 24th Regt. crossed the Buffalo River at Rorkes Drift on the 11th January, 79, my company, 'B' 2/24 Regt. being left at that post to guard the Commst Stores, hospital and pontoons on the Buffalo.

There were two buildings at Rorkes small farm, the larger one with an upper storey was used as the Commst Store, and the smaller actually a bungalow as a temporary hospital, the whole frontage including a stone cattle kraal was about 150 yards and the depth about 50 yards, no attempt had been made in the few days we had been there to connect the two buildings or the stone cattle kraal or put them in a state of defence for I don't think it was ever thought possible by anyone that the Zulus would defeat the column at Isandhlwana. Well such was the position on the 22nd

January, during that morning we distinctly heard firing from the direction of Isandhlwana but not one of us had the slightest idea that before the day was out we might be fighting for our very lives and the safety of the inhabitants of the whole of Natal, up to nearly two o'clock that day our work had gone quite normally but about that time our peace and quiet was knocked on the head by the arrival of two refugees from Zululand telling us that the camp at Isandhlwana had been over run by thousands of Zulus, that our ammunition [illegible] was cut, and that everyone except the few who were mounted and had been able to get away were killed and that a very large body of Zulus were marching on to us. We therefore at once set to work to put the Commissariat stores and hospital into a defensive state by loopholing the walls, and connecting the Commst and hospital by two boer wagons, and the front of the hospital with the stone cattle kraal with a line of sacks of Indian corn and oats. Lieut Gonville Bromhead, our splendid company commander, at once sent a message to Lieut Chard R.E. in charge of the pontoons on the Buffalo who immediately came to us, approved of the defence work we had done but thought our defences were too extended for the number of men available to defend them and suggested a line of biscuit boxes across the centre of our defence, this turned out to be a very wise step for shortly after the attack had developed we were forced to occupy this position and from which we had a perfect line of fire – only about 20 yards – to the front of the hospital where we found the dead next morning were lying four and five deep.

Shortly after 4 o'c, about 500 Zulus appeared from round the 'Oscarsberg' a big hill to our south, they advanced with a rush against our south wall where they were met with such a heavy fire from the Commst store that they were checked but at once took advantage of cover offered by the cookhouse and ovens, a great number without stopping moved to the left round the hospital and made a rush on our North West wall of mealie sacks but after a desperate struggle in which they held on to our bayonets until blown away leaving numbers of dead on the ground. The main body occupied the rocks and cover on the hillside and kept up a steady fire into our defences. Here let me say they were armed with a number of old smooth bore rifles, guns and also several Martini Henry rifles which they had taken from our dead at Isandhlwana and with ammunition from the boxes found on the dead mules at that camp, the mules having bolted when the camp was attacked thus preventing any one from getting at the boxes to open them.

About 6 o'c, the enemy set fire to the hospital and the few men who had been detailed to defend it fought bitterly to secure the rescue of the patients who were too ill to help themselves, but I am sorry to say a few men were killed and also Joseph Williams one of the defenders, the bravery of these men cannot be put into words each room was held to the bitter end. Victoria Crosses were awarded to Privates H. Hook, R. Jones, W. Jones and J. Williams, and Lieut Gonville Bromhead. These with Corporal Allen and Pte F. Hitch were also awarded the V.C.

I think I am right in saying that I am the only Colour Sergeant in the army that ever have 7 holders of the V.C. in his Company.

The fight continued until 4.00 on the morning of the 23rd Jany. when the enemy withdrew but re-appeared again about 7 o'c and then quickly disappeared.

The remainder of the Column from Isandhlwana reached us about 8 a.m. thus giving a temporary rest after twelve hours strenuous fighting but we had the great satisfaction of having won the fight.

I said at the beginning that our fighting strength was about 100, that of the enemy was estimated by Lieut Chard as 3000, by others between 3–4000, I think 3500 is nearly correct.

Our losses I regret to say were 17 killed and 10 wounded, that of the enemy was 351 killed, which we buried, and one man wounded who afterwards died, their wounded cannot have been between 3 to 400 which evidently they took away under cover of the night.

The results of this 'Defence' were, 1. that the Zulus never made a big stand again until Ulundi was fought on the 4th July '79 when they were so badly defeated that Cetewayo, their King, was taken prisoner and deported, and his warriors disarmed and dispersed. 2. That the whole of Natal was saved from invasion, murder, pillage & arson and perhaps worse.

I am sure you will all be interested to know that at the request of General Sir Alexander Wardrop the G.O.C. in C, Northern Command, my old Regiment, the 2nd Battalion the South Wales Borderers (late 2/24th Regt.)

has been requested to reproduce the "Defence of Rorke's Drift" at the Northern Command Tattoo to be held at Newcastle on Tyne from the 7th to the 14th July this year *

I want to say one word in conclusion it is this, that so long as a Regiment maintains its glorious traditions should a Squadron or a Company ever find itself in the same position as my Company did they will fight it out to the end – and will win –

Good Night

There are 10 Survivors of the "Defence", namely Sergt. Saxty, Privates Buckley, Cooper, Edwards, Jobbins, Lewis, Martin, Mason, Wood and myself

* He has also intimated his intention to invite the Survivors to attend the Tattoo.

6f. Bourne's copy of the transcript of his 1936 radio broadcast for the BBC, as published in *The Listener* magazine. Some words are underlined in pen in the original document [author's collection]

I Was There. Rorke's Drift, 1879 by Lieut-Colonel Bourne, O.B.E., D.C.M.
Sunday, 20th December 1936. 7.0–7.20 p.m.

Let me begin by telling you a little of my early days of soldiering and the sort of men we were in Rorke's Drift. I enlisted into the 24th Regiment in December 1872. I was 18 and I received the princely pay of sixpence a day, of which threepence halfpenny was deducted for messing and washing, leaving 1s. 5.½d. a week – <u>for luxuries.</u> And I went to bed hungry every night but quite happy, and it made a man of me.

The Regiment had just come home from India after fifteen years, and the "A" Company of any Regiment in those days was always called the Grenadiers' Company – supposed to be the biggest men. I think the Sergeant-Major must have been a wee bit humorous, as he posted <u>me</u> to <u>our</u> "A" Company although I stood only five feet six inches and was painfully thin.

The recruits appeared only on Church parade. And the first I attended I asked Partridge, the old soldier who was teaching me the traditions of the Regiment, and how to keep my equipment clean, where I should fall in, and I received the crushing reply "In the centre of the rear rank, where do you think" – the smallest place is in the Company.

Well, after five years of home service, in February, 1878, the Regiment received sudden orders to proceed to the Cape of Good Hope to take part in the Kaffir War. This was my first experience of active service, and shortly after, my Colonel promoted me to Colour Sergeant of "B" Company – 100 strong. I was only twenty three, very nervous, sensitive, and afraid of my new responsibilities.

Several men of the Company were of my own age, others older, and some old enough to be my father, but after a few months I felt more secure and thought I was getting along quite well. I also found myself "unpaid private secretary" to several men who could barely read and write, and I read and answered their letters home, feeling quite happy in our relations.

One day I heard a man named Wall, ask my Batman outside my tent "if the kid was in", and a day or two later I asked Partridge casually who "the kid" was, and received the answer, "Why, you are of course", and my stock slumped at once.

I think it does us all good to have our swollen heads reduced, but we were a very happy family. You can't live in tents, and on Mother Earth, for two years on Active Service without knowing your men intimately.

Well, the Kaffir War ended in June, 1878, and we were moved to Pietermaritzburg, Natal, to assist in the curtain being raised on the Zulu drama.

On the 11th of January we crossed the Buffalo River at Rorke's Drift – into Zulu country, our Commander-in-Chief was Lord Chelmsford. Our strength was four thousand five hundred men – including thirteen companies of my regiment, of the 24th, now the South Wales Borderers. One company was left behind at Rorke's Drift, to guard the hospital, stores, and pontoons at the Drift on the Buffalo River. This was my company, and at the time I was bitterly disappointed. I did not know we were going to have a battle to ourselves.

Well, we saw the main column under Lord Chelmsford engage the enemy at once, and I watched the action, along with my four sergeants, from a little hill by Rorke's Drift. Then we saw them move on again, and they disappeared.

And now I must tell you what happened to them during the next ten days, although I shall be telling you something that we didn't know ourselves, back at Rorke's Drift. They made their camp under a hill called Isandlwana, about ten miles away. Ten days later, on the 21st, first, Lord Chelmsford learned that the enemy was in force ahead of the camp, and he moved out on the morning of the 22nd with nearly half his force to attack them. But as he advanced they disappeared, and in his absence his camp was attacked and overwhelmed by fourteen thousand Zulus.

As regards the fighting in camp that day, little is known; so swift was the disaster that the few survivors who got away could give no reliable account of it, but the evidence of the dead who were afterwards found and buried where they lay told the unvarying tale of groups of men fighting back to back until the last cartridge was fired. After the war, Zulu witnesses all told the same story:–

"At first we could make no headway against the soldiers, but suddenly they ceased to fire, then we came round them and killed them with our assegais". According to one account, the last survivor was a drummer boy who flung his short sword at a Zulu. (* *This was the last occasion that band or drummer boys were taken on active service, as it was also the last occasion that the Colours were carried into action. Lieuts Melville & Coghill lost their lives in trying to save the Colours.)* Fully twelve hundred men were killed. And by half past one no white man was alive that day in Isandlwana Camp.

Well, of course, back at Rorke's Drift we knew nothing of this disaster, although my sergeants, and I, on our hill above it could hear the guns and see the puffs of smoke.

But an hour later, at 2 o'clock, a few refugees arrived and warned us what to expect.

One man whispered to me "Not a fighting chance for you, young feller". Up to that time we had done nothing to put our small post in a defensive position as our force in front was nearly five thousand strong and had six guns, and the last thing that we expected was that we should be saviours of the remainder of that force. The strength of our small garrison at the Drift was two combatant, and six departmental officers and one hundred and thirty three Non-Commissioned Officers and men, thirty six of whom were sick, leaving about one hundred fighting men. Remember that twelve hundred men had just been massacred at Isandlwana. Can you then be surprised that, flushed with their success, the Zulus were making for our small post confident that we should be easy victims to their savagery?

Well, having had the warning – but only two hours, as it turned out – we set to work to loophole the two buildings and to connect the front of the hospital with a stone cattle kraal by sacks of Indian corn oats, and to draw up two Boer transport wagons to join the front of the Commissariat Store with the back of the hospital. These proved excellent barricades, but by no means impregnable.

The native has often been credited with deep cunning, but luckily for us, if the Zulu possessed any he did not use it, for as the sacks connecting the hospital had to be laid on a slope of the ground, he could have safely crept along, cut the sacks open with his assegais, the corn would have rolled out and he could have walked in and I should not now be telling you this story today. When Lieutenant Chard of the Royal Engineers joined us he approved of what we had done, but considered that our inner space was too big, and suggested a line of biscuit boxes. This was done and proved of great value when the enemy set the hospital on fire.

I was instructed to post men as look-outs, and in the hospital, and at the most vulnerable points, and to take out and command a line of skirmishers.

Shortly after 3.30pm an officer commanding a troop of Natal Light Horse arrived, having got away from Isandlwana, and asked Lieutenant Chard for instructions. He was ordered to send detachments to observe the drift and pontoons, and to place outposts in the direction of the enemy to check his advance.

About 4.15pm the sound of firing was heard behind the hill on our front; the officer returned and reported the enemy close upon us. He also reported that his 100 men would not obey his orders and had ridden off. About the same time another detachment of 100 men belonging to the Natal Native contingent bolted, including their officer himself. I am glad to say he was brought back some days later, courtmartialled and dismissed from the service.

The desertion of these detachments of 200 men at first sight seemed to be a great loss, with only a hundred of us left, but the feeling afterwards was that we could not have trusted them, also that our defences were too small to accommodate them anyhow.

We knew now that whatever might happen we had to fight it out alone, and about 4.30 the enemy, from 500 to 600 strong, came in sight round the hill to our south, driving in my thin red line of skirmishers, and made a rush at our south wall. They were met, and held, by a steady and deliberate fire for a short time, but being reinforced by some hundreds, they made desperate and repeated attempts to break through our temporary defences, but were repulsed time and again. To show they had no fear and their contempt for the red coats, and small numbers, they tried to leap the parapet, and at times seized our bayonets, only to be shot down. Looking back, one cannot but admire their bravery.

About 7 o'clock they succeeded, after many attempts, in setting fire to the hospital. The small numbers we were able to spare defended it room by room, bringing out all the sick who could be moved before they retired. Privates Hook, R. Jones, W. Jones and J. Williams being the last to leave, holding the door with the bayonet as all their ammunition was expended.

Owing to the way the rooms communicated, and the burning of the house, it was impossible to save all. The Victoria Cross was awarded to these men, and they fully deserved it.

The Zulus had collected the rifles from the men they had killed at Isandhlwana, and had capture the ammunition from the mules which stampeded and threw their loads; so our own arms were used against us. In fact this was the cause of every one of our casualties, killed and wounded, and we should have suffered many more if the enemy had known how to use a rifle. There was hardly a man even wounded by an assegai – their principal weapon.

The attack lasted from 4.30 p.m. on the 22nd to 4.0 a.m. on the 23rd – twelve exciting hours – and when daybreak occurred the enemy was out of sight. But about 7 o'clock they appeared again to the south-west.

But help was at hand; Lord Chelmsford with the other half of his original force was only an hour's march away. On the previous afternoon he had learned of the destruction of his camp, at Isandlwana. A certain Commandant Lonsdale had chanced to ride back to the camp and been fired at by Zulus wearing our men's uniforms. He escaped by a miracle and was able to report the news to Lord Chelmsford.

Lord Chelmsford at once addressed his men and said:– "Whilst we were skirmishing ahead the Zulus have taken our camp; there are ten thousand in our rear, and twenty thousand in front, we must win back our camp tonight and cut our way back to Rorke's Drift tomorrow." The men of the 24th answered with a cheer, "All right, sir, we'll do it."

Well, they got back to the camp that night, but I cannot tell you now the grim and silent scene they found as they cautiously approached. The next day they resumed their march and appeared at Rorke's Drift, and our enemy retired. We were saved.

In his dispatch afterwards Lord Chelmsford said:– "To our intense relief the waving of hats was seen from hastily erected entrenchments, and information soon reached me that the garrison … had for twelve hours made the most gallant resistance I have ever heard of against the determined attack of some 3000 Zulus, three hundred and fifty of whose dead bodies surrounded the post."

As I've said, our fighting strength at Rorke's Drift was about 100 of all ranks and the Zulus 3,500. Our losses were 17 killed, 9 wounded, theirs 351 killed that we buried. Their wounded must have been between 400 and 500, which they removed under cover of the night.

There are two things which I think have made Rorke's Drift stand out so vividly all these years. The first, that it took place on the same day as the terrible massacre at Isandlwana, and second, that Natal was saved from being overrun by a savage and victorious foe.

We were just one company of the regiment which is now the South Wales Borderers, seven V.C.'s were awarded to this company, all in one company in the same action, which must be a record. I should like just to give you their names; I have told you the names of four of them already, the men who held the door in the hospital. The other three were Lieutenant G. Bromhead, Corporal Allen and Private F. Hitch. The Victoria Cross was also awarded to Lieutenant Chard, Royal Engineers, Surgeon Reynolds and Corporal Scheiss, but not one, I regret to say, of those V.C.'s. is alive today. In fact, there are only six survivors of Rorke's Drift alive today.

Ex-Privates W. Cooper, G. Edwards, E. Martin, W. Owens, H. Williams, and myself, and some of them are listening to me now.

Lieuts. Chard and Bromhead and the men, received the thanks of Parliament, the officers being promoted to the rank of Major. I was awarded the

Distinguished Conduct Medal with an annuity of £10 – the same as awarded to the Victoria Cross – and awarded a commission, but as I was the youngest of eight sons, and the family exchequer being empty, I had to refuse it that time.

Now just one word for the men who fought that night; I was moving about them all the time and not for one moment did they flinch, their courage and their bravery cannot be express in words, and for me they were an example all my soldiering days.

The following year Queen Victoria received at Windsor Castle a Colour Party of the Regiment, and decorated the Queen's Colour with a silver wreath of immortelles in memory of Lieuts. Melville and Coghill "for their devotion in trying to save the Colours on the 22nd January, (that was at Isandhlwana) and for the noble defence of Rorke's Drift." So if ever you have the great privilege of seeing the Colours of the South Wales Borderers uncase you will see the wreath.

The original wreath presented by Her Majesty is now in the Regimental Chapel of Brecon Cathedral.

You may have seen the famous picture of "Rorke's Drift" painted by that great French artist, de Neuville, and the original is in the Officers' Mess of the Second Battalion, now at Londonderry.

If there are any Service or ex-Service men listening, (*) may I say this to you; that if your company had found itself in the same position as we were, you would have done the same as we did, fought it out and won.

The following verse from Macaulay's "Lays of Ancient Rome" can, I think, be applied appropriately to the 24th Regiment on that fatal day, 22nd of January, 1879:–

"For how can man die better
Than facing fearful odds,
For the ashes of his fathers,
And the temples of his gods."

Good night.

(* I believe the 2nd Battalion of my old Regiment, commanded by Colonel Edwards are back from Pakistan tomorrow morning, are listening to me now on the High Seas aboard the 'Caledonian' off the coast of Wales).

6g. *Sunday Express*, 22 January 1938

Hero of Rorke's Drift Lives The Battle Over Again At 83

Sixty years ago eighty-eight men were sleeping the sleep of the valiant in the shadow of a little hill in South Africa. For fifteen hours B Company of the 24th Regiment, now the South Wales Borderers, had put up one of the most magnificent stands in the fighting history of England.

One of the eighty-eight who survived Rorke's Drift was Colour-Sergeant, now Lieut.-Colonel F. Bourne, of Stone Roof, Dorking, who was awarded the D.C.M.

Last week, talking to a Sunday Express reporter, he lived the battle over again.

He is eighty-three now.

"The odd thing," he said smiling, "was that it was our company that was left behind to look after the stores while the other twelve went into battle.

Overwhelmed

"Our main column, under Lord Chelmsford, camped at Isandhlwana. Ten days later they heard that the Zulus were ahead and Lord Chelmsford took half his force to attack them.

"While he was gone 14,000 Zulus descended on the unprepared 1,200 Britons, overwhelmed them when the ammunition was spent, and wiped out the lot.

"At two o'clock a few refugees arrived and told us the news. They said we were next.

"At half past four the triumphant Zulus came, first 600 of them, then more until there were 4,000 against 100!

"They charged right up to our parapet, even trying to leap over it and clutching our men's bayonets in their hands.

"They hurled all their assegais. Then they started to use the rifles and ammunition they had captured from our men at Isandhlwana. They fired the hospital.

"All night the battle went on, but we had only seventeen killed and nine wounded, and we had won. The Zulus retreated, leaving behind them 350 dead. We buried 351."

The last pair of figures sounded odd.

Colonel Bourne chuckled.

"I don't think the story of that one Zulu has ever been told," he said.

Left for Dead

"One Zulu who was alive had been left for dead.

"Later in the day Lieutenant Bromhead sent for me and said, very urgently. 'Where's that man who was here just now with a prisoner? Find that man and bring him here.'

"I went round asking. 'Who's the man who's got a prisoner?' They said, 'Ashton, of course.' Ashton was a lusty Irishman. I found Ashton.

"'What have you done with your prisoner?' I said. He pointed to a tree from which the Zulu's body was hanging.

"'I took him in to Lieutenant Bromhead,' said the innocent Irishman, 'and he told me to get the hell out of here with him, and I did.'"

6h. *Dorking County Post,* 10 May 1945

Deaths.

Bourne – On May 9th 1945, at Stoneroof, Dorking, Lt.-Col. Frank Edward Bourne, O.B.E., late 24th Regiment, believed to be the last survivor of Rorke's Drift 1879, aged 90 years. Funeral Service at St. Martin's, Dorking, on Monday, May 14th, at 2.30p.m. Interment private

7. Lieutenant Gonville Bromhead, 'B' Company, 2/24th Foot

7a. Bromhead's official letter of recommendation for the award of the Victoria Cross to members of the 2/24th. The sections in **bold** appear in the original in Bromhead's handwriting [National Archives, London, WO32/7390]

From/ Lieut. Gonville Bromhead 2/24th Regt:

To/ The Officer Commanding 2/24th Regt:

Rorke's Drift
15th February 1879

Sir,

I beg to bring to your notice the names of the following men belonging to my Company who especially distinguished themselves during the attack by the Zulus on this Post on the 22nd & 23rd January last; & whose conduct on this occasion came under my personal cognizance.

No. 1395 Private John Williams was posted by me together with Private Joseph Williams & Private William Horrigan 1/24th Regt. in a further room of the Hospital. They held it for more than an hour, so long as they had a round of ammunition left, when, as communication was for the time cut off, the Zulus were enabled to advance & burst open the door. They dragged out Private Joseph Williams & two of the patients by the arms, & assegaied them. Whilst the Zulus were occupied with the slaughter of these unfortunate men, a lull took place, during which Private John Williams – who with two patients were the only men now left alive in this ward – succeeded in knocking a hole in the partition, & in taking the two patients with him into the next ward, where he found

No. 1373 Private Henry Hook. These two men together, one man working whilst the other fought & held the enemy at bay with his bayonet, broke through three more partitions, & were thus enabled to bring eight patients through a small window into our inner line of defence.

In another ward, facing the hill, I had placed

No. 593 Private William Jones & No. 716 Private Robert Jones: They defended their post to the last, until six out of the seven patients it contained had been removed. The seventh, Sergeant Maxfield, 2/24th Regt: was delirious from fever. Although they had previously dressed him, they were unable to induce him to move. When Private Robert Jones returned to endeavour to carry him away, he found him being stabbed by the Zulus as he lay on his bed –

No. 1240 Corporal William Allen & No. 1362 Private Frederick Hitch, must also be mentioned. It was chiefly due to their courageous conduct that communication with the Hospital was kept up at all. Holding together at all costs a most dangerous post, raked in reverse by the enemy's fire from the hill, they were both severely wounded, but their determined conduct enabled the patients to be withdrawn from the Hospital, & when incapacitated by their wounds from fighting themselves, they continued, as soon as their wounds had been dressed, to serve out ammunition to their comrades during the night. –

I have the honour to be Sir

Your most obedient servant

G. Bromhead

Lieut. 2/24 Regt.

Commanding B. Company 2/24 Regt.

7b. A private letter from Bromhead to his friend, Captain Godwin-Austen, 2/24th [courtesy of the Royal Welsh Regimental Museum, Brecon, Acc. No. D87.72]

Rorkes Drift
19th Feb. 1879.

My dear Austin,

I can't tell you how grieved I was to hear on the return of the Column on the 23rd of January that your brother had been left in that fateful camp. He had been attached to B. Co. at Greytown, and we got on so jolly together that he told me he should ask the Col. to let him stay with the Company, but I am sorry to say it was not to be.

The night before the Column crossed the River it came out in orders that B Company were to remain here and your Brother was sent back to G Company and Griffiths who was Company Officer as usual was posted to the Company. Your Brother who was knocked up from over work at the ponts where he had been working day & night, to get the troops across the River had to go sick, but still he march with the Column. I have not got over the dreadful … we received yet, in fact can hardly believe it. We had an awful night of it here as you may fancy. We heard the Camp had been taken, and were also afraid that the Column had received a heavy blow, and the Zulus came at us in such force & with such fierce pluck. I thought we should never pull through it, but the Company behaved splendidly and as our ammunition held out and we held them back till daylight. We were on the Natal side of the Buffalo but can do nothing as far as I can see, till we are fitted up again. I hope they are going to send us out some more troops or you wont see many of us again. The Zulus are so strong we stand a poor chance against them, as it is we expect to be attacked any day. I hope the wound is better, and that you do not suffer from it.

Yours sincerely,

G. Bromhead.

7c. An extract from a private letter from Bromhead to one of his sisters [Royal Welsh Regimental Museum, Brecon, Acc. No. D87.721]

… I fear you will be very anxious about me as no doubt we are rather in a fix. I am getting over the excitement of the fight and the sickness and fury at our loss. It is not so much the poor fellows being killed as the way the savages treat them. Having been left alone we have built a mud fort, which I think we ought to hold against any amount of Zulus, till we get help from England …

… I send you a paper with the report of the fight and the remarks of the General on the behaviour of my company which are flattering. If the Government gives all the steps of the poor fellows killed I shall most probably get my company into the 1st Battalion who are to go home directly after the war is finished …

… I have not got over the wonder of there being one of us left. God was very good to us in giving us a little time to get up a defence, or the black fellows would have taken us by surprise, which they will find hard to do now …

7d. *The Times*, 30 April 1879

The following extract from the letter of an officer with the column under Lord Chelmsford who arrived at Rorke's Drift on the morning of January 23rd, will still be read with interest; –

"From the distance we saw the hospital in flames and thought all was over. The mounted men rode up carefully and were greeted with cheers by the little garrison. When Lord Chelmsford rode up Bromhead came out alone to make his report, and was received most enthusiastically by what was left of Lord Chelmsford's column. The men never stop their yarns about him, and we are full of admiration at the coolness, forethought, pluck, and determination which he showed. With hardly a man to spare, he still posted two men in the Commissariat rum stores to prevent any from helping themselves. During every lull in the attack he sallied out, disarmed the dead Zulus, and destroyed their weapons. In the middle of the night he went out with one man to see for himself how the reserve ammunition was holding out. Cautiously striking a match, to count the boxes, the Zulus saw it and fired; the lantern was smashed and the man killed."

7e. *Natal Witness*, c. September 1879

Victoria Cross presented to Major Bromhead.
... At half past eight we had a parade of all the troops in garrison, consisting of the 2-24th, the three squadrons of Dragoons, and the detachment of Royal Artillery with two guns, were drawn up in front of our headquarters, in three sides of a square; and then the General attended by his staff and many other officers rode on to the ground.

General Colley then called out for Brevet-Major Bromhead and Private Jones, who both came forward from the ranks; a letter from the Secretary of State for War to the General Commanding in South Africa was then read, and afterwards extracts from the London Gazette, giving the acts for which the Victoria Cross was to be presented.

Sir G. Wolesley having had the much-prized honours handed to him by Colonel Degacher, said: "Colonel Degacher and men of the 2-24th – The extracts just read describe very fully two acts for which Her Majesty the Queen has been pleased to order these two crosses to be awarded. The decoration is the highest one that a soldier can obtain, and is naturally highly prized in consequence. It is worn at the present time by many brave officers and men in our army; but none for better services to the State than those for which it is given to-day, in gallantly defending Rorke's Drift against overwhelming numbers of savages; the defence, I believe, is only an instance of what British soldiers can do when properly handled and led. That fight will always be remembered with pride by every British regiment, as well as by the 2-24th; and when so thought of I feel sure that the names of the two who now obtain the cross will be associated with it in the regimental annals, together with those other brave men who have also obtained the cross."

The General then pinned the crosses on their left breasts and wished them a long life, and many opportunities of gaining other medals …

7f. *Madras Weekly News* (India), 19 February 1891

The Late Major Bromhead, V.C.

It is with regret that we have to announce the death, from enteric fever, of Major Gonville Bromhead, V.C., of the 2nd Battalion South Wales Borderers, which melancholy event occurred at Allahabad on the evening of Monday last. The deceased took to his bed with the malady on the 31st January, and every hope was entertained of his recovery; but two days previous to his demise a sudden change for the worse took place, and notwithstanding the close attention paid by Doctors Donevan and De la Cour Corbett, and the nursing of Miss Hislop, the unfortunate officer gradually grew worse. It was then deemed advisable to wire to his elder brother, Colonel C.J. Bromhead, commanding the Borderers, who had but a few days previously left for Bombay en route to England, on retirement, who returned at once to Allahabad. About 2 p.m. on Monday, serious symptoms for the worse set in, and at 6-30 the same evening, Major Bromhead passed quietly away. The remains of the deceased officer were interred with full military honours on Tuesday evening, the attendance at the cemetery being very large, including Brigadier-General A.A.A. Kinloch, the District Staff and the whole of the officers of the garrison. The solemn *cortége* left the quarters of the deceased at 4-30, with the whole battalion of the South Wales Borderers, together with the full complement of officers. The firing party consisted of 200 rank and file of the regiment of which Major Bromhead belonged, under the command of Major Heaton, with the Band, whilst the coffin, bearing the deceased officer's helmet and sword covered with the Union Jack and almost hidden by wreath of flowers, was place on a gun carriage horsed by six bays of the 34th Field Battery. The chief mourner was the brother of the deceased, the pall-bearers being Colonel Clements, Major Browne, Captain Trower and Captain Weallens. The spectacle as the procession wended its way to the military cemetery headed by the band of the S.W. Borderers playing the "Dead March in Saul," was most solemn and imposing. Arrived at the gate of the cemetery, a large contingent of officers joined the procession, the last rites of the Church being performed by the Rev. Hesketh-Biggs. We might here mention that enteric fever is rather prevalent in Allahabad just now, another officer, Lieutenant Murray, of the Royal Engineers, being laid up at the Station Hospital with the same disease.

7g. *Bombay Gazette* (India), 3 April 1891

The Late Major Bromhead, V.C.

Colonel Glennie, commanding the 1st Battalion South Wales Borderers, writes in the Army and Navy Gazette: –

"It is with feelings of pain and regret that the officers of the 24th Regiment (the South Wales Borderers) have read a paragraph, published in the *World* newspaper of February 18 relative to the late Major Gonville Bromhead, V.C. The whole paragraph as applied to him is a shameful slur on the memory of a gallant officer, and is inaccurate in his name and all its facts. Gonville Bromhead was unfortunately deaf, but by no means dull-witted, and I never heard that he failed in any examination, indeed, when promoted Major, although a letter was sent to him stating he was not required to pass, he refused to take advantage of this privilege. The *World* calls him 'a big clumsy dull-witted subaltern' and 'clownish hero' but he was the reverse of all this. To those who know him, he was a thorough good-hearted fellow, bon camarade, an English gentleman. The name of Gonville Bromhead and the gallant deeds of B. Company, 2nd Battalion 24th Regiment on the night of January 22, 1879, will ever be remembered in his regiment, and, will be handed down to future generations notwithstanding the unfeeling remarks of the *World* newspaper."

Truth remarks that its contemporary's description of the late officer has excited keen indignation and publishes two letters on the subject. One officer of the 24th writes: –

A paragraph appeared in the *World* of the 18th inst referring to the death of Major Bromhead, V.C., in which the most unfeeling and untrue statements are made. "A big clumsy dull-witted subaltern" and a "clownish hero," are just about the very reverse of the truth. He was universally looked up to and respected as a man of infinite judgement and common sense – so much so that one of the names he earned was "Old Judgement." His opinion on any matter was eagerly sought and carried the greatest weight with all those fortunate enough to be brought in daily contact with him. As far as the ridiculous assertion that he could not pass examination, nothing could be wider from the truth. He did pass all his examinations up to Captain with ease. And would just as easily, have passed for his Majority had not the Horse Guards very kindly sent out a letter to India which arrived a few days before the examination took place, especially exempting him. Never was there a man more believed and respected. He was good at all games being one of the best cricketers in the regiment. On one occasion, he played for "The Army vs The Bar" at Aldershot. He had an excellent wit, with a very keen sense of humour and was one of the gentlest-hearted men that ever lived.

Another brother officer writes: –

I read with feelings of surprise and indignation the paragraph in the *World* newspaper, February 18th. Any one who had the pleasure of knowing the late Lieutenant Bromhead of some twelve years will understand right well how utterly false such remarks are.

Major Bromhead, V.C., was beloved by all ranks, and during the thirteen years I served with him I never heard him say an unkind word to or of any one. He was the quintessence of an English gentleman, gentle, kind, modest to a degree, retiring, the soul of honour – a most perfect character indeed.

He had the misfortune to be deaf, but he was an exceedingly well-read and well-informed man on all subjects, and I never saw a trashy book in his hand. He was a good game shot, and a few years ago quite the best slow bowler in the army.

It will be a long, long day ere his place will be refilled in the roll of the regiment which had the honour of claiming him.

8. 2-24/981 Private Charles Bromwich, 'B' Company, 2/24th Foot

8a. *Warwick Gazette*, 3 June 1893

A Warwick Hero.
Death of a Rorke's Drift Hero.

There died, on Saturday last, at 38, High-street, Warwick, a hero in humble life. Charles Bromwich, one of those concerned in the defence of Rorke's Drift, an act of heroism which is familiar as a household word with every Englishman, after surviving the dreadful experience of that memorable encounter between a handful of desperate British soldiers and an overwhelming horde of savage Zulus, passed peacefully away in his native town, at the age of 53. He had for two weeks occupied his death bed, and it is a remarkable circumstance that his wife, who has also been ill a long time, predeceased him only by a few days. Mrs Bromwich was buried yesterday (Friday) week, and Bromwich himself was borne to his last resting place on Tuesday afternoon. From Sergeant Thomas, of the Borough Police Force, an old comrade, we learn that Bromwich joined the then 24th Royal Warwickshire Regiment, 2nd Battalion, in 1858, and had seen a good deal of foreign service in India. From there he was invalided home, but on the Zulu war breaking out in 1879, he was ordered to the Cape, where he was destined to take his share in a deed of gallantry almost unexampled in the annals of the British army, a deed that made the English-speaking race all the world over thrill with pride and admiration. Things are soon forgotten in these busy times, but the defence of Rorke's Drift will never fade from the memory of the nation. There may be others who, like Private Bromwich, have retired into comparative seclusion, but their services to their countrymen in Cape Colony will never pass into oblivion …

… When Bromwich got his discharge from the army in 1880, he having completed over 21 years' service, he was in possession of four good conduct badges, and was granted a pension of 1s. per day. He was also decorated with the Zulu war medal and two clasps. For some time Bromwich was caretaker at the office of Mr. R.C. Heath (Under Sheriff), in New-street, but failing health compelled him to give up some time ago, and he died after two weeks' illness as already stated.

9. 25B/1184 Private Thomas Buckley, 'B' Company, 2/24th Foot

9a. *The Times*, 2 February 1924

Rorke's Drift Survivors.

A recent reference to the fact that there were two survivors of the defence of Rorke's Drift by the 24th Regiment South Wales Borderers, in the Zulu War, has prompted a military correspondent to write to The Times to say that there is another survivor. He is Mr. T. Buckley, a London man, who figures on the roll of those at the defence of the Drift as a private with the regimental number of 1184 in the B Company of the 24th Regiment. He is now 65. The other two survivors, Private John Williams, V.C., and Sergeant Evan Jones, are both Welshmen.

9b. *Natal Witness*, 21 January 1961

A Rorke's Drift Hero And Two Dogs Of The 2/24th Regiment. By Capt. G.F. Court.

One sunny May morning in 1930, Mallelieux and I sat on a park bench in Brook Green, Hammarsmith, London, chatting and watching very good tennis played by Chinese students on the public courts.

At the end of our bench sat a moustached elderly gentleman reading a newspaper.

Suddenly he uttered a loud "agh!" in a contemptuous voice, at the same time striking the paper angrily with his right hand, and glared at us over his spectacles, evidently much put out. Seeing us looking at him inquiringly, he spoke in a deep toned Irish voice saying: "I have just read here" – thumping the paper – "that a survivor of Isandhlwana has died in Natal. Every year I read of a survivor of this battle dying in Natal. I tell you that there were none, every man fought, died on the battle field. There were no survivors except a dog owned by our Colonel. The only living thing to come through the fight that day. I'm telling you."

"Are you speaking about the Zulu war battle of Isandhlwana, Sir?" I asked.

"Yes I am! The day of the battle I was at Rorkes Drift, Private Buckley of 'B' Company the 2/24th Warwickshire Regiment. Lieut. Bromhead commanded us." The old soldier proudly declared.

"Surely there were survivors, about forty Sir?" Mallelieux asked.

"There were none, those that got away left the field early in the fight. Some came to us at Rorkes Drift, a few stayed and fought with us: others rode on to Helpmekaar where two Companies of our First Battalion were posted. In the Regiment, we always said that Flip, a dog owned by Colonel Degacher, was the only living thing to survive, the other dog, Kreli, was never seen again."

"So there were only two dogs in the fight Sir?" I enquired.

"Yes, of my Regiment, but only one when the Regiment sailed from Cork to the Cape in January 1878, to engage in the Kaffir war. He was a Dalmatian, one of those black and white spotted dogs, owned by our C.O., Colonel Degacher. Flip was his name. The Regiment disembarked at East London and then went inland to King Williams Town to take part in the war with our First Battalion.

"The morning after a fight, we found a Kaffir dog tied up in a deserted kraal. He was a young yellow haired greyhound with kind black eyes. We named him Kreli, after the Kaffir king, our enemy. He chummed with Flip, they kept together through the war and he became a favourite in the Regiment.

"After the war we lay at the Kaboosie River for orders. When they came, it was, that the Regiment embark at East London for Natal.

"Orders were issued that no dogs could be taken, because by this time many had been collected by the men as pets.

"We entrained and left for East London on the new railway, with perhaps forty dogs of all breeds, sizes and colours galloping alongside the train, encouraged by men shouting, calling and cheering them on, and the dogs all barking and whining at being left behind. The dogs gradually fell out or they became tired, until after a few miles the only one left was Kreli the yellow dog, who continued to keep up with the train midst the cheers of the men, and barking of his chum Flip, who was on the train.

"At last the Colonel ordered the train to be stopped for Kreli, and he was helped on to rejoin Flip. The Colonel's kind act was loudly cheered by everyone.

"The Regiment landed at Durban and proceeded inland to Pietermaritzburg and then on to Helpmekaar to join Colonel Glynn's column about to invade Zululand, both dogs being with us.

"When we got to Rorkes Drift, my Company 'B', commanded by Lieut. Bromhead, was detached for line of communication duties. The main column entered Zululand and camped at Isandhlwana mountain.

"Early one morning Colonel Degacher left camp with six companies of the Regiment to fight the enemy. Flip and Kreli were left in camp with the company ordered to guard the camp together with five companies of our First Battalion commanded by Colonel Pulleine. The camp was attacked that day and all killed, no man survived.

"That night when our Colonel with six companies arrived back at the decimated camp to find everyone killed, the dogs were not found and it was assumed they had been killed.

"The following morning, Lord Chelmsford the Commander-in-Chief returned to Rorkes Drift with all that remained of Colonel Glynn's column, including the six companies of my Regiment under Colonel Degacher and camped.

"A few hours later Flip came into camp with a rope tied to his neck, and a severe spear wound in the shoulder. Everyone crowded to see and to cheer Flip, the only living thing to survive the battle where we lost a thousand killed that day.

"Apparently after being wounded a Zulu led Flip off, and the dog broke away and returned to his master. The yellow dog, Kreli, was not seen again. In the Regiment Kreli was not forgotten, we spoke of him affectionately for many years, this common kindly Kaffir dog that we found in one war and lost in another."

The old soldier indicated that was the end of the story.

Mallelieux said: "What became of Flip Mr. Buckley?"

"After the Zulu war the Regiment went to Gibraltar and afterwards to Burma, and Flip of course with the Colonel. When the Colonel retired from the army and went to live in the old family home in France, he took his dog, where he died of old age, so I was told."

We got up and introduced ourselves and thanked this old Irish soldier, hero of Rorkes Drift, for this story about Flip and Kreli. At the same time telling Mr. Buckley that we too had served in South Africa – Mallelieux at King Williams Town in Kaffirland and Pondoland in the Cape Mounted Rifles and myself in Pietermaritzburg in Natal and Zululand, a member of the Natal Police.

"This is very interesting indeed. I was in the siege of Ladysmith in the Imperial Light Horse." Mr. Buckley replied.

I added that I had been to Rorke's Drift and Isandhlwana several times.

"The devil you have!" Mr. Buckley exclaimed looking at me with a happy smile, "You are a lucky one."

We shook hands, said "Good morning," leaving the old hero opening up the paper, perhaps again to scan the item that made him angry – "Survivor of Isandlwana dies in Natal."

9c. *South Wales Borderers Regimental Journal,* March 1932

In the middle of February we learnt of the death of No. 1184, ex-Private Thomas Buckley, which occurred at Liverpool on 31st December, 1934. He was buried by the British Legion in that City.

Buckley enlisted in February 1877, and went through the Kaffir and Zulu Campaigns, and was one of the defenders of Rorke's Drift on 22nd 23rd January 1879. He remained with the 2nd Battalion when it went to India and Burmah, and was through the Burmah Campaign. He was discharged in 1889. He served in the South African Campaign 1899–1902 in the Imperial Light Horse, and again in the Great War with the Royal Air Force.

The Association kept in touch with him until 1933, when the letters sent to his last address were returned through the Dead letter office. Efforts were made to trace him but without result.

The medals he gained in the five Campaigns are in the Officers Mess of the 1st Battalion, to which Battalion he presented them in 1929.

10. 2076 Gunner John Cantwell, 'N' Battery, 5th Brigade, Royal Artillery

10a. Extract from a letter written by Cantwell in 1900, when seeking an increase in his pension from the Natal government [Pietermaritzburg Archives Repository, Pietermaritzburg, South Africa, NAB Ref. 1975/00]

2nd Avenue
Greyville
Nr. Durban

Sir,

I joined Her Majestys Service in 68 and served until 19th July 87 – where I left as a full N.C.O. of the R.A. with a very good discharge.

I am one of the heroes & defenders of Rorke's Drift, & am in receipt of the War Medal for, 77–78 + 79 – together with the Medal for Distinguished Service for gallantry at the defence of "Rorke's Drift" – presented to me by the hands of Her Most Gracious Majesty the Queen at Windsor 8th March 80 – also the Medal for Long Service & Good Conduct …

10b. *Natal Mercury* (South Africa), 15 August 1900

A Rorke's Drift Defender

Mr. John Cantwell, 54, married, died yesterday at Addington Hospital, after a long and painful illness. He was a pensioner of the Natal Government, and until recently convict guard at Durban Gaol. He was formerly sergeant in the Royal Artillery, and was in possession of medals for the Zulu War '77, '78, and '79, and was decorated by the Queen with medal for distinguished conduct in the field (defence of Rorke's Drift). He had also long service and good service medals. The funeral leaves Addington Hospital this afternoon at 3-30 for the Roman Catholic Church, when ex-members of Her Majesty's service will doubtless attend in large numbers.

11. Lieutenant John Rouse Merriott Chard, 5th (Field) Company, Royal Engineers

11a. A copy of Chard's first official report on the defence of Rorke's Drift. The sections in **bold** appear in the original in Chard's handwriting [National Archives, London, WO32/7737]

Rorkes Drift
25th January 1879

Sir,

I have the honor to report that on the 22nd inst I was left in command at Rorkes Drift by Major Spalding, who went to Helpmakaar to hurry on the Compy. 24th. Regt ordered to protect the ponts.

About 3.15 p.m. on that day I was at the ponts when two men came riding from Zulu-land at a galop, and shouted to be taken across the river.

I was informed by one of them, Lieut Adendorff of Lonsdales Regt (who remained to assist in the defence) of the disaster at Isandhlwana Camp, and that the Zulus were advancing on Rorkes Drift.

The other a Carabineer rode off to take the news to Helpmakaar.

Almost immediately I received a message from Lieut. Bromhead, commg. the Company 24th. Regt at the Camp near the Commt. Stores, asking me to come up at once.

I gave the order to inspan, strike tents, put all stores &c into the wagon, and at once rode up to the Commt. Store and found that a note had been received from the Third Column to state that the enemy were advancing in force against our post, which we were to strengthen and hold at all costs.

Lieut Bromhead was most actively employed in loopholing & barricading the store building and hospital and connecting the defence of the two buildings by walls of mealie bags and two wagons that were on the ground.

I held a hurried consultation with him and with Mr Dalton of the Commt. (who was actively superintending the work of defence, and whom I cannot sufficiently thank for his most valuable services) entirely approving of the arrangements made. I went round the position and then rode down to the ponts and brought up the guard of 1 Sergt + 6 men, wagon &c.

I desire here to mention the offer of the pont man Daniells and Sergt Milne 3rd. Buffs to moor the ponts in the middle of the stream and defend them from their decks with a few men.

We arrived at the post about 3.30 pm. Shortly after an officer of Durnford's Horse arrived and asked for orders. I requested him to send a detachment to observe the drifts and ponts to throw out outposts in the direction of the enemy, and check his advance as much as possible, falling back upon the post when forced to retire and assisting in its defence.

I requested Lieut Bromhead to post his men, and having seen his and every man at his post, the work once more went on.

About 4.20 pm the sound of firing was heard behind the hill to our South. The officer of Durnfords returned, reporting the enemy close upon us, and that his men would not obey his orders, but were going off to Helpmakaar, and I saw them apparently about 100 in number going off in that direction.

About the same time Captain Stephenson's detachment of Natal Native Contingent, left us, as did that officer himself.

I saw that our line of defence was too extended for the small number of men now left us and at once commenced a retrenchment of biscuit boxes.

We had not completed a wall two boxes high, when about 4.30 pm 500 or 600 of the enemy came in sight around the hill to our South and advanced at a run against the South wall. They were met by a well sustained fire but notwithstanding their heavy loss – continued the advance to within 50 yards of the wall, when they met with such a heavy fire from the wall, and cross-fire from the store that they were checked, but taking advantage of the cover afforded by the cook-house ovens &c kept up a heavy fire.

The greater number however without stopping moved to the left around the hospital and made a rush at our N.W. wall of mealie bags but after a short but desperate struggle were driven back with heavy loss into the bush around the work –

The main body of the enemy were close behind and had lined the ledge of rock and caves overlooking us about 400 yds to our South from where they kept up a constant fire and advancing somewhat more to their left than the first attack occupied the garden hollow road & bush in great force

Taking advantage of the bush which we had not time to cut down the enemy were able to advance under cover close to our wall and in this part soon held one side of the wall while we held the other.

A series of desperate assaults was made extending from the hospital along the wall as far as the bush reached, but each was most splendidly met and repulsed by our men with the bayonet. Corpl. Schiess N.N.C. greatly distinguishing himself by his conspicuous gallantry.

The fire from the rocks behind us, though badly directed, took us completely in reverse and was so heavy that we had suffered very severely, and about 6 pm were forced to retire behind the retrenchment of biscuit boxes.

All this time the enemy had been attempting to force the hospital and shortly after set fire to its roof.

The Garrison of the hospital defended it room by room, bringing out all the sick who could be moved before they retired –

Privates Williams, **Hook, R. Jones** and **W.** Jones 24th. Regt. being the last men to leave holding the doorway with the bayonet their own ammunition being expended.

From the want of interior communication and the burning of the house it was impossible to save all – With most heartfelt sorrow I regret we could not save these poor fellows from their terrible fate.

Seeing the hospital burning and the desperate attempts of the enemy to fire the roof of the stores, we converted two mealie bag heaps, into a sort of redoubt which gave a second line of fire all round Asst. Commy. Dunne working hard at this though much exposed, and rendering valuable assistance.

As darkness came on we were completely surrounded and after several attempts had been gallantly repulsed were eventually forced to retire to the middle and then inner wall of the Krall on our East. The position we then had we retained throughout.

A desultory fire was kept up all night and several assaults were attempted and repulsed; the vigour of the attack continuing until after midnight, our men firing with the greatest coolness did not waste a single shot; the light afforded by the burning hospital being of great help to us.

About 4 am 23rd. inst. the firing ceased and at daybreak the enemy were out of sight over the hill to the South West

We patrolled the ground collecting the arms of the dead Zulus and – strengthened our defences as much as possible

We were removing the thatch from the roof of the stores, when about 7 am a large body of the enemy appeared on the hills to the SW. –

I sent a friendly Kaffir who had come in shortly before, with a note to the Officer Commanding at Helpmakaar asking for help.

About 8 am the third column appeared in sight the enemy who had been gradually advancing, falling back as they approached I consider the enemy who attacked us to have numbered about 3,000 (three thousand).

We killed about 350 (three hundred & fifty)

Of the steadiness and gallant behaviour of the whole garrison I cannot speak too highly.

I wish especially to bring to your notice the conduct of

Lieut Bromhead 2/24th. Regt. and the splendid behaviour of his company B 2/24th.

Surgeon Reynolds AMD in his constant attention to the wounded under fire where they fell

Acting Commt. Officer Dalton to whose energy much of our defences were due and who was severely wounded while gallantly assisting in the defence

Asst. Commy Dunne

Actg store keeper Byrne (Killed)

Col Sergt. Bourne, 2/24th.

Sergt. Williams 2/24th. (wounded dangerously since dead)

Sergt. Windridge 2/24th.

Corpl. Schiess 2/3 Natal Native Contgt (wounded)

1395 Private Williams 2/24th.	**Private Hook 2/24th.**
593 Private **W.** Jones 2/24th.	**716 Private Jones 2/24th.**
Private McMahon A.H.C.	**Private Roy 1/24th.**

The following return shows the number present at Rorke's Drift 22nd Jany. 1879

	Officers	NCO + men	Sick Officers	Sick NCO + men	Total
Staff		1			1
Royal Artillery		1		3	4
Royal Engineers	1	1			2
3rd Buffs		1			1
1/24th. Regt.		6		5	11
2/24th. **B (Compy)** 17 casuals sick	1	81		17	99
90th. Lt. Infantry				1	1
Commt. & Transport Dept.	3	1			4
A.M.D.	1	3			4
Chaplain	1				
Natal Mounted Police				3	3
Natal Native Contgt.	1			6	7
Ferryman		1			1
	8	96	0	35	139

The following is a list of the killed

Sergt.	Maxfield	2/24	Regt.
Pte	Scanlon	"	"
"	Hayden	"	"
"	Adams	"	"
"	Cole	"	"
"	Fagan	"	"
"	Chick	"	"

1398 Pte Williams 2/24 Regt.
Pte Nicolls 1/24 "
" Horrigan 1/24 "
" Jenkins 1/24 "
Mr Byrne Commt Dept.
Trooper Hunter N.M. Police
" Anderson N.N.C.
1 Pte (Native) "

Total 15
12 wounded * of whom two have since died
viz, Sergt. Williams, 2/24th. Regt
Private Beckett, 1/24th. "

Making a total killed of 17

* List already forwarded by Medical Officer

Herewith is appended a plan of the buildings showing our lines of defence
The points of the compass referred to in this report are as shown in sketch approximately magnetic.

I have the honor to be
Your obedient servant
John R.M. Chard
Lieut R.E.

To Col Glyn CB.
Comg 3rd. Column

11b. *Batley Reporter and Guardian,* 1 March 1879

The Fighting at Rorke's Drift.

Among the letters received at Aldershot Camp, yesterday, from South Africa, was one from an officer attached to Colonel Glyn's column, who, writing on the 27th January, says: – "We arrived too late to be of service. The sight I witnessed at the Drift exceeds anything I saw during the Mutiny. I could hardly recognise Chard, for he had his tunic off, and was begrimed with powder. Broomhead and his people must have fought like demons. Their only protection against the Zulus consisted of meal bags, and they were so low that anyone who had pluck enough could have jumped over them …"

11c. *Natal Colonist* (South Africa), 17 May 1879

Rumoured Death Of Major Chard, R.E.

We were sorry to hear a rumour in town yesterday, based evidently on pretty liable authority, that Major Chard, R.E., had died at Helpmakaar of fever. It is quite unnecessary to remind our readers who Major Chard is. If it should transpire that the statement is correct, another very sad incident has to be added to the many melancholy events connected to the war.

11d. Extract from an unidentified 'rival' Natal newspaper, c. May 1879

Major Chard, R.E.

The *Colonist* on Saturday, stated it was sorry to hear, on good authority, that Major Chard, one of the heroes of Rorke's Drift was dead. The report, we are glad to say, was quite unfounded, and was brought to us on Friday. We found however, on enquiry at the proper quarters, that there was no foundation for it. Major Chard is in hospital, and is, we are glad to hear, recovering from the attack of fever, from which he has recently been suffering.

11e. *Natal Colonist,* 22 May 1879

Major Chard, V.C.

It is with very great pleasure that we are able to contradict the report of the death of this valiant soldier, to which we reluctantly gave currency, although, only as a report, not a fact, as amiable contemporaries assert. We are glad to state that he is now reported nearly well, and will shortly resume his duties. Such men can be ill spared.

11f. *The Mail,* London, 6 June 1879

Isandlana.
To the Editor.

Sir, In a letter which I have lately received from Major Chard, R.E., V.C., dated Ladysmith, April 13, there occurs the following passage: –

"The day after the column left the Drift I got an order to send my men at once to the camp (Isandlana) of the General. I took them out in the waggon and rode out myself, the orders for me not having been sent. When I arrived at the camp the troops (white men), were in column about a mile or so out of camp. Before Durnford came up there was scarcely anybody in camp. I could see crowds of Zulus moving on the distant hills. I looked at the orders, saw that I ought to be at Rorke's Drift, and seeing the Zulus moving so far to the left was afraid they might be going to make a dash at the Drift. On my way back I met Colonel Durnford about a quarter of a mile from camp, at the head of his mounted men. I told him what I had seen, and then took several orders from him all along his line."

This extract of a letter from an eye witness, whose name is a guarantee for the accuracy of the statement, seems to me to set to rest the disputed question as to whether Colonel Durnford was or was not responsible for the moving of the troops out of camp.

I do not know why this evidence was not produced before the Court of Inquiry; possibly it was because Major Chard was at the time prostrate with fever.

I have the honour to be, Sir, your obedient servant,

Henry D. Crozier, Major, Royal Engineers.
Taunton, June 4.

11g. *Bristol Mercury and Daily Post,* 20 September 1879

Major Chard.
A Cape Town correspondent of the Daily News writes on the 1st inst: – Major Chard, V.C., one of the heroes of Rorke's Drift, embarked on Saturday by the Egypt for England without any attempt whatever being made in the colony to acknowledge the services he rendered in January last. The colonists were too much occupied with feasting and congratulating their own volunteers – those who have never ceased to cry 'Let us return home' – to pay the slightest tribute of even respect to the man who saved Natal from fire and the sword.

11h. *Western Morning News,* 18 November 1879 [Chard is speaking on the occasion of the presentation of a Sword of Honour in Plymouth]

Public Welcome and Presentation to Major Chard, V.C.
"… I cannot but ever feel grateful to those brave fellows to whose devoted gallantry I owe the fact of my being here to-day … You all know how they behaved, and how one and all, they proved themselves ready to sacrifice their lives, if necessary, for their Queen and their country … I read in the paper as I came down in the train to-day of how Bromhead and myself had a tankard of beer together after the morning of Rorke's Drift; the story is very true, except about the tankard. You may imagine there were very few tankards there. We had a bottle of beer together, and you may fancy how we congratulated each other on coming safe out of that business …"

"… The Zulus were an enemy that it was some credit to us to have defeated; they showed a courage that could not be excelled by anybody, and their military organisation and their discipline might have given a lesson to more civilised nations. Cruelly savage as they were the Zulus were a gallant enemy, and I cannot understand for one moment how Englishmen could for one instant credit the report that appeared and the stories that were circulated of cruelties perpetrated, or, at all events, permitted, by British officers. I don't think it necessary for me to say they were false …"

11i. An account of the defence of Rorke's Drift, compiled at the personal request of H.M. Queen Victoria. Submitted to the Queen at Windsor Castle, 21 February 1880. The subheadings shown in **bold** are actually written in the margin of the original document [The Royal Archives, Windsor, by kind permission of Her Majesty Queen Elizabeth II]

RORKE'S DRIFT.

(**Start from Durban.**) Early in January 1879, shortly after the arrival of the 5th Compy. Royal Engineers at Durban, an order came from Lord Chelmsford directing that an officer, and a few good men of the R.E., with mining implements, etc., should join the 3rd Column as soon as possible.

I was consequently sent on in advance of the company, with a light mule wagon, containing the necessary tools, etc., and in which the men could also ride on level ground; with a Corporal, 3 Sappers and one Driver, my batman, who rode one, and looked after my horses.

The wagon was driven by a Cape black man, with a Natal Kaffir lad as vorlooper.

(Bad Roads.) The roads were so bad, that in spite of all our exertions, our progress was slow, and although we got a fresh team at PieterMaritzburg, we did not reach Rorke's Drift until the morning of the 19th Jany. 1879.

(Arrive at Rorke's Drift) The 3rd Column was encamped on the other side (left bank) of the river Buffalo, and the wagons were still crossing in the Ponts.

I pitched my two tents on the right (Natal) bank of the river, near the Ponts, and close to the store accumulated there for keeping them in repair.

(3rd Column leave Rorke's Drift.) On the 20th Jany., the 3rd Column broke up its camp on the Buffalo River and marched to Isandhlwana, where it encamped, and the same evening, or following morning,

(Durnford arrives at Rorke's Drift) Colonel Durnford's force arrived and took up its camp near where the 3rd Column had been.

(Ponts) There were two large Ponts at the river, one of which only was in working order, and my sappers were during this time working at the other, which was nearly finished, to get it also in working order.

(My Sappers ordered to Isandhlwana) Late in the evening of the 21st Jany., I received an order from the 3rd Column, to say that the men of the R.E., who had lately arrived, were to proceed to the camp at Isandhlwana at once.

I had received no orders concerning myself.

I reported this to Major Spalding, who was now in command at Rorke's Drift, and also pointed out to him that the sappers leaving, there were no means at my disposal for putting the Ponts in working order, or keeping them so.

Major Spalding had also received no orders respecting me, except that I was to select a suitable position protecting the Ponts, for Capt. Rainforths Compy. 1/24th to entrench itself.

I consequently asked, and obtained, permission from Major Spalding, to go to the camp at Isandhlwana and see the orders. –

(Take sappers to Isandhlwana.) On the morning of the 22nd January, I put the corpl and 3 sappers in the empty wagon, with their field kits, etc., to take them to the camp of the 3rd Column; and also rode out myself.

The road was very heavy in some places, and the wagon went slowly; so I rode on in advance, arrived at the Isandhlwana camp,

(Arrive at Isandhlwana) went to the Head Quarter tent, and got a copy of the orders as affecting me, & found that I was to keep the Ponts &c. in working order, & also the road between Helpmakaar and Rorke's Drift, and the orders also particularly stated that my duties lay on the right bank of the river Buffalo.

A N.C.O. of the 24th Regt. lent me a field glass, which was a very good one, and I also looked with my own,

(See the Enemy) and could see the enemy moving on the distant hills, and apparently in great force.

Large numbers of them moving to my left, until the lion hill of Isandhlwana, on my left as I looked at them, hid them from my view. The idea struck me that they might be moving in the direction between the camp and Rorke's Drift, and prevent my getting back, and also that they might be going to make a dash at the ponts.

(Meet Durnford) Seeing what my duties were, I left the camp, and a quarter of a mile, or less, out of it, met Col. Durnford R.E., riding at the head of his mounted men.

I told him what I had seen, and took some orders, and a message all along his line, at his request.

At the foot of the hill, I met my men in the wagon, and made them get out, and walk up the hill with Durnford's men.

(Return to Rorke's Drift) I brought the wagon back with me to Rorke's Drift, where on arrival I found the following order had been issued. The copy below was given me, & preserved from the fact of its being in my pocket during the fight.

COPY

Camp Rorke's Drift
22nd Jany. 1879

Camp Morning Orders

1. The force under Lt Col Durnford, R.E., having departed, a Guard of 6 privates and 1 NCO will be furnished by the detachment 2/24th Regt. on the Ponts.

A Guard of 50 armed natives will likewise be furnished by Capt. Stevenson's detachment at the same spot. – The Ponts will be invariably drawn over to the Natal side at night.

This duty will cease on the arrival of Capt. Rainforth's Company, 1/24th Regt.

2. In accordance with Para 19 Regulations for Field Forces in South Africa, Capt. Rainforth's Company, 1/24th Regt., will entrench itself on the spot assigned to it by Column Orders per. – dated –

(sd). H. Spalding, Major,
Commanding.

The Guard as detailed was over the Ponts.
Capt. Rainforth's company had not arrived.

(Report to Spalding) I went at once to Major Spalding on arrival, told him what I had seen, and pointed out to him that in the event of an attack on the Ponts, it would be impossible with 7 men (not counting the natives) to make an effective defence.

(According to the orders, Capt. Rainforths compy. should have been already at Rorke's Drift.) Major Spalding told me he was going over to Helpmakaar, and would see about getting it down at once.

Just as I was about to ride away he said to me "Which of you is senior, you or Bromhead"?

I said, "I dont know."

He went back into his tent and looked at an Army list, and coming back, said –

(Left in commd by Spalding.) "I see you are senior, so you will be in charge, although of course nothing will happen, and I shall be back again this evening early."

I then went down to my tent by the river, had some lunch comfortably, and was writing a letter home, when my attention was called to two horsemen galopping towards us from the direction of Isandhlwana.

(2 Fugitives from Isandhlwana arrive.) From their gesticulations, and their shouts, when they were near enough to be heard, we saw that something was the matter, and on taking them over the river, one of them, Lieut. Adendorff of Lonsdale's

(Lt Adendorff N.N.C.) Regiment Natal Native Contingent, asking if I was an officer, jumped off his horse, took me on one side, and told me, that the camp was in the hands of the Zulus, and the army destroyed; that scarcely a man had got away to tell the tale, and that probably Lord Chelmsford and the rest of the column had shared the same fate.

His companion, a Carbineer, confirmed his story.

He was naturally very excited, and I am afraid I did not, at first, quite believe him, and intimated that he probably had not remained to see what <u>did</u> occur.

I had the saddle put on my horse, and while I was talking to Lieut. Adendorff, **(message from Bromhead.)** a messenger arrived from Lieut. Bromhead, who was with his Company at his little camp near the Commt. Stores, to ask me to come up at once.

I gave the order to inspan the wagon, and put all the stores, tents, &c., we could into it. I posted the sergt. and six men on the high ground over the

Ponts, behind a natural wall of rocks, forming a strong position from which there was a good view over the river & ground in front, with orders to wait until I came or sent for them.

The guard of natives had left some time before and had not been relieved. **(Ride up to Rorke's House.)** I gallopped up at once to the Commissariat Stores, and found that a pencil note had been sent from the 3rd Column by Capt. Allan Gardner to state that the enemy were advancing **(News of Enemy Advancing)** in force against our post. –

(work commenced) Lieut. Bromhead had with the assistance of Mr Dalton, Dr Reynolds and the other officers present, commenced barricading; and loopholing the Store building and the Missionary's house, which was used as a Hospital, and connecting the defence of the two buildings by walls of mealie bags, and two wagons that were on the ground.

(Native Contingent) The Native Contingent, under their officer, Capt. Stephenson, were working hard at this with our own men, and the walls were rapidly progressing.

(Letter sent by Bromhead to O.C. Helpmakaar.) A letter describing what had happened had been sent by Bromhead by two men of the Mounted Infantry, who had arrived fugitives from Isandhlwana to the Officer Commanding at Helpmakaar.

These two men crossed the river at Fugitives Drift, with some others, and as they have since reported to me, came to give notice of what had happened, to us at Rorkes Drift, of their own accord, and without orders from anyone.

(Consult with Bromhead & Dalton) I held a consultation with Lieut. Bromhead, and with Mr Dalton, whose energy, intelligence and gallantry were of the greatest service to us, and whom, as I said in my report at the time, and I am sure Bromhead would unite with me in saying again now, I cannot sufficiently thank for his valuable services.

I went round the position with them and then rode down to the Ponts where I found everything ready for a start, ponts in midstream, hawsers & cables sunk &c.

(Daniells and Sergt. Milne 3rd Buffs) It was at this time that the Pontman Daniells, and Sergt. Milne, 3rd Buffs, who had been employed for some time in getting the ponts in order & working them under Lieut. MacDowell, RE (killed at Isandhlwana), offered to defend the Ponts, moored in the middle of the river, from their decks with a few men.

(Sergt. Williams 24th) Sergeant Williams 24th and his little guard were quite ready to join them.

(Arrive at Commt. Store.) We arrived at the Commissariat Store about 3.30 p.m.

(Some of Durnford's Horse arrive) Shortly afterwards an officer of Durnford's Horse reported his arrival from Isandhlwana, and I requested him to observe the movements, and check the advance, of the enemy as much as possible until forced to fall back.

I saw each man at his post, and then the work went on again.

(Fugitives) Several fugitives from the camp arrived, and tried to impress upon us the madness of an attempt to defend the place.

Who they were I do not know, but it is scarcely necessary for me to say that there were no officers of H.M. Army among them.

They stopped the work very much – it being impossible to prevent the men getting around them in little groups to hear their story.

They proved the truth of their belief in what they said, by leaving us to our fate, and in the state of mind they were in, I think our little garrison was as well without them.

(Lt. Adendorff.) As far as I know, but one of the fugitives remained with us – Lieut. Adendorff, whom I have before mentioned.

He remained to assist in the defence, and from a loophole in the store building, flanking the wall and Hospital, his rifle did good service.

(Sergt. Windridge 24th Regt.) There were several casks of rum in the Store building, and I gave strict orders to Sergt. Windridge, 24th Regt., who was in charge, (acting as issuer of Commt stores to the troops), that the spirit was not to be touched, the man posted nearest it was to be considered on guard over it, and after giving fair warning, was to shoot without altercation anyone who attempted to force his post, and Sergt. Windridge being there was to see this carried out.

Sergt. Windridge showed great intelligence and energy in arranging the stores for the defence of the Commt. store, forming loopholes, &c.

(Rev. Geo. Smith) The Revd. George Smith, Vicar of Estcourt, Natal, and acting Army Chaplain, went for a walk (before the news of the disaster reached us) to the top of the Oscarberg, the hill behind Rorke's Drift.
(Mr Witt.) Mr. Witt, the missionary, went with him, or met him there. They went to see what could be seen in the direction of the Isandhlwana camp.
(Smith) He saw the force of the enemy which attacked us at Rorke's Drift, cross the river in three bodies – and after snuff-taking, and other ceremonies, advance in our direction. – He had been watching them for a long time with interest, and thought they were our own Native Contingent.

There were two mounted men leading them, and he did not realise that they were the enemy, until they were near enough for him to see that these two men also had black faces.

He came running down the hill, and was agreeably surprised to find that we were getting ready for the enemy. Mr. Witt, whose wife and family were in a lonely house not very far off, rode off, taking with him a sick officer, who was very ill in the hospital, and only just able to ride.

Mr Smith, however, although he might well have left, elected to remain with us, and during the attack, did good service in supplying the men with ammunition.
(Sound of Firing) About 4.20 p.m. the sound of firing was heard behind the Oscarberg.

The officer of Durnford's returned reporting the enemy close upon us, and that his men would not obey his orders but were going off to Helpmakaar,
(Durnford's Horse leave) and I saw them, about 100 in number, going off in that direction.

I have seen these same men behave so well since, that I have spoken with several of their conduct – and they all said as their excuse, that Durnford was killed, and it was no use.
(Native Contingent Desert.) About the same time Capt. Stephenson's detachment of Natal Native Contingent left us – probably most fortunately for us.

I am sorry to say that their Officer, who had been doing good service in getting his men to work, also deserted us.

We seemed very few, now all these people had gone, and I saw that our line of defence was too extended,

(Retrenchment made) and at once commenced a retrenchment of biscuit boxes, so as to get a place we could fall back upon if we could not hold the whole.
(Private Hitch 24th) Private Hitch 24th was on top of the thatch roof of the Commt. Store keeping a look-out.

He was severely wounded early in the evening, but notwithstanding,
(Corpl. Allen 24th) with Corpl Allen 24th who was also wounded, continued to do good service, and they both when incapacitated by their wounds from using their rifles, still continued under fire serving their comrades with ammunition.
(Attack commenced 4.30 p.m.) We had not completed a wall two boxes high when, about 4.30 p.m., Hitch cried out that the enemy was in sight, and we saw them, apparently 500 or 600 in number, come around the hill to our South (the Oscarberg) and advance at a run against our South wall.

We opened fire on them, between five & six hundred yards, at first a little wild, but only for a shot or two, a chief on horseback
(Private Dunbar 24th) was dropped by Private Dunbar 24th, the men were quite steady, and the Zulus began to fall very thick.

However it did not seem to stop them at all, although they took advantage of the cover, and ran stooping with their faces near the ground. It seemed as if nothing would stop them, and they rushed on in spite of their heavy loss, to within 50 yards of the wall, when they were taken in flank
(Zulus checked) by the fire from the end wall of the store building, and met with such a heavy direct fire from the mealie wall, and Hospital at the same time, that they were checked as if by magic.

They occupied the Cook house ovens, banks and other cover, but the greater number, without stopping, moved to their left around the Hospital, and made a rush at the end of the Hospital,
(1st Assault) and at our N.W. line of mealie bags.

There was a short but desperate struggle, during which Mr. Dalton shot a Zulu, who was in the act of assegaing a corpl. of the Army Hospital Corps, the muzzle of whose rifle he had seized, and with Lieut. Bromhead and many of the men behaved with great gallantry.

The Zulus forced us back from that part of the wall immediately in front of the Hospital, but after suffering very severely in the struggle were driven back into the bush around our position.

(Main body of Enemy) The main body of the enemy were close behind the first force which appeared, and had lined the ledge of rocks and caves in the Oscarberg overlooking us, and about three or four hundred yards to our south, from where they kept up a constant fire. Advancing somewhat more to their left than the first attack, they occupied the garden, hollow road, and bush in great force.

The bush grew close to our wall & we had not had time to cut it down.

The enemy were thus able to advance under cover close to our wall, and in this part, soon held one side of the wall, while we held the other.

(Series of Assaults) A series of desperate assaults was made, on the Hospital, and extending from the Hospital, as far as the bush reached; but each was most splendidly met, and repulsed by our men, with the bayonet. Each time as the attack was repulsed by us, the Zulus close to us, seemed to vanish in the bush, those some little distance off, keeping up a fire all the time.

Then, as if moved by a single impulse, they rose up in the bush as thick as possible, rushing madly up to the wall, (some of them being already close to it), seizing, where they could, the muzzles of our men's rifles, or their bayonets, and attempting to use their assegais and to get over the wall.

A rapid rattle of fire from our rifles, stabs with the bayonet, and in a few moments the Zulus were driven back, disappearing in the bush as before, and keeping up their fire. – A brief interval, and the attack would be again made, and repulsed in the same manner.

Over and over again this happened, our men behaving with the greatest coolness and gallantry.

It is impossible for one individual to see all, but I particularly myself noticed the behaviour of Col. Sergt. Bourne 24th, Sergt. Williams 24th, Corpl. Scheiss N.N.C., Corpl. Lyons 24th, Private McMahon A.H.C., Privates Roy, Deacon, Bush, Cole, Jenkins 24th, and many others.

Our fire at the time of these rushes of the Zulus was very rapid – Mr. Dalton dropping a man, each time he fired his rifle, while Bromhead and myself used our revolvers.

The fire from the rocks and caves on the hill behind us

(Fire from Oscarberg takes us in reverse.) was kept up all this time and took us completely in reverse, and although very badly directed, many shots came among us and caused us some loss – and at about 6 p.m.

(Enemy extends his attack) the enemy extending their attack further to their left, I feared seriously would get in over our wall behind the biscuit boxes.

I ran back with 2 or 3 men to this part of the wall and was immediately joined by Bromhead with 2 or 3 more. The enemy stuck to this assault most tenaciously and on their repulse; and retiring into the bush, I called all the men inside our retrenchment – and the enemy immediately occupied the wall we had abandoned and used it as a breastwork to fire over.

(Mr Byrne killed) Mr. Byrne, acting Commissariat Officer, & who had behaved with great coolness and gallantry, was killed instantaneously shortly before this, by a bullet through the head, just after he had given a drink of water to a wounded man of the N.N.C.

(Enemy fire and Break into Hospl.) All this time the enemy had been attempting to force the Hospital and had at length set fire to its roof and got in at the far end.

I had tried to impress upon the men in the Hospital the necessity for making a communication right through the building – unfortunately this was not done.

Probably at the time the men could not see the necessity, and doubtless also there was no time to do it.

Without in the least detracting from the gallant fellows who defended the Hospital, and I hope I shall not be misunderstood in saying so – I have always regretted, as I did then, the absence of my four poor sappers, who had only left that morning, for Isandhlwana and arrived just to be killed.

(The gallant Defence of the Hospital.) The garrison of the hospital defended it with the greatest gallantry, room by room, bringing out all the sick that could be moved, and breaking through some of the partitions while the Zulus were in the building with them.

(Private Williams, Hook, R. Jones, W. Jones 24th.) Privates Williams, Hook, R. Jones & W Jones being the last to leave and holding the doorways with the bayonet their ammunition being expended.

Private Williams' bayonet was wrenched off his rifle by a Zulu, but with the other men he still managed with the muzzle of his rifle to keep the enemy at bay.

(Reynolds) Surgeon Reynolds carried his arms full of ammunition to the Hospital, a bullet striking his helmet as he did so.

But we were too busily engaged outside to be able to do much, and with the Hospital on fire, and no free communication, nothing could have saved it.
(Sergt. Maxfield killed.) Sergeant Maxfield 24th might have been saved, but he was delirious with fever, refused to move and resisted the attempts to move him.

He was assegaied before our men's eyes.

Seeing the Hospital burning, and the attempts of the enemy to fire the roof of the Store, (one man was shot, I believe by Lt Adendorff, who had a light almost touching the thatch)
(Redoubt of Mealie Bags.) we converted two large heaps of mealie bags into a sort of redoubt, which gave a second line of fire all around, and formed a strong position to hold, and rally round, in case the store building had to be abandoned, or the enemy broke through elsewhere.
(Dunne.) Asst. Commy Dunne worked hard at this; from his height, being a tall man, he was much exposed, in addition to the fact that the heaps were high above our walls, and that most of the Zulu bullets went high.
(Trooper Hunter N.M.P. Killed.) Trooper Hunter, Natal Mounted Police, escaping from the Hospital, stood still for a moment hesitating which way to go, dazed by the glare of the burning Hospital, and the firing that was going on all around. – He was assegaied before our eyes, the Zulu who killed him immediately afterwards falling.
(Dalton severely wounded.) While firing from behind the biscuit boxes, Dalton, who had been using his rifle with deadly effect, and by his quickness and coolness had been the means of saving many men's lives, was shot through the body.

I was standing near him at the time, and he handed me his rifle so coolly, that I had no idea until afterwards of how severely he was wounded. – He waited quite quietly for me to take the cartridges he had left out of his pockets.

We put him inside our mealie sack redoubt, building it up around him.
(Good shooting of Pte. Dunbar 24th) About this time I noticed Private Dunbar 24th make some splendid shooting, seven or eight Zulus falling on the ledge of rocks in the Oscarberg to as many consecutive shots by him.
(Corpl Lyons 24th) I saw Corpl. Lyons hit by a bullet which lodged in his spine, and fall between an opening we had left in the wall of biscuit boxes. I thought he was killed, but looking up he said,

"Oh, Sir! you are not going to leave me here like a dog?" – We pulled him in and laid him down behind the boxes – where he was immediately looked to by Reynolds.

(Corpl Scammle N.N.C.) Corpl. Scammle of the Natal Native Contingent, who was badly wounded through the shoulder, staggered out under fire again, from the Store building where he had been put, and gave me all his cartridges, which in his wounded state he could not use.

(Pte Jenkins 24th) While I was intently watching to get a fair shot at a Zulu who appeared to be firing rather well, Private Jenkins, 24th, saying look out Sir, gave my head a duck down just as a bullet whizzed over it. – He had noticed a Zulu who was quite near in another direction, taking a deliberate aim at me.

For all the man could have known, the shot might have been directed at himself.

I mention these facts to show how well the men behaved and how loyally worked together.

(Corpl Schiess N.N.C.) Corpl. Schiess, Natal Native Contingent, who was a patient in Hospital, with a wound in the foot, which caused him great pain, behaved with the greatest coolness and gallantry throughout the attack, and at this time creeping out a short distance along the wall we had abandoned, and slowly raising himself, to get a shot at some of the enemy who had been particularly annoying, his hat was blown off by a shot from a Zulu the other side of the wall.

He immediately jumped up, bayonetted the Zulu and shot a second, and bayonetted a third who came to their assistance, and then returned to his place.

(Darkness.) As darkness came on we were completely surrounded. The Zulus wrecking the camp of the company 24th and my wagon which had been left outside, in spite of the efforts of my batman Driver Robson (the only man of the Royal Engineers with us), who had directed his particular attention to keeping the Zulus off this wagon in which were, as he described it, "our things."

They also attacked the East end of our position, and after being several times repulsed, eventually got into the kraal,

(Enemy drive us out of Kraal.) which was strongly built with high walls, and drove us to the middle, and then to the inner wall of the kraal – the enemy occupying the middle wall as we abandoned it.

This wall was too high for them to use it effectively to fire over, and a Zulu no sooner showed his head over it, than he was dropped, being so close that it was impossible to miss him.

(Troops from Helpmakaar.) Shortly before this, some of the men said they saw the red-coats coming on the Helpmakaar road.

The rumour passed quickly round – I could see nothing of the sort myself, but several men said they could.

A cheer was raised, and the enemy seemed to pause, to know what it meant –

But there was no answer to it, and darkness came on.

It is very strange that this report should have arisen amongst us, for the two companies 24th from Helpmakaar, did come down to the foot of the hill, but not, I believe, in sight of us.

They marched back to Helpmakaar on the report of Rorkes Drift having fallen.

After the first onslaught, the most formidable of the enemy's attacks was just before we retired behind our line of biscuit boxes, and for a short time after it, – when they had gained great confidence by their success on the Hospital.

Although they kept their positions behind the walls we had abandoned, and kept up a heavy fire from all sides until about 12 o'clock, they did not actually charge up in a body to get over our wall after about 9 or 10 o'clock.

After this time it became very dark although the Hospital roof was still burning – it was impossible from below to see what was going on, and Bromhead and myself getting up on the mealy sack redoubt, kept an anxious watch on all sides.

(Enemy in force all around.) The enemy were now in strong force all around us, and every now and then, a confused shout of "Usutu" from many voices, seemed to show that they were going to attack from one side and immediately the same thing would happen on the other, leaving us in doubt as to where they meant to attack.

(Fire slackens) About midnight or a little after the fire slackened, and after that, although they kept us constantly on the alert, by feigning, as before, to come on at different points, the fire was of a desultory character. Our men were careful, and only fired when they could see a fair chance. The flame of the burning hospital was now getting low, and as pieces of the roof fell, or hitherto unburnt parts of the thatch ignited, the flames would blaze up illuminating our helmets & faces. – a few shots from the Zulus, replied to by our men – again silence, broken only by the same thing repeatedly happening.

This sort of thing went on until about 4 a.m. and we were anxiously waiting for day break and the renewal of the attack, which their comparative, and at length complete silence, led us to expect.

(Daybreak.) But at daybreak the enemy were out of sight, over the hill to our South West.

(A plucky Zulu) One Zulu had remained in the kraal and fired a shot among us (without doing any damage) as we stood up on the walls, and ran off in the direction of the River. Although many shots were fired at him as he ran, I am glad to say the plucky fellow got off.

(patrol around) Taking care not to be surprised by any ruse of the enemy, we patrolled the ground around the place, collecting the arms, and ammunition, of the dead Zulus.

(Curious Wounds) Some of the bullet wounds were very curious.

One man's head was split open, exactly as if done with an axe.

Another had been hit just between the eyes, the bullet carrying away the whole of the back of his head leaving his face perfect, as though it were a mask, only disfigured by the small hole made by the bullet passing through.

One of the wretches we found, one hand grasping a bench that had been dragged from the Hospital, and sustained thus in the position we found him in; while in the other hand, he still clutched the knife, with which he had mutilated one our poor fellows, over whom he was still leaning.

(Strengthen the Defences.) We increased the strength of our defences as much as possible, strengthening and raising our walls, putting sacks on the biscuit boxes, &c, and were removing the thatch from the roof of the Commt. Store, to avoid being burnt out in case of another attack,

(Enemy re-appear) when at about 7 A.M., a large body of the enemy, (I believe the same who had attacked us), appeared on the hills to the South West.

I thought at the time that they were going to attack us, but from what I now know from Zulus, and also of the number we put hors de combat, I do not think so.

I think that they came up on the high ground to observe Lord Chelmsford's advance; for from there, they could see the Column, long before it came in sight of us.

(Friendly Kaffir sent to Helpmakaar) A frightened & fugitive Kaffir came in shortly before, and I sent for Daniells the Pontman, who could speak Zulu a little, to interview him.

Daniells had armed himself with Spalding's sword, which he flourished in so wild and eccentric a manner, that the poor wretch thought his last hour was come.

He professed to be friendly, and to have escaped from Isandhlwana, and I sent him with a note to the officer commanding at Helpmakaar, explaining our situation, and asking for help; for now, although the men were in excellent spirits, and each man had a good supply of ammunition in his pouches or pockets, we had only about a box and a half left besides, and at this time we had no definite knowledge of what had happened, and I myself did not know that the part of the Column with Lord Chelmsford had not taken any part in the action at Isandhlwana, or whether in the Camp being taken he had fallen back on Helpmakaar.

The enemy remained on the hill, and still more of them appeared, when about 8 A.M.

(3rd Column appears.) the Column came in sight, and the enemy disappeared again. There were a great many of our Native Levies with the column, and the number of red coats seemed so few, that at first we had grave doubts that the force approaching was the enemy.

We improvised a flag, and our signals were soon replied to from the Column.

The mounted men crossed the Drift, and gallopped up to us, headed by Major Cecil Russell, and Lieut. Walsh, and were received by us with a hearty cheer.

(Lord Chelmsford arrives) Lord Chelmsford, with his staff, shortly after rode up, and thanked us all with much emotion for the defence we had made.

The column arrived, crossing by the Ponts, and we then had a busy time in making a strong position for the night.

I was glad to seize an opportunity to wash my face in a muddy puddle, in company with Private Bush 24th, whose face was covered with blood from a wound in the nose, caused by the bullet which had passed through & killed Private Cole 24th.

With the politeness of a soldier, he lent me his towell, or, rather a very dirty half of one, before using it himself, & I was very glad to accept it.

(A bottle of beer with Bromhead.) In wrecking the stores in my wagon, the Zulus had brought to light a forgotten bottle of beer, and Bromhead & I drank it with mutual congratulations on having come safely out of so much danger.

(My wagon driver's escape.) My wagon driver, a cape (coloured) man, lost his courage on hearing the first firing around the hill. – He let loose his mules, and retreated concealing himself in one of the caves of the Oscarberg.

He saw the Zulus run by him and, to his horror, some of them entered the cave he was in, and lying down commenced firing at us.

The poor wretch was crouching in the darkness; in the far depths of the cave, afraid to speak or move, and our bullets came into the cave, actually killing one of the Zulus. – He did not know from whom he was in the most danger – friends or foes, – and came down in the morning, looking more dead than alive.

The mules were recovered; they were quietly grazing by the riverside.

(My vorlooper's escape) On my journey homewards, on arriving at the railway station, Durban, I asked a porter to get me some Kaffirs to carry my baggage to the Hotel. – He sent several, and the first to come running up was my vorlooper boy, who had taken me up to Rorke's Drift. – He stopped short and looked very frightened, and I believe at first thought he saw my ghost.

I seized him, to prevent his running away, and when he saw that I was flesh and blood, he became reassured. He said he thought I had been killed, and upon my asking him how he thought I got away. He said (the solution of the mystery just striking him), "I know, you rode away on the other horse".

As far as I could learn and according to his own story – the boy had taken the horse I rode up from the river to the Commt. stores, and wild with terror, had ridden it to PieterMaritzburg without stopping, where he gave it over to the Transport people – But having no certificate to say who he was, they took the horse from him and would not give him any employment.

(Escapes from the Hospital) During the fight there were some very narrow escapes from the burning Hospital.

(Private Waters 24th.) Private Waters, 24th Regt. told me, that he secreted himself in a cupboard, in the room he was defending, and from it shot several Zulus inside the Hospital. – He was wounded in the arm, and remained in the cupboard until the heat and smoke were so great, that they threatened to suffocate him. – Wrapping himself in a cloak, or skirt of a dress, he found in the cupboard, he rushed out into the darkness, and made his way into the cookhouse. – the Zulus were occupying this, and firing at us from the wall nearest us.

It was too late to retreat, so he crept softly to the fireplace and, standing up in the chimney, blacked his face and hands with the soot. – He remained there until the Zulus left.

He was very nearly shot in coming out, one of our men at the wall raising his rifle to do so at the sight of his black face, and strange costume – but Waters cried out just in time to save himself.

He produced the bullet that wounded him, with pardonable pride, and was very amusing in his admiring description of Dr Reynold's skill in extracting it.

(Gunner Howard, R.A.) Gunner Howard, R.A. ran out of the burning hospital, through the enemy, and lay down on the upper side of the wall in front of our N Parapet. The bodies of several horses that were killed early in the evening were lying here, and concealed by these, by Zulu bodies & the long grass and bushes, he remained unseen with the Zulus all around him until they left in the morning.

(Private Beckett 24th) Private Beckett, 24th Regt. escaped from the hospital in the same direction – he was badly wounded with assegais in running through the enemy.

He managed to get away and conceal himself in the ditch of the Garden – where we found him next morning.

The poor fellow was so weak from loss of blood that he could not walk, and he died shortly afterwards.

(Mealie bag walls replaced.) Our mealie-bag walls were afterwards replaced by loopholed walls of stone, the work making rapid progress upon the arrival of half the 5th Compy. R.E. with Lieut. Porter.

As soon as the sappers arrived, we put a fence around, and a rough wood cross over, the graves of our poor men who were killed.

(Monument to the dead) This was afterwards replaced by a neat stone monument & inscription, by the 24th, who remained to garrison the place.

I have already, in my report, said, how gallantly all behaved, from Lieutenant Bromhead downwards, and I also mentioned those whom I had particularly noticed to have distinguished themselves.

(Number of Enemy killed.) On the day following, we buried 351 bodies of the enemy in graves not far from the Commt Buildings – many bodies were since discovered and buried, and when I was sick at Ladysmith one of our Sergeants, who came down there invalided from Rorke's Drift, where he had been employed in the construction of Fort Melvill – told me that many Zulu bodies were found in the caves and among the rocks, a long distance from the Mission house, when getting stone for that fort.

As, in my report, I underestimated the number we killed – so I believe I also underestimated the number of the enemy that attacked us – and from what I have since learnt I believe the Zulus must have numbered at least 4,000.

As the Revd. Geo. Smith said in a short account he wrote to a Natal Paper –

"Whatever signs of approval may be conferred upon the defenders of Rorkes Drift, from high quarters, they will never cease to remember the kind and heartfelt expressions of gratitude, which have fallen both from the columns of the Colonial Press, and from so many of the Natal Colonists themselves."

And to this may I add, that they will ever remember with heartfelt gratitude, the signs of approval that have been conferred upon them, by their Sovereign, and by the People and Press of England.

JOHN R.M. CHARD
Captain & Bt Major, RE
January 1880.

11j. *Western Morning News*, 6 November 1880

Major Chard on the Zulus.
Defence of Rorke's Drift.

Major Chard, R.E., V.C., lectured in the Plymouth Free School last evening in connection with the Christ Church, Plymouth, winter evening entertainments on "My Life in Zululand." The school was crowded …

… In charge of a detachment of Engineers, together with a company of the 24th Regiment, under Lieut. Bromhead, he was in January ordered to Rorke's Drift on the Buffalo river. He pitched his tents on the right bank of the river. On the 20th of the month the third column broke up its camp on the other side, and moved to Isandula. On the following morning, Colonel Durnford arrived, and encamped close to where the third column had been. He was left at the river in charge of the crossing arrangement, which consisted of two ponts, similar to the floating bridges we saw on the rivers here, and were moved by ropes. On the evening of the 21st he received an order for his sappers to join the head-quarter column as soon as possible. Having received no order respecting himself, he could not make out exactly what he had to do, and not being able to get on with the work he had in hand, because his men had been taken away, he got permission to go out with his men the following morning to the camp at Isandula to see the orders. He took the men out, and they reached the camp early in the morning. While he was there he could see the Zulu attack developing on the distant hills. Large numbers of the enemy were moving, and moving as far to the left that, as he stood looking at them, he thought it quite possible they might be going to make a dash for the Drift, where he was supposed to be. Having seen what his orders were, and that he had no business to be where he was, he moved back to Rorke's Drift. The sappers, poor fellows, only reached the camp just in time to be killed. He met Colonel Durnford arriving in the camp as he left, and told him what he had seen, took several orders from him, and returned to his own station.

Isandula, Major Chard, said, was a long hill, rising abruptly from west to east. The camp was on the southern slope; the road from Rorke's Drift passed over the western part of the hill, and a small koppie on the right of the hill was the place where the last stand was made by Durnford and the mounted men under him. What happened they all know, some 770 white men were killed, and about forty escaped over the river.

It was on the same day at about quarter past three as he was sitting in his tent at the riverside that he saw two men coming at a gallop from the direction of the Zulu side, who told him what had taken place at the camp. The mission station where the camp and stores were, was about a quarter of a mile from the riverside and the punts were some distance above the Drift and in deeper water. Illustrating the position of the mission station by a diagram on the black board, Major Chard showed the station with its kraals, garden and other enclosure, situated in an oblong patch of ground under a hill, with a ridge of rocks shelving off in front. Major Bromhead, who was in the upper side of the station with his company had heard of the massacre at the same time as he, from men who crossed lower down and on the other side of the mountain at a place known as Fugitive's Drift.

The part of the Zulu army which attacked them was that part which during the action had been in reserve. They came straight on from the action, crossed the river the other side of the mountain, and, after crossing, went through some customary, snuff taking, and so on, which were customary among them.

Mr Smith, who was a chaplain of the forces, had in the morning gone up in the top of this hill to see what was going on at the camp. They knew there was an action proceeding, but had no idea of what the result was to be. Mr Smith saw the Zulus come down to the river, and had an idea that they were our own Native Contingent. In fact, he was observing how well the men marched, and how beautifully everything was going on. He stood watching them on top of the hill until they came near enough for him to see that the two mounted men who were leading them had black faces, when of course he at once knew they were Zulus. He came running down to the camp, and was agreeably surprised to find that they were getting ready to receive them by connecting the mission house and kraal at one end and the hospital at the other into an oblong enclosure, the walls of which beyond the stout walls of the kraal, were formed of biscuit boxes and bags of mealies. Before they had quite finished the Zulus came in sight round the point of the hill. They had been firing, and as soon as the sound became distinct enough our Native allies, who had been very active in building up the walls, bolted altogether.

He was sorry to say their officer did the same immediately after, and he was a white man. When they left it was seen that the whole position could not be held, the wall being 35 yards long, and the buildings 70 feet and 38 feet wide. Accordingly, a wall of biscuit boxes was built, dividing the enclosure in two about half-way between the hospital and the kraal. They had nearly completed it when a private of the 24th, who was on the top of one of the buildings shouted, "Here they come," and they saw coming round the hill on the southern side a sort of advance guard about 600 strong. A steady fire was opened upon them at about 700 yards, and they dropped tremendously thick, but it did not seem to stop them in the least, until a cross-fire from the Mission House, which projected beyond the line of the walled enclosure, took them in flank, and then some of them took shelter behind some new buildings to the left of the Mission House, while the greater part moved round to the other side of the enclosure. It had been difficult before to keep the men who lined the wall on that side from coming round 'to have a shot,' but there was a tremendous struggle there.

The Zulus drove our men from the wall under the hospital, but were kept at bay by the heavy fire from the cross-wall. They then commenced a series of attacks extending from the end of the hospital, and at the same time a large number who were in the clefts of the hill fired on us. Attack after attack was repulsed by the use of the bayonet and rapid firing, before which the Zulus crouched down in the bush and were lost sight of. Presently, as if moved by a common impulse, they were up again, many of them close to the wall. This they did several times.

About six o'clock they managed to force an entrance into the outer end of the hospital. There was a wounded Kafir soldier there, and our men heard them questioning him for a long time, after which they murdered him. Elated by their success they extended their attack as far up as the mission house, where there was a place quite open, and it seemed for a time that they would break in. After that attack was repulsed, he withdrew all the men inside the cross-wall. The Zulus frequently got over the outer wall, but never occupied the enclosure, they were shot down quickly. After dark they completely surrounded the position and came on at all sides. They were repulsed for some time, but then they forced their way into the kraal and drove our men back to the kraal wall, so that the position finally held was a rectangular space between the mission-house and the kraal wall. The roof of the mission-house was thatched, and after repeated attempts had been made by the Zulus to set it on fire, bags of mealies were formed into a sort of little redoubt inside the enclosure, on which they could have fallen back if the attempts to burn the hospital were successful. "This sort of thing," went on until about midnight. After that there was not much more attempted in the way of getting over the walls; but the Zulus still kept on firing until about four o'clock. Then the fire ceased at dawn the enemy disappeared, and at eight o'clock the advance guard of Lord Chelmsford's force appeared in sight, very soon came up and "we were at ease," (Loud applause).

In describing the panic among the natives and in Natal which ensued, Major Chard made a favourable exception in favour of the Natal Pioneers, who like most of the tribes that were any good had been organised by the late Colonel Durnford, and who stuck to the English. After the temporary defence of Rorke's Drift had been replaced by a stone wall, on the 10th of February Major Chard was struck down with fever, and with two other officers, both of whom died, was sent back to Helpmakaar and Ladysmith. Under the excellent care of Dr. Hyde, who was in practice at Ladysmith, he recovered, and it was while he was becoming convalescent that he learned from Dr. Hyde's native servants, some of whom were Zulus, most of what he knew about Zulu customs …

11k. *New York Tribune* (United States of America), 3 November 1897

Col. John R. M. Chard Dead.
Hero of the Defense of Rorke's Drift, South Africa, Expires.

London, Nov. 2. – Col. John Rouse Merriott Chard, V.C., the hero of the famous defense of Rorke's Drift, South Africa, in January, 1879, died at Taunton yesterday evening.

Col. John Rouse Merriott Chard was born in 1847, and obtained his commission in the Royal Engineers in 1868. He was a Lieutenant when he went to Natal in January, 1879. Jan. 22 he was placed in charge of the commissariat post, at Rorke's Drift, at the head of eighty men of the Eightieth Regiment of Infantry. Suspecting that an attack on the spot was imminent, Lieut. Chard caused a barricade to be hastily thrown up. The soldiers used the commissariat stores as a breastwork. About 3,000 Zulus attacked the post soon after dark, and the fighting lasted late into the night. The Zulus' attacks were made with great rapidity; six times they forced themselves within the barricade, only to be repulsed at the point of the bayonet. They finally withdrew, leaving 351 of their dead within or near the barricade. It is estimated that the Zulus lost in all about 1,000.

111. *Civil and Military Gazette,* Lahore (India), 29 December 1897

The Defence of Rorke's Drift.
Chard's Own Story.
By an officer who knew him well.

The general order issued by Lord Chelmsford after the defence of Rorke's Drift was as follows;

"The Lieut.-General commanding Her Majesty's forces in South Africa has much satisfaction in publishing for general information the subjoined official report of the gallant defence of Rorke's Drift Post, made on January 22nd and 23rd. The Lieut.-General feels sure that the gallant conduct of the garrison will receive most ample recognition, and trusts the example set by a few brave men and the success that attended their noble efforts will be taken to heart by all under his command. The odds against them were nearly thirty to one: but taking advantage of the material which lay to hand, and hastily constructing with it such cover as was possible, this heroic little garrison was enabled to resist during the space of twelve hours the determined attacks made upon them, and further inflicted heavy loss upon the enemy, the killed alone being more than three times their own number." It was difficult to get Chard,

The most modest of men,

to speak concerning the defence of Rorke's Drift, but it was the writer's privilege on one occasion to hear the whole story from his own lips, and the following incidents read in conjunction with the account of the defence, as given in his official report, will prove of interest, and are, at least, worthy of being placed on record now that the chief actor in that arduous fight has gone to his final rest.

On the morning of the 22nd January Chard arrived with six sappers (all of whom lost their lives in the disaster which followed) at the camp at Isandula, and, had he been allowed to have his own way, would himself have remained there, and without doubt, would have lost his life in consequence. He had been ordered to proceed there with his six men, whom he was to leave at the camp, and then to return to Rorke's Drift himself. Having reported their arrival he was on the point of leaving for the return journey, having a waggon driven by a Kaffir with him, when he saw the attack by the Zulus commencing and at once went to Colonel Durnford, who was in command, and asked if he might be allowed to remain to take part in the fight. Durnford asked him what his orders were, and upon his replying that he had been instructed to return to Rorke's Drift without delay, told him that he must obey his orders. With a feeling of disappointment Chard accordingly left the ill-fated camp with his waggon for Rorke's Drift – about ten miles distant. He had not proceeded far, however, when he saw the Zulus in large numbers working round under cover of the hills in order to surround the camp, and at one time thought that he should be cut off. The driver of his waggon was of the same opinion and showed that he was more than half inclined to abandon his charge and bolt. Chard, seeing this, drew his revolver and threatened to shoot him if he did so without his permission, being resolved to save the waggon if possible. Needless to say they pushed on as rapidly as possible, Chard finding it necessary to repeat his threat more than once, and succeeded in reaching Rorke's Drift in safety.

No one at the latter place, least of all Chard, himself, dreamed of the possibility of disaster overtaking the force at Isandula, and when the two men – referred to in his report – arrived at the ponts with the news, he was at first inclined to disbelieve them; but when, almost immediately afterwards, he received the message from Bromhead asking him to go up to the commissariat stores at once, he surmised that something serious had taken place which was confirmed on his arrival on seeing the note received from the third column, ordering the post to be strengthened and held at all costs. The work, already in progress, was pushed on rapidly, and the ammunition, of which there was practically an unlimited supply, stored in the most suitable positions. Orders were also given for holes to be knocked in the partition walls of the hospital, but, owing to want of time, this was unfortunately not done, with the result that many helpless men had afterwards perforce to be left to a horrible fate. Had there been time to carry out the order Chard was convinced that all the sick in the hospital would have been saved.

Chard was busily engaged in supervising the work of defence, when it was reported to him – too late, however, for any action to be taken – that Captain Stephenson with his detachment of the Natal Native Contingent – about one hundred and fifty men – had deserted the post. He considered this act of such dastardly cowardice that he would have probably shot that officer if he had been on the spot at the time. As events turned out, it was perhaps the best thing that could have happened, as the presence of men with such craven hearts would have materially weakened the defence, and had there been any hanging back or want of vigour in repelling the Zulu assaults as Chard himself said, "God only knows what would have happened!" It was dusk when

The first big rush

took place, and Chard at first thought all was over. The Zulus, the flower of King Cetewayo's army, fresh from Isandula, flushed with victory and thirsting from the blood, came on with tremendous force, supremely confident that the post would be rushed with little difficulty; our men, moreover, were excited and commenced to fire rather wildly, as was only natural, it being the first time that most of them had seen a shot fired in anger. But after the first rush had been successfully met, their self-confidence was revived, they speedily steadied themselves, and during the remainder of the engagement fired with the utmost coolness and steadiness, and no words can express the admiration felt for their heroic behaviour by the chief actor in that night's work. There was little talking, each man feeling that he was engaged in a struggle for life, and that it was no place for words. The stillness of the night was broken only by the reports of the rifles and the cries of the Zulus, a dramatic scene truly, the description of which is calculated to make every Englishman worthy of the name glow with pride in belonging to the same race as that little band of heroes. The enemy took advantage of all cover, and those who sheltered themselves by the bush (which had not been cleared for want of time) beyond the garden in the hollow of the road, proved particularly troublesome, and could not be seen at all as darkness came on. It was for this reason that the light afforded by the burning hospital proved of such great value. When the building was fired, one of its inmates, a lunatic sergeant, was seen to charge wildly into a mass of Zulus and was cut to pieces before the eyes of his comrades. Another man lost his life during the retirement on the inner entrenchment of biscuit-boxes (which were filled with biscuits, having been obtained from the commissariat stores); he was the last to leave and was closely followed by the enemy. The poor fellow soon realized that he was racing for his life, and our men dared not fire on his pursuers for fear of hitting him: fate was against him and he fell, assegaied through the back, just outside the entrenchment; the next instant the Zulu who caused his death was shot down. When

The Zulus drew off,

the ground round the position was patrolled, and the dead bodies of our men were found to be terribly mutilated. Chard was himself slightly wounded during the night, receiving a scratch on his hand; he did not, however include himself in the list of wounded. His native servant turned up after the fight was over and informed him that he had been in hiding in the cookhouse whilst it was taking place. The Zulus had several times been within a few feet of him, but he was not discovered and so miraculously saved his skin. Chard was essentially the right man in a "tight place" of this kind, being quite free from that fussy nervousness which is so apt to generate nervousness in others, and never interfering unnecessarily in the work of those under his command, characteristics which he retained to the end of his life. Quiet but thoroughly self-reliant, of resolute determination when his mind was made up, he was not the man to give up any post left in his charge without a severe struggle, especially after having been ordered to hold it at all costs. He used to say that he fought Rorke's Drift many times over, as the events of that night were so firmly impressed on his memory, that for several nights after he dreamt that the affairs was happening again that he was once more in command of that gallant band of men who so nobly upheld the honour of the country on the 22nd January 1879.

12. 25B/906 Private John Connolly, 'G' Company, 2/24th Foot

12a. Extract from letter from Captain Liddell of HMS *Tamar* about Connolly [Royal Archives, Windsor, RA VIC/034/64, by kind permission of Her Majesty Queen Elizabeth II]

Case inquired into & following statement made, at Lady Frere's request, to Capt. Liddell, R.N. of H.M's Transport "Tamar" – by John Conolly – invalided home –

Government House,
Cape Town.

Statements of John Conolly
Private 2nd Battalion, 24th Regiment as to the manner in which he escaped at Rorkes Drift 22.1.79.

"I am 20 years of age having been born at Castletown, Berehaven, County Cork in 1859.
My father, of the same Christian name, was a fisherman at that place.
Enlisted 24.11.76 at Newport Monmouth, where I was working as a labourer.
I came out in the Himalaya last year leaving Portsmouth Feb 2.
Having been injured in the left leg at the knee when loading a waggon at Tugela River (5.1.79) I was in the Hospital at Rorke's Drift under treatment – and in bed, when the position was attacked by the Zulus on the 22nd January.
Attack commenced about 5 p.m. but my bad leg prevented me from being of the slightest use in the defence.
Attack was made on the hospital at 6.30 p.m. but the men defending it having expended all their ammunition, they retreated to the main body, leaving the hospital in charge of 2 men.

There were 7 invalids in the hospital 5 with fever (3 belonging to the 24th, 1 to Natal Contingent and 1 to Police) 1 belonging to the Natal Contingent having an assegai wound in the thigh, and myself.
State appearing hopeless, I crawled out of the window by placing mealie bags and at 7.30 p.m. made for the bush by sitting down and pushing myself along feet first. After going 50 yards I got into the bush and laid down to keep out of sight.
The hospital was set on fire at 7.45. The Zulus kept passing me all night, but either did not see me or thought me dead.
Our own men kept firing into the bush till 4 a.m. from a distance of 150 yards, but I was not hit by any bullet.
About 5 a.m. on the 23rd, I crawled back into the entrenchment and then learnt that all the 5 poor patients had been burnt to death, the wounded patient escaped."

The Surgeon states that, the injuries sustained by John Conolly is of so serious a character that it will permanently interfere with his earning a livelihood, as he will be lame all his life.

His mind was at first a good deal affected by melancholia and he still suffers from attacks of the same.

William W Liddell
Captain

HMS "Tamar,"
May 3rd, 1879.

12b. *Herald of Wales, Swansea Herald & Monmouthshire Recorder*, 26 February 1887

A Reminiscence of Rorke's Drift.
An Awful Night.
One of the Defenders Interviewed

… South Africa has been the scene of more than one disaster to British arms, but it has also been the field of heroism, and the story of Rorke's Drift – where 84 men, some hale and some ill, held their own against many thousands of mad and drunken savages throughout the night of January 22nd, 1879, – will ever find a place among records of valour in this and other tongues.

There is in Swansea at the present time one of those who went through that memorable fight, and, at our request, he has favoured us with a description of the event. In the course of an interview he said: – My name is John Connolly, and I am a native of Castleton Bay, Ireland. I enlisted in the Second Battalion of the 24th Regiment at Newport, on the 24th October, 1875. I was drafted to Brecon, and thence to Dover. On the 10th March, 1877, I landed with the rest of the regiment in East London, South Africa. We afterwards had service in Basutoland against the Kaffirs, and when the Zulu War broke out we formed a part of Lord Chelmsford's force.

Q: Was Chelmsford popular with his men?

A: Yes, but he had a small force and a large country to operate in. The Zulus were fine men and brave enough for savages, and if they had been armed as we were they would have knocked saucepans out of us.

Q: Do you remember Isandhlwana?

A: Yes. I wasn't there, or I shouldn't be here. My regiment was cut up to a man. I was in hospital at Rorke's Drift. We heard all about the fight, and how our men were served. The Zulus killed everybody they could lay their hands on, and it was said that some of our band boys were tossed by them in the air in order that they might fall on spears and be transfixed.

Q: How were you in hospital at Rorke's Drift?

A: I met with an accident by the Tegula River, and had my knee dislocated. This caused me to be attached to the company at Rorke's Drift. G. Company was my company, and they were all cut up and killed at Isandhlwana. I had been something like a fortnight at the hospital before this occurred.

Q: Can you describe the station at the Drift?

A: The Drift was a farm, a house with a thatched roof. This was used as a hospital; we were eleven in the hospital, and 84 all told, under the command of Lieuts. Chard and Bromhead and Surgeon Major Reynolds. About 30 yards from the farm house was a barn, and around the buildings were a few trees. The barn was used for housing the ammunition and commissariat stores. Some of the men in hospital were down with brain and other fever. I was all right in health, but could not move in consequence of my leg.

Q: When did you hear of the Isandhlwana disaster?

A: About 4 o'clock in the evening of the 22nd two mounted policemen who had escaped, came tearing by and told us the Zulus were making for the place in great force. The company could not retire because of the hospital patients; they would not leave them behind, so it was decided to face the blacks and fight to the end whatever it may be.

Q: What was done in order to prepare for the fight?

A: Orders were given to form barricades immediately. Corn sacks and biscuit and compressed meat boxes were brought out, – they were about the only things we had – and the windows were all filled up and loopholed, especially towards the hill, over which the Zulus had to come.

Q: What time did they arrive?

A: About five o'clock, or a little past. The chaplain and a few of the men went on scouting duty on the hill, saw them coming and reported it. Presently down they came in droves, hooting, yelling and howling. Many of them were drunk, for they had collared and drank all the spirits in the camp, and then they seized the medicines and drank them too. A good many of them were poisoned by the drugs. About two or three thousand surrounded us. We kept firing at them as fast as we could, but they did not seem to care, they came right up to the loopholes, and some of them caught hold of the bayonets on the rifles. A good many of them had rifles and ammunition which they had just captured, and they contrived to make it warm for us.

Q: But you managed to hold the farm?

A: Yes up till about 7.30. You know it was summer there in January, and the days were fairly long, but the night was closing in then, and they came nearer. Then some of our rifles began to jam: they were Martinis and Enfields, and many of our men were crying in temper because their rifles were useless. They could not get the spent cartridges out, and a rifle is less dangerous than an assegai if it won't go off.

Q: You were at a disadvantage, then?

A: Yes, and the Zulus got into the farm. They had got possession of three rooms, and we in the hospital had to do the best we could to get to the barn, while the others fought the Zulus hand to hand.

Q: How did you get out?

A: Another young fellow named Jones, of Pontypool, who had brain fever, helped me out through a window, and I crawled in a sitting posture backwards towards the barn. We were bound to leave the farm, as the Zulus had set it on fire. A man named Maxwell, belonging to my company who had brain fever, was burned alive; also a young man named Richards, belonging to the Rhondda Valley.

Q: You got to the barn?

A: Yes, but we were in danger of being shot by our own men who were defending it. We were almost in more danger from them than the Zulus, as the air was alive with bullets. The men who had been fighting in the farm then ran to the barn, as some of their rifles had jammed, and their ammunition was spent and they left the Zulus in possession.

Q: What did you do on getting to the barn?

A: Everything seemed hopeless, but it was decided to fight to the last, – it was our only chance. The sick and the others then got their rifles and cartridges, and fired for dear life. I had a rifle and cartridges and got by one of the loopholes, and kept firing away as best I could, though my leg gave me great pain. The farm continued blazing away all night, and by this means we could see the Zulus. If it hadn't been for this we should not have seen them so well.

Q: How long did the fight continue?

A: Until about half-past three or four o'clock in the morning. It was then getting light, and the Zulus drew off. It was a good job they did, for I was told we had only 600 rounds left, and that would not have lasted long. They were coming back again in force about half-past five, but Lord Chelmsford had heard of our position, the blaze from the farm was seen for miles around, and a contingent of mounted infantry came to our relief. The Zulus saw them swimming across the Buffalo river, and retired. The mounted infantry reached us about 6.30.

Q: What was the result of the night's conflict?

A: Well, we had 35 killed and wounded, and they counted about 900 Zulus dead on the ground around us.

Q: What became of you then?

A: I, together with the others who were in hospital, remained at Rorke's Drift for a few days, and, after being in hospital at Pietermaritzburg for some time, came home on crutches in 1879.

Q: Have you a pension?

A: Yes, 1s. a day. In 1880 I received the following testimonial:–

Private John Connolly.

To the officers, non-commissioned officers, and men of the 2nd Battalion of H.M. 24th Regiment. As the time has now arrived when you must take your departure from the Colony, we, the Mayor and Town Council, as representing the burgesses of Durban, Natal, cannot allow you to leave the land whose frontier your heroism has kept inviolate without delaying your footsteps for a moment upon the shore, while we place upon enduring record, this expression of our admiration of your deeds, and our lasting gratitude to you for the heroic services performed by you in the defence of this colony, when menaced by an invasion of overwhelming numbers of Zulus, on the night of the 22nd January 1879.

It is not yet a year since, in the shadows of the evening, a company of your regiment saw approaching, from the slopes of the Buffalo River, the darkest cloud of invasion that had ever lowered over the wild frontier of British dominion in Africa.

The storm which then gathered around you held in it all the fierce power caught from a recent victory gained over your brethren who had fallen fighting at a vast disadvantage on the sad and fatal field of Isandhlwana.

Reckless of loss, confident in its numbers and strength, that wild wave of savage invasion burst upon your hastily improvised defences, and surged against the scanty defenders as the sun went down; all through the night the savage but dauntless foe renewed again and again his attempts to break your line – a line which was weak in all save courage, loyalty, and duty. No need for us to repeat now the story of Rorke's Drift.

As the daylight faded away above the height of Helpmakaar it left your simple and untried soldiers holders of an unknown post; when daylight broke again over the Zulu hills, Rorke's Drift had become a name of pride to those who speak the English tongue over the earth, and each and all of that little garrison had become heroes. Out of the gloom of a great disaster the star of your victory shone resplendent, and Natal, saved by your heroism, dried the tears of her anguish in the glory of your victory.

Take, then, officers, non-commissioned officers, and soldiers of the 2nd Bat. 24th Regiment, the thanks which, we, burgesses of Durban and colonists Natal, heartily offer you.

Wherever your future fortunes and destinies of the Empire you serve may call you be assured you will carry with you the honour, the admiration, and the gratitude of those who now bid you farewell.

W.H. Currie, Mayor

Durban, Port Natal, Jan. 13th, 1880.

Q: What have you been doing since?

A: Anything I could get. I have got on fairly well until latterly, but for the last six weeks I haven't been able to get a stroke of work. I have a wife and two children, and were it not for some assistance I had from Mr. Burnie last week we should have been without bread. I am willing to do anything, but things are so slack. If you can get me employment I shall be eternally grateful.

We then asked Connolly to give us a specimen of his calligraphy which he did. He writes a good hand, and the Head Constable has investigated his case and pronounced it to be thoroughly genuine. Connolly is a steady, straightforward, deserving man, and, surely in our numerous works, some employment can be found for one who, in his country's service, has assisted in making one of the most heroic passages in our history. His address is 13 Seyborfach-street, Pentre, and any offer of employment may be addressed either there or to the office of this paper. We trust this intimation will have the effect desired, and that a deserving man will not be allowed to remain, together with his young family, in a state of abject poverty for the want of work.

12c. *Cardiff Times*, 10 November 1906

One of the 24th.
Death of a Rorke's Drift Hero at Swansea.
On Thursday afternoon there died at Brynhyiryd, near Swansea, John Conolly, one of the heroes of Rourke's Drift, who in Lady Butler's famous painting is represented as being carried from the burning hospital by Sergeant Hook, V.C., who died in Gloucester last year. He was invalided home in 1880 with a broken knee, from which he has suffered severely ever since. Recently, through the efforts of Capt. Colquhoun, his pension of 1s. a day was increased to 1s. 6d: a fund was raised for his assistance, and the United Service Brigade attended to some of his wants.

13. 2-24/2310 Private Anthony Connors, 'B' Company, 2/24th Foot

13a. Extract from Connors' army discharge registers, Royal Hospital, Chelsea [National Archives, London, WO116/120]

Claims to pension submitted to Chelsea Board on 14th September 1880.

24th Regiment 2nd Battn Private Anthony Connors, age 28 years

Disability or Cause of Discharge: 'Gunshot wound – left thigh at Rorke's Drift. Accidentally shot by a comrade when on duty slaughtering cattle. Will seriously affect powers. N.B. The cattle were killed by being shot through the head.'

14. 25B/2453 Private William Cooper, 'F' Company, 2/24th Foot.

14a. *West Sussex Gazette*, 12 April 1934

A Defender of Rorke's Drift.
It is said that there are only five or six survivors of the 130 men of the 24th Regiment of Foot (South Wales Borderers) who defended Rorke's Drift. One is William Cooper, of Cocking. Another is Lt.-Col. F. Bourne (Dorking); and, according to a published list of names, others are A. Saxty, C. Wood, and J. Jobbins. With about 150 old comrades, they were guests at the ceremony of laying up the colours of the 1st Batt. the South Wales Borderers (24th Regiment) in Brecon Cathedral on Easter Sunday.

Mr. Cooper enlisted, at the age of 18, on December 10, 1872, and served twelve years. He agrees that historians have not magnified the horror of January 22, 1879, when 3,000 Zulus attacked the post at Rorke's Drift, where a hospital and a store depot had been established. Col. Bourne, who enlisted about the same time as Mr. Cooper, was a Colour-Sergeant at Rorke's Drift. The colours were presented to the 1st Batt. on June 21. 1886, and history recalls how, at Isandhlwana, Lts. T. Melvill and N.J.A. Coghill lost their lives in attempting to save the Queen's Colours. The wreath placed with the colours in the regimental chapel at Brecon Cathedral was the wreath placed on the Queen's Colours by Queen Victoria on July 28, 1880, in commemoration of the gallant conduct of the officers mentioned, and in recognition of the noble action of 'B' Company, 2nd Batt. at Rorke's Drift. A silver replica of the wreath is carried by both battalions. On December 18, 1918, the colours were carried across the frontier into Germany, and new colours were presented in 1933.

At the memorable ceremony Mr. Cooper, who is 78, could find only one man 'who could give me a year or so in age,' Four Chelsea pensioners were there, but they were not Rorke's Drift men. Mr. Cooper was warm in praise of the hospitality and generosity he and others who had travelled a great distance received from officers and men, and told a 'W.S.G.' representative that the ceremony impressed him very much because it was something like 50 years since he last saw the colours. The re-union dinner at the Wellington hotel,

Brecon, on the previous night was also a great occasion. It was then stated that it was hoped, before long, to get the battle honours inscribed on the colours.

For 30 years Mr. Cooper was employed by Messrs. Mann, Crossland and Paulin, the brewers, at Croydon, but for 18 years he and Mrs. Cooper have lived in retirement in a Cocking cottage facing the Downs. They lost their son in the Great War, and their only daughter is the wife of Mr. E. Curtis, who is Mace Bearer at Worthing, and was formerly a Police-Sergeant at Midhurst. Mr. Curtis is an ex-guardsman, and his son is in the R.A.F.

14b. *West Sussex Gazette,* 26 February 1942

Suicide at Eighty Six.

The circumstances of the death of William Cooper (86) a pensioner, 6 Cranmer-road, West Worthing, were investigated by the Deputy Coroner (Mr. F.G. Stevens) on Friday. The widow said that her husband had had trouble with his eyes for some years. Generally he was cheerful, but he worried about the war. He had never suggested taking his life. He was in normal health when he went to bed on February 18. She did not hear him get up, but when she went down in the morning found him lying in the scullery. Ernest Cook, a neighbour, said that he was called in by Mrs. Cooper and found Mr. Cooper lying in the scullery with his head in a gas-cooker. There was a strong smell of gas and witness turned off the taps and opened the window. P.C. Storey said that when he went to the house deceased was quite dead. There was an abrasion behind his ear and a pool of blood. Dr. W.O. Pitt said that death was due to carbon-monoxide poisoning. The Coroner recorded a verdict of 'Suicide from gas poisoning, whilst the balance of his mind was disturbed.'

14c. *South Wales Borderers Regimental Journal,* c. 1942

Obituary.

No. 25th Bde. 2453 ex-Private William Cooper, died at Worthing, Sussex, on the 19th February, at the age of 86. He was at Rorke's Drift on the night of 22nd and 23rd January, 1879. He belonged to F. Coy., but formed one of a ration party sent to B. Coy. the day before from Isandhlwana. He is number 113 in Lieutenant Chard's roll published in the History of the Regiment and in No. 7 of the Journal.

It is regretted that his family did not inform us of the death until May, as it is the unanimous wish of the Regiment to show respect to such veterans, consequently no representatives were present at the funeral. It would have been quite easy to have sent representatives as more than one of our units were then stationed in the vicinity.

15. Acting Assistant Commissary James Langley Dalton, Commissariat & Transport Department.

15a. Dalton's letter to Surgeon General Woolfryes testifying to the actions of Surgeon Reynolds at Rorke's Drift [National Archives, London, WO138/3]

Dy Surgeon General

Agreeably to your request I beg to make the following statement with reference to the part taken by Surgeon Reynolds A.M.D. On the afternoon of the 22nd January last when intelligence of the disaster at Isandhlwana reached Rorkes Drift it was resolved by Lieut. Bromhead, in conversation with Surgeon Reynolds and myself to hold the Post at all costs and we at once set about connecting the Hospital and Commst. Store by means of two breast works of mealie bags.

Surgeon Reynolds was most energetic in causing the Hospital to be barricaded and loopholed in anticipation of the threatened attack and both in voice and jesture encouraged the men to hasten the completion of the work.

On the repulse of the first attack the defenders of the Hospital ran short of ammunition and shouted loudly for more. All the other officers and men being hotly engaged, Surgeon Reynolds (who was with the main body behind the Retrenchment of biscuit boxes) instantly volunteered to convey the ammunition, and filling his folded arms and pockets with as many cartridges as he could carry he ran from behind the entrenchment of biscuit boxes across the intervening space, a distance of about 25 yards, and swept by the enemy's crossfire, to the Hospital, receiving a bullet through his helmet in the crossing. Having succeeded in supplying the defenders of the Hospital with the ammunition he returned at once across the same exposed space to attend to the wounded.

P.M.Burg 28th March 1879
J.L. Dalton
A.A.C.

15b. *Carnarvon and Denbigh Herald,* 24 May 1879

The 'Cape Times' correspondent at Durban, having acknowledged the receipt of the news of the decoration of Chard and Bromhead with the Victoria Cross, says: – "While decorations are going about, however, it is to be hoped that the noble fellows who won laurels at Rorke's Drift will not be left out in the cold. I have the story on the best authority, and can therefore vouch for its accuracy, as far as any man can vouch for what he has not witnessed with his own eyes. On the fatal day of Isandhlwana, when the first alarm reached Rorke's Drift that the enemy were coming, Chard was busy at the front, a mile away from the post.

In the garrison there was a Mr Dalton, holding an acting commissariat appointment, who, as a sergeant in the 85th Regiment, had received in former years a course of instruction in field fortification, of which he had mastered the general principles. Applying now his knowledge of this art, Dalton proceeded, with such help as he could obtain, to put up roughly-constructed walls of mealie bags, flour bags, biscuit boxes, and any other material at hand. When Chard reached the post, Dalton explained what he had done, and his work met with entire approval of the engineer officer, who proceeded to complete the defence of the post. It was Dalton, who afterwards deliberately formed up the men, and gave the word of command for the first volley at 600 yards. In the severe fight which ensued, Dalton was wounded, defending a corner of the rude fortification, which he considered the key to the position; and while he was being carried away, he impressed upon Lieutenant Chard the importance of holding this corner to the last. His sagacity was justified by the result. Dalton's name is honourably mentioned in Lieutenant Chard's admirable report."

15c. A letter written by John R.M. Chard in response to a request from Commissary General Strickland for corroboration of Dalton's bravery prior to a recommendation for a VC being made [National Archives, London, WO32/7386]

Durban
20th Augt 1879

My dear Sir Edward,

I had endeavoured in my report of the attack on Rorke's Drift 22–23 Jany 1879, to express my admiration of Mr Daltons conduct on that occasion, and my sense of the great importance of the service rendered by him – but I have very much pleasure in writing as you request the following short account of his services as noticed by myself. –

– It was in a very great degree owing to the exertions of Mr Dalton that we were enabled to put the place in so short a time in the state of defence which imperfect as it was was undoubtedly the means of our repulsing the Zulu attack. –

– When the fugitives from Isandhlwana passed by with their terrible news & expressions of the madness of an attempt at defence, Mr Dalton's calm treatment of their remarks and his example of cool determination were of the greatest service in inspiring our little garrison with confidence. –

He was amongst the foremost of those who received the first attack at the corner of the Hospital, where the deadliness of his fire did great service, and the mad rush of the Zulus met its first check, and where by his cool courage he saved the life of a man of the Army Hospl. Corps, shooting the Zulu who having seized the muzzle of the man's rifle, was in the act of assegaing him. –

Throughout the attack he was ever present, using his rifle with deadly effect, making sure of each man & picking off those who were annoying us with their fire, or who coming on to the attack were on the point of causing us some loss. After shooting one of these & while his rifle was empty he was seriously wounded by a shot through the body. He handed me his rifle & spoke so calmly that although I saw he was disabled I had no idea until afterwards of the severity of his wound. – For all through the night although he must have been suffering intense pain he still continued to give the same example of cool courage.

Believe me
Dear Sir Edward
very faithfully yours
[signed] John R. M. Chard
Capt & Bt. Maj R.E.

To Sir Edward Strickland K.C.B

15d. *Natal Witness,* 16 October 1879

The Arrival of the 2-24th.

The spectators in Church Street could not make out why one company of the noble 24th suddenly raised a deafening cheer on coming to the Club House.

The fact was that B Company, the gallant defenders of Rorke's Drift, under Major Bromhead, V.C., had recognised among the spectators Assistant Commissary Dalton, one of the leaders in that night.

May we ask why Mr. Dalton, who originated the defences at Rorke's Drift, and who was wounded while gallantly leading a portion of the men, has not yet received the Victoria Cross?

15e. *Illustrated London News,* 6 December 1879

Sub-Assistant Commissary Dalton, V.C.

Along with Major Chard, Major Gonville Bromhead, and Surgeon Reynolds, the name of Mr. James Langley Dalton, Sub-Assistant Commissary, will be remembered for the heroic defence of Rorke's Drift, with a hundred men against three thousand, throughout the night of Jan. 22, after the disastrous affair at Isandhlwana. The *Gazette* a fortnight ago recorded that her Majesty the Queen has bestowed the Victoria Cross upon "this officer, to whose energy much of the defence of the place was due." It is officially stated, more particularly, that "he actively superintended the work of defence, and was amongst the foremost of those who received the first attack at the corner of the hospital, where the deadliness of his fire did great execution, and the mad rush of the Zulus met its first check, and where by his cool courage he saved the life of a man of the Army Hospital Corps by shooting the Zulu, who, having seized the muzzle of the man's rifle, was in the act of assegaing him." Mr. Dalton was severely wounded during the contest, "but still continued to give the same example of cool courage." This testimonial of "conspicuous gallantry," as the official writer calls it, is equal to any praise of that kind earned by officers or soldiers in the late campaign. Mr. Dalton, we are informed, entered the service in 1849, as a private soldier in the 85th Regiment, in which he served twelve years, till he volunteered to the Commissariat Staff Corps. He completed his term of twenty-one years, and was pensioned as a first-class staff-sergeant. He was granted the medal for long service and good conduct before his discharge. On leaving the army he settled in Natal, but on the outbreak of the war, he applied for employment in the Commissariat, in which he was given a temporary appointment as Acting Assistant Commissary. He was employed in the duties of that office at the Rorke's Drift dépôt, when the Zulus attacked the post, and he then performed the acts of "conspicuous gallantry" above described. He has since received a commission in the Commissariat and Transport Department as Sub-Assistant Commissary.

15f. *The Times,* 17 March 1880

Court Circular
Windsor Castle, March 16

... Assistant-Commissary James Langley Dalton, V.C., arrived at the Castle to-day, and had the honour of an interview with the Queen.

15g. *Eastern Province Herald* (South Africa), 10 January 1887

James L. Dalton, V.C.

"Years following years, steal something every day
At last they steal us from ourselves away."

With much regret we have to chronicle today the demise of Mr. J.L. Dalton, V.C., a gentleman who has played an important part in comparatively recent South African history. Deceased, who was 53 years of age, served for some considerable time with the 85th Regiment, and had military experience in many parts of the Empire. After retiring from the Army, he resided for a time in Port Elizabeth, but in the early part of 1879 again resumed service with the expedition against the Zulus. On the night of the 22nd January, when at Rorke's Drift, the enemy in great force attacked a small party of men stationed there. On the occasion deceased exhibited conspicuous bravery, and materially assisted in repulsing the Zulus, and it has always been maintained, averted a serious disaster to the Colony of Natal. His services were rewarded by the presentation of the Victoria Cross and the offer of a commission in the Army. The Cross was presented at Fort Napier, Maritzburg by General Clifford, C.B., amid surroundings well calculated to make it impressive to participators and spectators alike. Mr. Dalton went to England, but shortly afterwards resigned his officer's commission and retired into private life. During the Egyptian campaign, however, he had further service as a volunteer, and obtained the rank of Captain. Subsequently he returned to South Africa, and, until recently, was engaged in gold mining affairs in the Transvaal. About three weeks ago he came to Port Elizabeth and stayed with his old comrade in arms, Mr. Williams, of the Grosvenor Hotel. He exhibited few signs of illness, and, until Friday seemed in fairly good health. On that day, however, he kept his room, and seems to have expired suddenly in bed about seven o'clock in the evening. The matter was reported to the Resident Magistrate and the District Surgeon, and an enquiry will be held to-day.

The remains were interred yesterday afternoon in the Catholic Cemetery, the Rev. Father Kelly officiating at the grave. It was anticipated by many people that deceased would have had a military funeral, but the affair was a very quiet one. Major Dears, Dr. Ensor, Mr. James Lyons, Mr. Gleeson, and a number of others, who, we imagine, respected the character of deceased, followed the body to its last resting place. Had it been the fate of deceased to die in some town where he was thoroughly known the memory of Mr. Dalton would have been honoured in a different fashion.

However, it is not every brave soldier who meets a soldier's death or receives a soldier's burial. The country he secured will probably soon forget him – as she has nearly forgotten others who lie in the hills and valleys of the Crimea, on Spanish Sierras, on arid Indian plains, in the wilds of Ashantee, in Zululand, in Egypt. Nineteenth century life seems to permit few opportunities of cultivating either a heroic or an extra patriotic spirit, but he has few of the characteristics of the Anglo Saxon who will not accord to the memory of brave men a tribute of generous praise. Yesterday the little burying ground in Russell Road received the remains of as brave a soldier as ever wore Her Majesty's uniform.

16. 25B 1467 Private George Deacon (George Deacon Power), 'B' Company, 2/24th Foot

16a. *Eastern Counties Times and Recorder*, 29 June 1928

Rorke's Drift Veteran.
A Life of Patriotic Service.
Tales of Zulu Battles.
(Special to the "Recorder")

In the back room of a house in Thorold-road, a 'Recorder' representative, accompanied by Mr. W. Maxfield Mead, discovered a veteran soldier of the South African campaigns who was engaged in the battle of Rorke's Drift when a small body of British troops were attacked by an overwhelming horde of Zulus.

The veteran is Mr. G. D. Power, and the story of his life is as thrilling as any book of fiction, but it is also tinged with deep tragedy. Mr. Power is 76 years of age.

Our representative found him sitting in a high backed armchair, with a fork in one hand and cloth in the other. He was helping his daughter to wash up knives and forks from a meal.

At the entrance of our representative and his companion, he raised his head in their direction. He then held out his hand. It was intended for his visitors for an exchange of greetings but he held it away from them. He was blind – totally blind.

Despite his affliction and his age, Mr. Power has preserved a wonderful appearance. He is of chiselled features, with a high forehead and has silvery grey hair. This wonderful old man is cared for by his daughter, Miss Helena Power, who gave up her career as a nurse to look after her father.

Mr. Power suffered from diabetes and afflicted with cataract in both eyes, each of which were removed. Mrs. Power died in August, 1926, when a small annuity from an uncle ceased. The income of Mr. Power is now 26s. 10d. for the paying of rent (£1.) and maintenance of two persons.

Mr. W. Maxfield Mead who is well-known for his benevolent actions is trying to obtain help for this particularly hard case.

Mr. Power in telling us the story of his life, did so in a firm voice in which there was not a falter.

"I was born in the Parish of Kensington," commenced Mr. Power, "August 23rd, 1852. My father was on the Great Western Railway, and I went to Westbourne Park School for a time. From there I went to a better school at Notting Hill. I left school in 1865.

A Stupid Boy.

"I was one of those stupid boys," said Mr. Power smiling, "very anxious to go to work instead of remaining at school. I did not know the world and I wanted to get out into it. I entered the service of the Great Western Railway in the Provident Office. I did not stay in the office long and left to go into the goods department at Paddington. I did not remain there very long.

Fenian Memories.

"On November 7th, 1870, I joined the Royal Regiment of Artillery at Woolwich. I did drilling of recruits and drilled with the Prince Imperial. I remained in the Artillery until I sailed from Portsmouth in 1872 for Gibraltar and Europa Point. I remained there until early in 1875 and came home with the 15th Brigade. I again went to Woolwich but was transferred to Purfleet to guard the magazine. That was the time when the Fenians were about and there was the fear of the magazine going up. From the box in which was the sentry, there was a bell which had to be rung each half an hour to let it be known that the sentry was not asleep. At Purfleet we had an upset when Richard Coates committed a murder and we were removed.

Purchased Out.

"We were sent to Tilbury, where I stayed until I left the regiment being purchased out by my father for £30. I obtained a job with the L.N.W.R., but I gave it up and walked to Chatham and joined up with the 24th Regiment. I saw the sergeant-major and he asked me whether I had been a soldier before. I said I had not and in doing that I lost £15, because I could have got half of my purchase money back for rejoining within twelve months.

Refused Rank.

"I did not like the regiment because I did not like a foot regiment. They told me that if I liked I could be a sergt.-major of the battalion but I did not try because of it being in a foot regiment. The sergt.-major kept a close watch over me, but I did not try to get away.

"We sailed from Portsmouth in the early spring, in the old 'Himalaya,' for the Cape. We went up to East London. Then we shipped for Durban, Natal and when we got there we went into the bush to fight Sandilli. This chief had always made trouble and our expedition was punitive. We got into the bush and we continued to pursue the chief until we killed and buried him. We then had to settle with the Isidingi tribe. They were never really quiet and I don't suppose they are now.

"From the Prieri bush we proceeded to Kish Kama Hoke, where we went to fight Kreli. We were with Sir Bartle-Frere, High Commissioner of the Cape, and he sent an ultimatum to the Zulus which expired on June 11th, 1879. The terms of the ultimatum demanded the surrender of the murderers of British residents. We settled with Kreli. I was wounded in the knee and in the head but I did my duty. The whole regiment was then ordered to muster at King William's Town where we shipped for Durban.

We took the train to East London and then we were taken by surf-boats to the 'Simoon,' man-o'-war.

"Well, we got to Durban and when we had hardly settled down we were ordered to go immediately down country. This took us till January 11th, the date of the expiration of the ultimatum to the Zulu king, Cetewayo. At Greytown we dyed our helmets khaki from the bark of a tree, which was known to the officers, and which we boiled. I helped to dye the helmets. When that was done, we went to Rorke's Drift. On the way we lost our captain in the bush and I believe, because we only had a lieutenant in command we were put behind to look to the supplies. Rorke's Drift was called so after a Norwegian missionary. We took charge of the Drift and Lord Chelmsford took charge of the column in Zululand.

Zulus – Thick as Grass.

"The Dutchmen told Lord Chelmsford that the bush was alive with Zulus – as thick as the grass – and that not a man would come back alive. The column had about 1,500 white men all told.

"On 22nd January, Lord Chelmsford took the column out and we were left in camp.

"Suddenly we heard heavy firing in Zululand and from the camp we could see the Zulus swarming. Some of them had seen the camp and they came at us about 3 o'clock and gave us pepper. We stuck to our guns and killed an enormous number of them. I helped to bury 350. The second Battalion were out with Chelmsford's men.

Ruse.

"Later we saw the column returning from Isandhlwana. We signalled to them but at first they would not come as they thought it was a ruse. However, we did convince them we were British soldiers – the remnants of the force at Rorke's Drift. Lord Chelmsford sent mounted scouts.

"We stayed at Rorke's Drift three months. After that we went up country towards Ulundi.

Vaulted to Death.

"Early in the fall we had with us the Prince Imperial and he wanted to sketch. He was athletic and always vaulted into the saddle of his horse. He went out to sketch in a mealie field when the Zulus descended upon them. The Prince Imperial vaulted into the saddle, but it gave way and his horse bolted, leaving him behind. When he was found he had 117 assegai wounds on him. But they had not ripped him open.

"There seems to be a superstition among the Zulus," said Mr. Power, "that a white man is not really dead until he has been ripped open.

Joined Police.

"Well, after that the regiment went to India, but I remained behind and went on to Bloemfontein and Kimberley. I then joined the Bechuanaland Police. I did not stay long. There was some more trouble and I joined up with Major Nesbitt's Light Horse and went against the Tambookie and then to Basutoland. Later I came home.

"I then joined the police of the Great Eastern Railway and for 23 years wore an inspector's cap. 14 years of which I was chief inspector. Whilst in the service of the Great Eastern Railway I was present when King Edward made journeys and also King George."

Mr. Power has three medals for his service in Africa including the Khedive Star.

16b. Extract from an unidentified newspaper, c. 1931

Old Soldier Shows His Medals.
2s. 4d. A Day Pension For A Rorke's Drift Hero.
'No Complaints.'
Experience That Made a General's Hair White.

Blind, paralysed, and bed-ridden, an old soldier who fought in one of the most famous defences in British military history is [illegible] a week.

He is Mr George Power of Hill Crescent, Ilford. When a [illegible] member of the heroic garrison at Rorke's Drift which, during the Zulu War, defied the ceaseless onslaughts of Cetewayo's troops, fresh from their victory at Isandhlwana

Now 79 years of age, he lives on an Army pension of 2s. 4d a day, plus his old age pension.

When I called on him to-day (writes a "Star" reporter) I found him to be a fine specimen of the English soldier, with his handshake still powerful despite the affliction which keeps him lying all day on his back.

His one joy in life is showing his medals. He keeps them locked in a black tin box which none but he must open.

His constant companion and helper is his daughter Helena. When his blind fingers groped and could not find the lock to his medal box, she offered to open it for him.

"No, my dear, I must open it myself," he protested.

"Bill" (as his daughter calls him), "will not let anyone assist in showing his medals," said Miss Power.

One by one he handed them to me – the Khedive Star, the South African Medal, the Queen's Medal with bar, testifying to many years spent under scorching suns.

"I enlisted when I was 18, under a false name, so that my father should not trace me," he said. "In January, 1879, I landed in South Africa with the 2/24th Regiment. We marched straight away out in the direction of Rorke's Drift, knocking out several native chiefs on the way, and burying them.

"On arrival at Rorke's Drift, B Company, which was mine, was detailed to garrison the post and maintain the provision supply of the column which was marching into Zululand under Lord Chelmsford.

"One morning I was standing outside the post baking little loaves in a field kitchen. Suddenly a few stragglers limped past our sentries with the news that half Lord Chelmsford's column had been destroyed at Isandhlwana.

"Our meagre defences were quickly thrown into as good a state as possible, and at 2 o'clock the Zulus attacked from across the Buffalo River. They were as thick as grass, outnumbering us by thirty to one. For twelve hours a rifle scarcely left my hand. They gave us pepper.

"For a minute or two we stopped to bandage a wounded comrade, or to give him a drink of water, then back to our loopholes. Our rifles got so hot with the constant firing that the barrels became bent, and the rifles useless.

"I was stationed in the store-room, and several times a few of the Zulus forced their way inside. They did not live long. And when they got on our mealie bags we soon put 'em off.

"The Zulus did everything except the one thing that might have carried Rorke's Drift. They did not think of ripping up our mealie bags with their assegais.

"When dawn came – the most dreadful dawn a soldier ever saw – we were still leaning against our loopholes, grimly determined to make the best use of the few rounds of ammunition that were left.

"Fortunately, Lord Chelmsford relieved us with the other half of his column. His hair had gone white in a night."

Private Power was a member of the party sent out to recover the body of the Prince Imperial, who was surprised and killed by Zulus while sketching.

He saw service at Bloemfontein, Kimberley, Bechuanaland, Basutoland and Egypt.

He bears his present circumstances with quiet fortitude, and, like a soldier who is asked, "Any complaints?" he answers, "No complaints, sir."

17. 25B/971 Private Thomas Driscoll, 'B' Company, 2/24th Foot

17a. *South Wales Argus*, 22 January 1929

Ebbw Vale Hero.
Experiences of Private Thomas Driscoll.

Ebbw Vale may be proud of the fact that one of their inhabitants is ex-private Thomas Driscoll (familiarly known as Tom Tambourine), one of the survivors of Rorke's Drift. Driscoll is living at the Cambrian workman's home, Briery Hill, Ebbw Vale and has reached the advanced age of 73. He is now very feeble, suffers from indifferent health and is practically blind. He is in receipt of a pension from the war office, also the old age pension, he is a bachelor and has no relatives living.

Mr. Driscoll was born at Lower High Street, Dowlais, and went to the Catholic School there. At the early age of 12 he went to work at Dowlais

Works, he served 13 years in the army and was discharged in 1888. For 40 years he was working as a labourer under the Ebbw Vale Company. Shortly after the death of Queen Victoria, he met with a severe accident at No.1 Mill, the property of the Ebbw Vale Company, when a portion of the roof fell on him and broke his right ankle, he was incapacitated for nearly six months. He enlisted in the 2nd Battalion of the 24th Regiment on December 6th 1876.

In Feeble Health.

A South Wales Argus representative who interviewed Driscoll at the Cambrian Workman's Home, found him in a very feeble condition and suffering from bad health, but he informed the reporter that they were fighting from 3.30 on January 22nd to daybreak the next morning. Driscoll said he could well remember the Zulus firing the hospital. They had to exist for two days on a few biscuits and corned beef. Driscoll has done no work since 1925. He had the misfortune to be knocked down by a motor-car in the street at Ebbw Vale during last year and was taken to the Tredegar Infirmary where he remained for two months. This accident severely shook the old man, and he has never completely recovered. Driscoll has been made a life member of the local branch of the British Legion, but owing to his failing eyesight, rarely attends the institute.

17b. *South Wales Argus*, c. June 1931

Death of Gwent Hero of Zulu War.
Survivor Of Epic Battle.
Death of Ebbw Vale Man Who Fought at Rorke's Drift.

Mr. Thomas Driscoll, the last of the Ebbw Vale survivors of the gallant stand made by the 24th Regiment (the South Wales Borderers) at Rorke's Drift, died on Tuesday at the age of 77 years.

Mr. Driscoll's sight failed him some months ago and he was rarely able to get out.

Mr. Driscoll was born at Lower High-street, Dowlais, and went to school there until he was 12, at which age he started work at Dowlais Works. He enlisted in the 2nd Battalion of the 24th Regiment on December 6, 1876, and served for 13 years.

The Epic Fight

When seen by a *South Wales Argus* reporter some time ago, Mr. Driscoll recalled the epic fight on January 22, 1879, at Rorke's Drift. He could well remember the Zulus firing the hospital. The defenders had to exist for two days on a few biscuits and tinned beef, and they fought from 3.30 on January 22 until daybreak next day.

Thirty years ago Mr. Driscoll met with an accident at the No.1 Mill of the Ebbw Vale Company, and six years ago he was knocked down by a motor-car. He never completely recovered.

Mr. Driscoll, who lived at the Cambrian Workmen's Home, Briery Hill, Ebbw Vale, worked for the Ebbw Vale Company for 40 years as a labourer. He was unmarried.

18. 25B/1421 Private James (Charles) Dunbar, 'B' Company, 2/24th Foot

18a. *Natal Mercury*, c. 1938

Survivor of Rorke's Drift.
Mr. Charles Dunbar interviewed.
Simple Tale of Heroic Fight.

"Yes I was at Rorke's Drift.

"I remember the rest of the crowd marching off to Isandhlwana with the colours flying and bands playing. And I don't mind telling you that those bands were a silly idea – you could hear them for miles.

"Sure, I'll tell you what I remember of the defence of Rorke's Drift, but there's not much to tell."

The speaker was Mr. Charles Dunbar (writes a woman representative of 'The Natal Mercury.') As we sat in the dining room of the Centenary Home for Aged Men I listened to the simply told description of one of the most heroic episodes in our history.

No glowing words laid stress on the gallantry of that stand – it might have been the tale of a slight skirmish, for all the emphasis laid on heroism.

"I was with the Second Twenty-fourth – the South Wales Borderers," said Mr. Dunbar, "and when we arrived at Rorke's Drift from Helpmakaar we found a deserted store. Our job was to remain in charge of all the provisions, and I can tell you we were thankful later for all those mealie bags.

News of Isandhlwana

"The first news we had of the disaster at Isandhlwana was from a man who rode in and shouted, 'Isandhlwana is wiped out – there isn't a man left,' and I remember saying to myself, 'Well, how the hell are you here?'

"We had a little Wesleyan parson with us, and I can still hear him say, 'We've got bags of mealies and biscuits. We can build barricades and we'll hold this place. Something will turn up.'

"We worked like Trojans at those barricades and then we waited."

I asked Mr. Dunbar to describe the fight against such desperate odds, but he replied: "There's nothing to tell, for we just fired away. That little parson was great. He kept shouting, 'Keep it up, boys. We'll keep them off – we've plenty of ammunition.'

"What we wanted was rum. You have plenty of courage after rum, and I think we got some that night.

"The store, which had been turned into a hospital, had a thatched roof, and the Zulus set fire to that. Four of our men went in and brought out most of the sick fellows, with the roof blazing away. That was brave, that was.

"Another thing I remember that night," said Mr. Dunbar, "was a big Zulu getting hold of my rifle through the loophole. I blew his head off, but otherwise there's not much to tell."

When I asked Mr. Dunbar how many Zulus attacked Rorke's Drift, he replied, "How the – can you count Zulus in the dark? They were shouting and bawling all night. I certainly don't know how many there were, but there were quite enough, anyway.

"In the morning we got ourselves together and had breakfast. Then we waited for news, and eventually we saw some men in red straggling down from Isandhlwana, where they had spent the night among the dead. We got flags out and when I saw Chelmsford he looked 15 years older."

Spectacular Life

Mr. Dunbar will be 88 years old in May, and his life has been more full of incident than the most spectacular film. When he was 13 he ran away from home because – in his own words – "My father was very religious.

"I had to march to church, blow the organ, sing in the choir, go to Sunday School, read a few verses from the Bible, and go to Church at night. One day I got hold of a book about pirates and fighting, and the next thing I knew I was cook and cabin boy on a coaster."

He served four years as apprentice in the famous Black Ball Line, and then joined the American Navy. He returned to England, fell in love with a girl in Liverpool, joined the Army and was sent out to South Africa, and that was the last he ever saw of his sweetheart.

"I've been in every war in this country since 1877," Mr. Dunbar told me. "Gaika, Zulu, Basuto, Matebele, it's all the same to me. Then the Boer War, where I was in the siege of Mafeking, and in the last War I started off by being drill instructor in Port Elizabeth, and ended up in German West. After the War I got a job in the special water police in Durban, and then became a guard down at the docks."

"I had a bit of money," said Mr. Dunbar, "so for 18 months I did nothing. Then I heard about this Home and here I am."

As I said good-bye to the fine old veteran, I had a sneaking feeling that if anyone had come in then and said, "Well Charlie, what about this war in China?" he would have straightened up and answered, "Sure, my boy – when do we go?"

19. Assistant Commissary Walter Alphonsus Dunne, Commissariat & Transport Department

19a. *Weekly Irish Times*, 8 March 1879

Private Letters from Zululand.

We have been permitted, through the courtesy of the writer's family, to publish the following extracts from letters received, within the last few days, from a young officer who took part in the gallant defence of the post at "Rorke's Drift:" –

Camp, Rorke's Drift, Natal
January 20th 1879

... I have not had a moment I could call my own to tell you of my adventures in coming here on horseback from Luneburg – how I had to swim a river, how the next day my horse sank up to the girths in mud, and how finally I completed in safety the ride of over one hundred miles. When I got here I was so done up that I could do nothing for two or three days, but I soon came round again, and now feel as well as ever. As has been long expected war has begun with the Zulus, and we are beginning another campaign with greater difficulties to face than the last. I am in charge of the commissariat of the column, which is a very serious responsibility entailing a great amount of work and anxiety, the roads and transport are so bad. So far things have gone well. In addition to this column are two others of about equal strength entering Zululand. This column crossed the River Buffalo this morning, taking food &c. for fifteen days. I remain here in charge of the depot, which is protected by some of the 2-24th Regiment and 400 natives. This is the first quiet day I have had for some time, and I was very glad when they moved off from the camping ground. It was a busy and picturesque scene to look on – the rows of tents and waggons, with crowds of oxen and men winding to and fro. The waggons were carried across the river on pontoons; the men went in boats. From our side of the river the view was very fine and impressive, as the strains of the band and the notes of the native war song were wafted on the breeze. Now the spot is deserted. There is a large farm house for commissariat stores, outside of which grain is raised high in bags, covered with tarpaulin. Inside boxes of biscuits are piled to the roof, with tea, coffee, meal, sugar, flour, &c. We are in the midst of a fine country, and the weather is cool, but there has been a great deal of rain, which is a disadvantage, as it cuts up the roads and damages our supplies … A part of our column had a small engagement the other day, the first of the war, and captured 400 head of cattle, some sheep, goats and horses. Some of the 4th Foot are expected here shortly …

Camp, Rorke's Drift, Natal
24th January 1879

… As you may have seen in the papers alarming accounts of the sad reverse which has happened to a part of our force. I hasten to let you know that I am quite safe and well. The Zulus lured the General and most of his column away for some miles from his camp, and then another large body, which had not been seen, fell on the camp and about 500 men left behind, and killed nearly all of them. Twenty officers are missing. We got notice here of the disaster, and that the Zulus were coming towards us. We fortified the store with bags and boxes, and in about two hours they attacked us. The soldiers fired steadily and continuously on them, but they came on to within about a few yards, where they were shot down in scores. We were surrounded on all sides, and they remained all night, but when morning broke they had disappeared, leaving 370 dead on the ground. Soon after the General returned with the column, and we were rejoiced to see them. The men fought splendidly, and the first words the General spoke were – 'I congratulate you all on the gallant defence you have made'. Everything was lost that was left in the camp, so that the officers and men have scarcely a thing besides what was on their backs …

19b. *Wellington Gazette, a Military History of Our Own Times*, 15 July 1879

In the last Chapter we ventured to urge upon the Government the propriety of bestowing upon Commissary Dunne the Victoria Cross, as a reward for

1. Fifty-two men of the 2/24th who defended Rorke's Drift, photographed at Pinetown, Natal. It is quite probable that this was the group who were personally presented with an Illuminated Address by the Mayor of Durban in January 1880 shortly before the battalion left South Africa. Amongst those identified are; far left C/Sgt Bourne, and Private Minehan, front row looking left, Gonville Bromhead, VC, then front row – Sergeants Saxty, Gallagher, Taylor and George Smith – who is often incorrectly identified as Joseph Windridge (Windridge had been reduced to the rank of private some months before).

2. 'Told he was dead', Arthur Howard, Royal Artillery, from the *Daily Mirror*, February 1930.

3. Frederick Hitch, VC, B Company, 2/24th, from *Chums* magazine, March 1908. Hitch is shown here minus his Victoria Cross, which was lost/stolen in 1902. He received an official replacement in late 1908.

4. Lieutenant Colonel Frank Bourne, OBE, DCM, (from the *Western Mail*, c. 1937). Formerly Colour Sergeant with B Company, 2/24th, Bourne is believed to have been the last survivor of the defenders. He died on 9 May 1945, age 90.

5. Corporal William Wilson Allan, VC, B Company, 2/24th.

6. John Chard, VC, wearing his newly presented Victoria Cross, poses with a group of fellow officers of the Royal Engineers at St Paul's Mission Station, Zululand. From left to right back row – Lt. William James, Capt. Walter Parke Jones, commanding 5th (Field) Company, Capt. and Bvt Major John Chard, VC; seated on floor left to right – Lt. Reginald da Costa Porter, Lt. Charles Commeline.

7. The crossing over the Mzinyathi (Buffalo River) at Rorke's Drift, photographed at the end of June 1879. The mission station is just visible on the rise to the left. Fort Melvill, hastily constructed after iSandlwana, but now abandoned, covers the crossing.

8. An unknown Zulu man in the full ceremonial regalia of an ibutho, c. 1879. Although the context of this photograph is unknown, this costume is similar to that worn by the uThulwana in national ceremonies.

9. A Zulu man, wearing the isicoco head-ring, a circlet of fibre and gum bound into the hair which was adopted when a man first married, and which marked his status as the head of a homestead. The uThulwana and its associated amabutho were of roughly this age at the time of the battle.

10. Ngcongcwana kaMaqoboza Zulu, a royal induna and a favourite of King Cetshwayo. Ngcongcwana is said to have fought at Rorke's Drift; he later accompanied the king to London in 1882, when this photo was taken, and was killed in July 1883 during the Zulu civil war.

11. Assistant Commissary Walter Alphonsus Dunne, *Illustrated London News, 1879.*

12. A dramatic sketch of Henry Hook defending the doorway whilst Private Williams rescues hospital patients, from *Leeds Mercury*, November 1897.

13. Acting Assistant Commissary James Langley Dalton, VC. 'In the garrison there was a Mr Dalton, holding an acting commissariat appointment, who, as a sergeant in the 85th Regiment, had received in former years a course of instruction in field fortification, of which he had mastered the general principles. Applying now his knowledge of this art, Dalton proceeded, with such help as he could obtain, to put up roughly-constructed walls of mealie bags, flour bags, biscuit boxes, and any other material at hand.'

MR. AUGUST HAMMAR, C.E.

14. August Hammar – Swedish engineer and friend of Otto Witt, who found himself at Rorke's Drift on the morning of 22 January 1879.

HERO OF RORKE'S DRIFT.

Col. Chard.

15. 'Death of Colonel Chard – Hero of Rorke's Drift', from the *Dundee Courier*, 3 November 1897

16. Lieutenant Gonville Bromhead, 2/24th. (Ron Sheeley collection)

17. Prince Dabulamanzi surrenders, 12 July 1879. 'He is about thirty-five years of age, has a fine commanding presence, and a bright, good-natured, intelligent face. He rides about our camp mounted on a Cape pony, wearing a pea jacket and an old silver-laced Yeomanry forage cap. His mounted *aide-de-camp* is in appearance a fine young fellow, and his equipment is unique, being armed with a carbine and assegais, and clothed in a soldier's old shirt' – Doctor Doyle Glanville, MD.

18. 'By nine o'clock, when darkness had set in, they got to close quarters, and were gripping our bayonets through the spaces left between the bags for firing. It was "touch and go" at that time, and how they were kept out was almost miraculous.'

19. Patrick Hayes, B Company, 2/24th, *News of the World*, 1939.

20. Henry Hook, VC, B Company, 2/24th. *The Penny Illustrated,* January 1900.

21. Sergeant Henry Gallagher, B Company, 2/24th, and his wife Caroline.

22. 'Charles' Dunbar, B Company, 2/24th, photographed in 1938. Dunbar enlisted in Newport in 1877 using the forename of James. His place of birth has been recorded as Scotland in some sources, but others suggest he may have been born in Canada. His father was stated to be living in Pittsburgh, USA in 1900.

23. 'The man whom Plymouth delights to Honor', a contemporary caricature of John Chard, VC.

24. Five of the last defenders photographed at the Northern Command Military Tattoo, Gateshead in 1934. From left to right – Alfred Saxty, Caleb Wood, Frank Bourne, John Jobbins, William Cooper.

25. Prince Dabulamanzi kaMpande and his attendants, photographed at King Cetshwayo's coronation in 1873; the prince was a close associate of King Cetshwayo's white adviser, John Dunn, from whom he learned to shoot and appreciate fine guns – note the varied firearms in the picture, including a quality double-barrelled gun carried by the prince himself.

26. 'He drew a capital picture of the fight': one of the first impressions of the battle drawn by Pte Mellsop, 2/24th, showing the relative positions of the buildings and barricades, and stressing the height of the mealie-bag redoubt.

Corporal Anderson, NNC, who, whilst fleeing, was shot by one of the defenders shortly before the Zulus arrived, lies dead outside the perimeter in the bottom left of the picture. (RRW Museum, Brecon)

27. The Rorke's Drift bible, showing the inscribed flyleaf, presented to John Chard, VC by the Ladies Rorke's Drift Testimonial Fund in 1881. (Private collection)

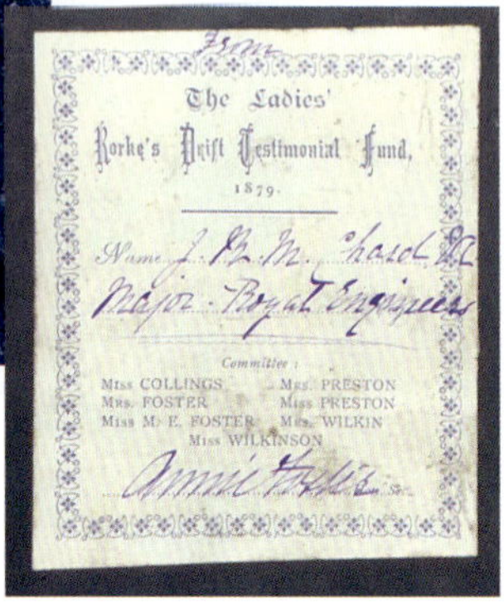

28. Victoria Cross and South African campaign medal awarded to John Chard, VC.

29. The military cemetery at Rorke's Drift, as depicted in the illustrated London press at the time; the stone obelisk was carved by Pte Mellsop, 2/24th using bits of old bayonets as chisels.

30. The exact site of the mass graves where the Zulus were buried after the battle is uncertain, although this spot was identified as a possibility at the time of the centenary in 1979.

31. The oldest of the known and marked Zulu mass graves at Rorke's Drift – the inscription reads: 'In proud memory of the Zulu warriors who fell at the battle of Rorke's Drift, 22nd January 1879, some of whom lie buried here'.

32. The Zulu attack continued after darkness. 'The Zulus came right up to the bags, and I could hear them outside, and could also see many by the burning hospital, and told the men very often to fire away and pot them off.'

33. A rather romanticised Victorian print depicting the fight along the front wall. It does however, give a good impression of the height advantage that the rocky ledge provided the defenders.

34. '... he shot my father who was standing within two or three yards of him, through the body, the bullet entering his stomach below the left side and coming out above the right hip. My father ran away, and as he was doing so Peula shot at him again twice, the first shot struck him above the left hip, the second passed through his right elbow and left wrist' – Mzingeli, son of Dabulamanzi, who witnessed his father's murder in 1886.

35. A modern view of the military cemetery at Rorke's Drift. The high retaining wall was built in the mid 1880's whilst Otto Witt was still at the mission station.

36. Capt and Bvt Major Gonville Bromhead, VC, B Company, 2/24th. (Ron Sheeley collection)

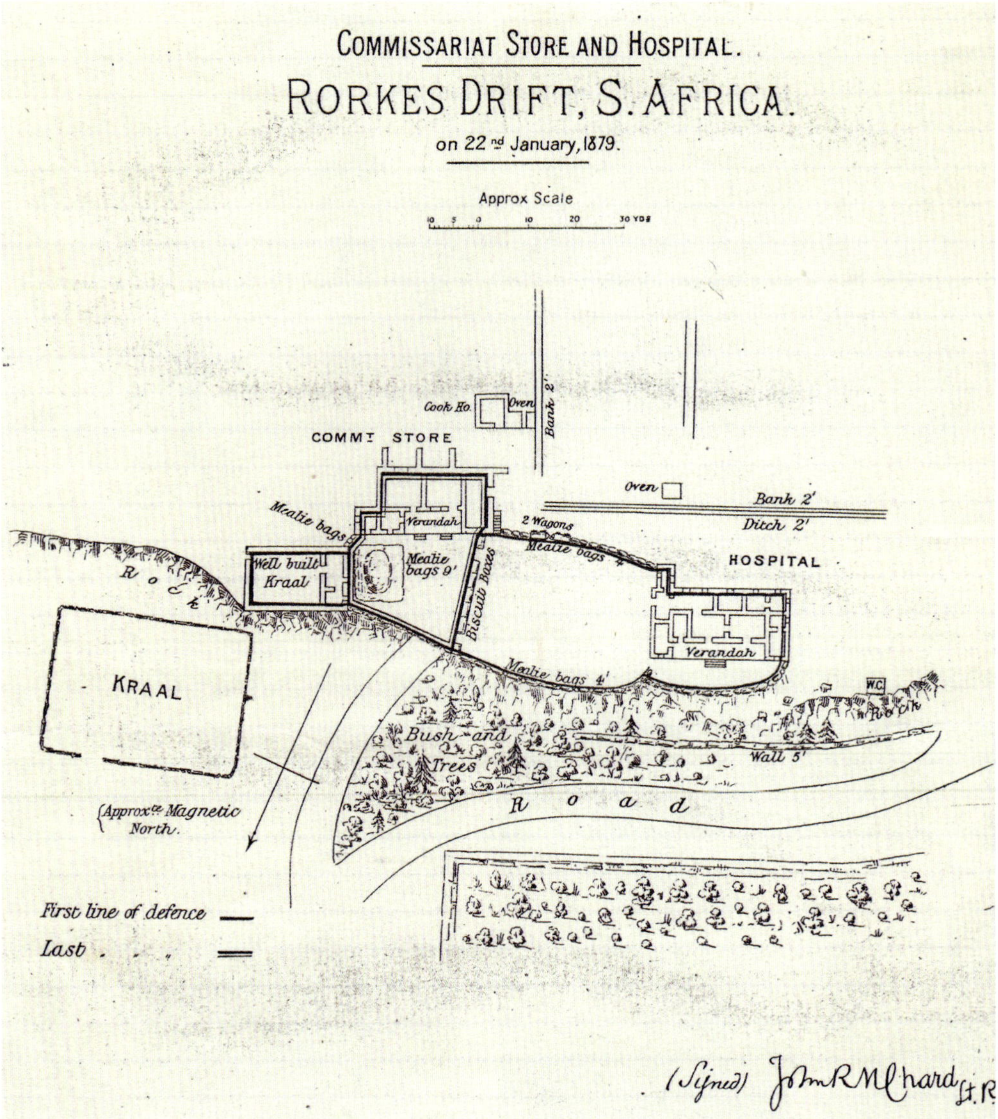

37. A copy of John Chard's plan of the defences at Rorke's Drift, *Royal Engineers Journal*, 1880. Note the internal layout of the hospital – showing doors and windows; this layout varies in each of Chard's surviving contemporary plans of the building, and whilst it is tempting to try and sequence the defence and subsequent evacuation of the hospital, some doubt must remain as to the original internal construction of the building. Chard was, of course, attempting to map the building after the battle when it had been gutted by fire.

38. A contemporary Victorian painting of the battle which, unusually, stresses the perspective of the attacking Zulus; this detail depicts the attack on the hospital veranda.

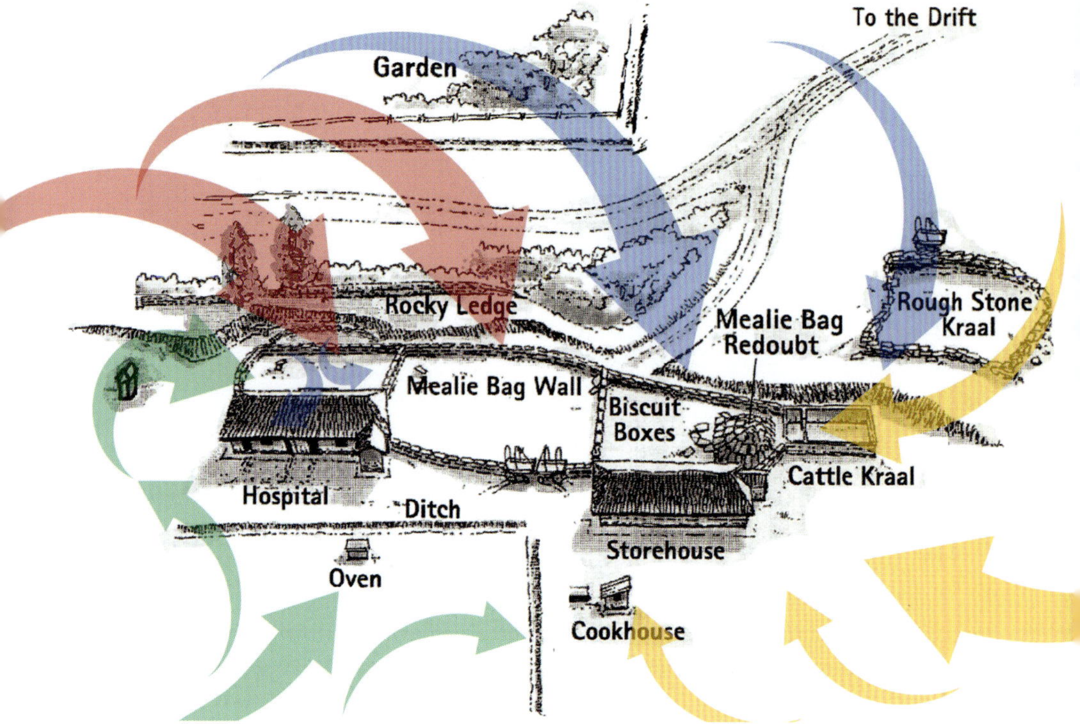

39. Map showing the Zulu attack at Rorke's Drift.

Green: About 4.30pm. The iNdluyengwe swoop around the Shiyane and run straight towards the nearest barricades. They are caught by heavy fire from the back wall, where some of Bromhead's best shots are positioned, and the majority veer off around the side of the hospital to attack the front of the building.

Red: From 4.30 to 6 pm. The main force, consisting of the uThulwana, the iNdlondlo, and the uDloko amabutho, arrive and attack the far end of the defences in front of the hospital, breaching the initial line of mealie bags and, after several attempts, forcing the defenders back to the small 'dog leg' wall. The front of the hospital is then left exposed and the Zulus attempt to break in. Meanwhile Zulu sharpshooters firing from the slopes of the Shiyane pick off several of the defenders.

Blue: About 6 pm. The Zulu attack extends – from the shelter of the garden – along the front wall. They take possession of the rough stone kraal and from there launch several assaults against the cattle kraal. The Zulus force their way into the hospital and set fire to the roof – forcing the few remaining defenders and patients to fight their way out by whatever route they can find.

Yellow: After 6 p.m. Chard orders the defenders to retreat to the biscuit box line, leaving the hospital exposed, and take up their final defensive position. The Zulus occupy the abandoned mealie bag wall – the Zulu sharpshooters come down from the Shiyane and take up position in and around the garden where they fire directly at the defenders. Slowly the entire position is surrounded. The Zulus finally capture half of the cattle kraal.

his bravery at Rorke's Drift. Since the publication of that chapter we have had the privilege of reading a letter addressed by that gallant young Officer to his Father; and though it may be, as he says, telling a twice-told tale, yet the description he gives of that terrible night is so graphic, is worded so modestly, and is so characteristic of the man, that no apology can be required for quoting it *in extenso*:–

"My Dear Father, Here I am back again at this post which has become so well known. The garrison has not yet removed into the new fort, which is closer to the river, about a mile from this. You asked me lately to send you some further particulars of the attack, and, though it is like telling a twice-told tale, I will try to give you some ideas of it. Broomhead and I had just finished lunch, and the day being warm, we were taking things easy under an awning which we had rigged up, and enjoying the view, which is very extensive from this point. The little force left him were variously employed. Everything looked peaceful and quiet, when suddenly we perceived at some distance in Zululand a large number of mounted men coming towards the river preceded by a lot of native women and children and oxen. We proposed to go down to ascertain what they were, but had not gone far when we were called back by one of the men, who said that a mounted orderly wished to see the officer in command. We returned at once, and met a mounted man in his shirt sleeves riding towards us. His first words were 'the camp is taken by the Zulus;' we could not take in the full meaning of the words at first, but he soon made it clear to us that a great disaster had happened to the force defending the General's camp, and that Zulus were advancing in our direction. The men were at once ordered to fall in, the tents were struck, and it was decided to put up a breastwork and defend the post to the last. Mr. Dalton was the first to suggest the use of grain bags, biscuit boxes, &c. We had 300 of the Native Contingent with us who were most useful in assisting to move bags, &c. into position. Chard came up from the river and superintended the work, which was quite in his line as an Engineer Officer. I was particularly struck by the coolness of the men, some of whom were very young. Every man had to work hard, for we did not know the moment the enemy might appear. A wall had been made all round, taking in the hospital and store, when I went to look at the arrangements at the former place, I saw at once that this was the weakest point, but just then a shot was fired outside. Running round I saw one of the outposts hastening back, and, at the same time, one Zulu was seen on the top of a high hill about 100 yards from the store. Immediately they heard the shot our natives took their bags and baggage and made off in a business manner. Nothing could stop them. So Chard had the space to be held curtailed by drawing a line of biscuit boxes across the middle. This, I consider, saved us subsequently from destruction, for it afforded shelter for the men when they were obliged to retreat, on the hospital being taken. The Zulus appeared very soon round the foot of the hill before-mentioned in a black mass, coming on without a sound at a steady trot. They were thus about 800 yards away, and our men immediately opened fire on them. The smoke from the rifles obscured the view, but I was told many of the enemy dropped here. In a very short time they appeared close to the hospital, and from all sides they came on and soon surrounded us completely. The greatest numbers and the real attack was made on the hospital, which they soon carried. Those of the sick who were able to move escaped by running back to the second entrenchment, the remainder of the poor fellows were assegaied in their beds. All this had not occurred without loss on both sides, numbers of Zulus having fallen close to the hospital, and on our side a couple of men were shot dead, one of them quite close to me, but I did not know it till I looked round and saw him, we were now in the thick of the fight, and the Zulus made several rushes right up to the wall, but were each time driven back by the destructive fire of our men, soon the hospital was seen to be on fire, and men began to fall. The Doctor had to attend them without having any proper appliances for all his equipments were in the hospital. I scarcely knew how the time passed, we dreaded the approach of darkness, but as it came on the blaze from the burning hospital lit up everything and enable the men to fire with unerring effect. We scarcely dared hope to finally drive off the determined savages, so as a last resource Chard got us to make a redoubt of mealie bags. In this, 'which was about 8 feet high of circular form and hollow inside,' we decided to make our last stand if our other defences were carried. As the night went on the fight continued slackening at times, when all was still as death, every man on the alert, and when a rush came, a withering volley soon stopped the onset. As dawn approached there was a long pause, and dead silence, when the light appeared, to our joy, not a Zulu was to be seen except the dead and wounded strewing the ground. After a time we ventured out, and were surprised to see the number of killed who lay in rows as if mowed down. They were almost entirely naked, and carried assegais and old muzzle loaders, many of which were collected and destroyed. A large body of men were now seen on the other side of the river, and we gave ourselves up for lost, for a moment thinking they were a fresh body of Zulus coming to avenge the defeat pf the past night, but to our great relief it turned out to be the General's column returning. On the approach we gave vent to our feelings in loud cheers, which were returned by the others. Trusting you will be satisfied with this hasty sketch, and love to all,

I am, my dear Father, your affectionate Son,

Walter Dunne.

Rorke's Drift, Natal, 14th April 1879."

19c. A letter by John R.M. Chard written in response to a request from Commissary General Strickland for corroboration of Dunne's bravery prior to a recommendation for a VC being made [National Archives, London, WO32/7386]

To Sir Edward Strickland K.C.B.
Durban
20th Aug 1879

My dear Sir Edward,

I have very much pleasure in writing at your request the following short account of Mr Dunne's services on the occasion of the attack on Rorke's Drift 22–23 Jany. 1879 –

Mr Dunne from the first gave valuable assistance in superintending and working at our defences, and with Mr Byrne was greatly instrumental to forming the retrenchment of biscuit boxes which was in all probability the means of our successful defence, & that at a time when the firing in the distance being heard, there was every necessity for the work being completed as quickly as possible. –

At one time during the attack, & when the Hospital was burning, it appeared as if the enemy would also succeed in setting fire to the Commt Store – and it became of the greatest importance to have some point to rally round in case they succeeded. – It was then that we formed our inner defence of the two heaps of mealies in sacks – Mr Dunne worked hard at this until the little redoubt was completed; his height, in addition to the fact of standing on the heaps which were high above our outer walls, causing him to be much exposed. – The enemy's fire was very heavy at the time, and in addition to any shots aimed at those working, from the usual Zulu fault of firing high, the place was one of particular exposure.

Believe me
Dear Sir Edward
very faithfully yours
John R. M. Chard
Capt & Bt. Maj R.E.

19d. Extract from the *Army Service Corps Journal,* February 1892 [by kind permission of Lt. Col. Ian Bennett]

Reminiscences of Campaigning in South Africa, 1877–81. Chapter III.

The force that was to invade Zululand in three columns from three different points on the border, under command of Lord Chelmsford, numbered 12,000 men, including the Native contingent, but Cetewayo's army was known to be about 30,000 strong, well drilled, organised in regiments and held under strict discipline.

I was attached to No. 3 Column, commanded by Colonel Glynn, C.B., under the personal supervision of Lord Chelmsford, who accompanied it, and was instructed to form a Supply Depôt at Rorke's Drift, the site of a Swedish Mission Station on the banks of the River Buffalo, 12 miles from Helpmakaar. The house and school of the mission, which had been abandoned, were utilised as a hospital and store respectively. The strength of No. 3 Column was over 2,000 whites and 2,500 natives, composed as follows: – one Battery of Royal Artillery, N/5 R.A., one Company of Royal Engineers 1st and 2nd Battalions of the 24th Regiment, one Squadron of Mounted Infantry, one Squadron of Natal Mounted Police, the Natal Carabiniers, Newcastle Mounted Rifles, Buffalo Border Guard and the 3rd

Regt. of Natal Native Contingent under European officers. The Transport comprised 1,500 oxen, 70 mules, 220 waggons, and 82 carts.

The quantity of Supplies to be stored was very large and my work was very arduous, the staff placed at my disposal for supply duties being very inadequate; but I did not then fully understand the magnitude of the task before us. An Acting Commissariat Officer (Assistant Commissary Dalton), a civilian clerk, Mr. Byrne, and Corporal Attwood of the Army Service Corps were all the assistants I had at first. I mention their names as they all took a gallant part in the defence of Rorke's Drift Post and are now no more. To these were subsequently added 2nd Lieut. Griffiths, of the 24th Regiment, a most promising young officer, and a sergeant and three privates as issuers, etc.

The once quiet Mission Station was now a busy scene. Heavily laden ox-waggons constantly came and went, accompanied by the usual yelling, whip cracking, and bellowing; piles of corn bags, biscuit boxes, etc. rose up; detachments of troops were continually arriving and pitching their tents – all the bustle of a large camp and depot was apparent.

On the 10th January, 1879, the first portion of the Column crossed the river and encamped on the Zulu side, and for the next ten days was engaged in road making. On the 20th the remainder of the Column crossed with the exception of the small garrison left to guard the Depot; the camps were struck and a general advance was made to Isandhlwana, about 12 miles distant, where a fresh camp was formed. On that day we said good-bye to friends and comrades, so many of whom we were destined never to meet again in this world – all of them, both officers and men, as fine fellows as the British Army has ever numbered in its ranks.

Our post at Rorke's Drift seemed silent and lonely after they had left; but we expected to join them soon, and to hear of some fierce but successful fight with the enemy. Alas for human hopes and expectations! Before daylight on the 22nd January, Lord Chelmsford advanced in force from Isandhlwana, leaving his camp there in charge of Lieut. Colonel Pulleine, of the 24th Regiment, who had under his command about 800 of all ranks, including five companies of 1st 24th and one company of 2nd 24th. Colonel Durnford, RE., arrived at the camp later on the same morning with about 500 of the Native Contingent and took over the command. What followed at the camp was learnt afterwards by putting together the accounts given by the few survivors and from the Zulus themselves after the war.

Early in the morning reports were brought in of bodies of the enemy being in sight. The troops turned out to meet them a mile or two from the camp, but were soon obliged to fall back, for fresh regiments of the enemy were continually arriving at the scene. About 11 a.m. a force of 20,000 Zulus advanced simultaneously to the attack and gradually surrounded the defending force, developing the movement with great swiftness and bravery, undaunted by their heavy losses. The Native Contingent gave way before their determined assault and fled, thus exposing the rear and flank of the British force, whose ammunition was nearly all expended, while they found themselves unable to obtain a fresh supply, as they were cut off from the camp. A desperate hand to hand fight now ensued. The Zulus suffered enormous losses; but numbers prevailed. Surrounded on all sides by crowds of the enemy the small British force was finally overwhelmed: very, very few escaped from that dreadful melee.

How Melville and Coghill of the 24th tried to save the colours, and how they were overtaken and killed in the river is well known. How groups of men formed back to back and fell to a man where they stood was shown only too well by their corpses when the battle-field was revisited.

On that ill-fated day, 51 officers and 786 non-commissioned officers and men, including both regulars, police and volunteers, were killed. The 24th suffered most, having lost 21 officers and 433 men. Twelve days' supplies for the Column and all the transport fell into the hands of the Zulus, besides two guns, hundreds of rifles and large quantities of ammunition. It was one of the most complete disasters that had ever occurred to a British force. In the meantime we at Rorke's Drift were all unconscious of the tragedy which was being enacted only twelve miles away.

The story of the engagement at Rorke's Drift has already been graphically told by the gallant Chard; but there are probably many readers of the Journal who have never read it.

The little garrison consisted of one company of the 2nd 24th Regiment, under Lieut. G. Bromhead, and a number of details, regulars, police and volunteers, making a total of 138 officers, non-commissioned officers and men, besides 300 of the Natal Native Contingent under an officer named

Stephenson. They were variously employed on their different duties on that morning. Lieut. Chard, RE, who commanded the post, was down at the river repairing the "pont," which had got out of order; poor young Griffiths, too eager for fighting to remain at Rorke's Drift, where there seemed to be no prospect of seeing any, had asked permission to ride out to Isandhlwana and had left the night before – never more to return! Bromhead and I were resting after luncheon under an awning which we had formed by propping up a tarpaulin with tent poles; everything was peaceful and quiet, when, suddenly, we noticed at some distance across the river a large number of mounted natives approaching, preceded by a lot of women and children and oxen. We were going down to find out what they were, but had not gone many steps when we were called back by one of the men who said that a mounted orderly wished to see the officer in command. Turning back at once we met a mounted man in his shirt sleeves riding hurriedly towards us. His first words were "The camp is taken by Zulus!" When I heard the words a strange feeling, which I cannot account for, came over me that I had heard of this somewhere before. Though we could not realise it fully at first, we soon gathered the truth that a great disaster had befallen that portion of No. 3 Column which was left to defend the camp at Isandhlwana, and that the Zulus, flushed with victory, were advancing to attack our post.

Dalton, as brave a soldier as ever lived, had joined us, and hearing the terrible news said "Now, we must make a defence!" It was his suggestion which decided us to form a breastwork of bags of grain, boxes of biscuit, and everything that would help to stop a bullet or keep out a man. An ox-waggon and even barrels of rum and lime juice were pressed into the service.

Bromhead at once ordered the men to fall in; outposts were thrown out, tents were struck, ammunition was served out, and the work of putting up the barricade was begun by all hands. Other preparations were also made: a water barrel was filled and brought inside, and several boxes of ammunition were opened and placed in convenient places. It was well for us that we had the help of the 300 natives at this juncture, otherwise the work could not have been accomplished in time. Chard had now come up from the river and heartily superintended the progression of the fortification, making many improvements. The men knew what was before them – a struggle for life;

but they one and all displayed the greatest coolness, though some of them were very young soldiers. On all faces there was a look of determination which showed that they meant to "do or die."

In about two hours a wall breast high had been made nearly all round, taking in the hospital and store. When I went to look at the progress made at the former place, I saw that this was the weakest point, for there was nothing but a plank to close the opening at one part; but before anything could be done to strengthen it a shot was fired outside. Turning round, I saw one of the outposts running back, and at the same moment a single Zulu appeared, standing out against the sky on the top of a high hill which rose up about 100 yards in rear of the store.

Immediately they heard the shot our 300 natives took up their assegais and made off towards Helpmakaar, followed by their officer! Chard, seeing that we could not now hold the original line, immediately had the space curtailed by drawing a row of biscuit boxes, two high, across the middle. This probably saved us later from destruction, for it afforded shelter for the men when they were obliged to retreat on the hospital being taken.

Very soon the Zulus appeared round the foot of the hill in a black mass, coming on without a sound at a steady trot. The men on that side, without waiting for any word of command, opened fire on them at once at about 800 yards range and dropped many of the foremost, causing the remainder to swerve away to their left and thus round to the front of our position. Soon they were all round us, and all sides of the square became hotly engaged. The store, which had been loopholed, afforded shelter to some of the men, who were able to do great execution on that side; but the heaviest attack was made on the hospital, which was soon captured after a very stubborn resistance on the part of the few men defending it who were forced back by numbers, fighting all the time with their bayonets, Ptes. Williams, Hook, and R. and W. Jones, of the 24th, greatly distinguishing themselves in their efforts to save the sick. Those of the sick who were able to move escaped by running back to the second line of boxes; but some of the poor fellows were stabbed to death with assegais in their beds.

All this had not occurred without loss on both sides, numbers of the Zulus having fallen, and on our side Pte. Cole ("old King Cole") and another man of the 24th had been shot dead, and three of four wounded. The doctor,

Surgeon Reynolds, was busy attending the wounded as they fell. Early in the fight Mr. Byrne was shot through the head, and later Dalton, when firing standing at full height, received a bullet in the chest, but the wound fortunately did not prove fatal.

About five o'clock some of us who were on the look out for help from Helpmakaar, noticed a cloud of dust on the road some miles away, and we felt little doubt that the two companies of the 24th quartered there were coming to our aid. The news passed round like wildfire, putting new spirits into all, and was welcomed with loud cheers, which must have astonished the Zulus. But the dust was dispersed by the wind, and the longed for help never came.

As darkness came on we saw that the hospital had been set on fire; but this proved fortunate, for the blaze gave light through the greater part of the night, thus enabling the men to take better aim. Several times the foremost Zulus rushed right up to the barricade, but were always driven back with heavy loss, many being stopped only by the bayonet. The men behaved with splendid coolness and bravery. It was a soldier's battle – each man fighting for his own hand; and well did they avenge the slaughter of their comrades at Isandhlwana.

However, the position was a desperate one and our chance of escape seemed slight indeed, so Chard decided to form a sort of redoubt of mealie bags, where a last stand could be made. We laboured at this till we dropped with exhaustion; but succeeded in building it up to about eight feet on the outside, and here the wounded were brought for protection. It was hard work, for the bags of mealies weighed 200 lbs. each. Overhead, the small birds, disturbed from their nests by the turmoil and smoke, flew hither and thither confusedly.

As the night wore on the attack slackened from time to time; all firing ceased for the moment and profound silence reigned, broken only by the words of command of the Zulu leaders, which sounded strangely close. How we longed to know what they said! Every man was then on the alert straining eyes and ears to detect the rush which was sure to follow, only to be checked each time by a withering volley. Luckily the supply of ammunition was very plentiful and it was served out as required, the chaplain, the Rev. George Smith, being very active in helping to distribute it.

Towards morning there was a longer pause than usual, causing us to wonder what devilment the Zulus could be planning; but when the pale dawn, glimmering in the east, lit up the scene they had disappeared! Without a sound to betray their movements they had gone – beaten; carrying their wounded with them: all except a few whose case was hopeless. Then the garrison gave vent to their feelings in ringing British cheers, while the hearts of all were full of gratitude to God for their escape from what seemed certain death.

The scene we beheld was a strange and sad one! On one side stood the blackened walls and still smoking ruins of the hospital. Around it and in front of that side of the barricade lay the bodies of Zulus in rows, as if literally mown down, showing how brave had been the assault and how unerring the fire that had laid them low. Inside, were our own dead comrades – stark and cold, one still kneeling in a natural position against the wall– while the wounded excited pity by their sufferings, patiently borne. The ground was strewn with trampled grain which had run from bags pierced by bullet or assegai, and every face was black with smoke and sweat of toil and battle.

No words of mine can do justice to the gallant soldiers who kept overwhelming numbers of those brave savages at bay all through the afternoon and long hours of the night with a steadiness which has never been surpassed. I am glad to say several of them in due time were awarded the Victoria Cross; but every private present deserved a special reward. Our casualties were 17 killed and 10 wounded.

We could not believe that the Zulus would quietly accept their defeat, so we set to work to repair, as far as possible, the damage that had been done during the fight, and to prepare for another attack. One party proceeded to tear down the thatch from the roof of the store, which might easily be set alight; another collected and destroyed the muskets and assegais strewn about the ground, while a third had the painful task of decently laying out our dead in a corner of the enclosure. We walked round the scene of the fighting, finding everywhere dead Zulus – all "ring kop," that is married men, who alone wear a black ring woven into the hair of the head.

While this was going on a pale white face suddenly appeared like a ghost from some small out-buildings, where the Commissariat ovens had been established. "Who and what is it?" we asked. To our intense astonishment it proved to belong to a man of the Artillery, who, in some unexplained manner, had been out all night while the fight had been raging round him, and who, strange to say, had escaped the notice of the Zulus. Just then one of the apparently dead Zulus rose up, fired his musket at us and walked away! We were too surprised for the moment to do anything to stop him, and, though a couple of shots were fired after him, he got away round the base of the hill.

About 7 a.m. our attention was drawn to a large column of men advancing towards us some miles off in Zululand. We all scanned them anxiously, fearing that they might be a fresh body of the enemy, and we felt, and said to each other, that in that case our doom was sealed. Even at that distance there was something strangely silent and solemn about them which depressed our hearts. In time suspense was turned into relief when, through glasses, we could descry the familiar red jackets of the infantry, and then once more the little garrison burst forth into wild cheering, while many helmets were waved aloft, for there could now be no doubt that this was the Column returning under Lord Chelmsford. But they, seeing in the distance the smoke still rising up from the ruins of the hospital, feared that the post had been captured, and that the signalling which they saw was a ruse of the enemy.

Approaching cautiously at first, a mounted officer, when re-assured, galloped up and anxiously inquired if any of the men from the camp at Isandhlwana had escaped and joined us. Sadly we answered "No!" Overcome by emotion at the terrible certainty conveyed by that short word, he bent down to his horse's neck trying in vain to stifle the sobs which broke from his overcharged heart. No wonder his grief mastered him, for he had passed during the night by that camp where hundreds of his brave comrades lay slaughtered, and the hope that some portion might have fought their way through was crushed for ever.

Lord Chelmsford next rode up. No one could envy him then, for in defeat, as in success, all thoughts centre on the commander. His first words were, "thank you all for your gallant defence." Then the main body of the Column began to arrive. Strange arrival! No train of waggons to park – no tents to pitch – weary and sad they looked from fatigue, hunger and anxiety. Fortunate it was that we were able to provide them with food, for they had been without any for eighteen hours.

They had no change of clothes, no blankets, no great coats, no cooking utensils, except what we could lend them. Empty sacks suddenly became most valuable: slit open at the bottom and with holes made for the arms, they were worn by the men in lieu of great coats, and under different circumstances it would have been laughable to see British soldiers gravely mounting guard in such a costume. But one sees strange things on active service.

The day after the fight our dead were buried near the foot of the hill, not far from the spot where they nobly fell. The little cemetery was afterwards enclosed by a wall and a monument erected, on which was recorded their names and how they died fighting for "Queen and Country." For the bodies of the Zulus two huge excavations were made in front of the hospital and therein were interred 351 corpses.

Death has already thinned the ranks of the survivors of the little band that fought at Rorke's Drift: Bromhead, who was beloved in his regiment; Dalton, the lion-hearted, and Corporal Attwood, who received the Distinguished Conduct Medal, having since passed away.

The Garrison having been increased to 800 men and strengthened by two guns, the remainder of the Column left next day en route for Pietermaritzburg, whither Lord Chelmsford proceeded direct to telegraph home for reinforcements, and to make arrangements for a fresh advance on their arrival.

Pending the arrival of tents and blankets, most of the Garrison at Rorke's Drift had to sleep on the ground without shelter, crowded together within the barricade, and as heavy rains came on, which turned the ground into deep mud, their wretched plight may be imagined. Fever and dysentery broke out which the Medical Officer had no means of combating, for all the medicines had been destroyed in the Hospital when it was burnt by the Zulus. Things improved after a time, but not before many men had been laid low. I, too, sickened with typhoid fever and was sent off, early in March, in an ambulance to Helpmakaar, where a field hospital had been established …"

W.A. Dunne, Lt. Col., A.S.C.

19e. *Catholic Press* (Australia), 27 August 1908

Death of Colonel W.A. Dunne.

A few months ago an heroic soldier of the British army came here to Rome gravelly stricken by illness. He was the last of the survivors of the heroic defence of Rorke's Drift, and 30 years ago his name was in many mouths for the distinguished bravery he had shown. He fought in a dozen campaigns against Kaffirs, Gaikas, Galekas, Zulus, Boers, and he saw considerable service in Egypt and the Sudan; he was mentioned frequently in despatches, and in 1896 he received the C.B. for his many services to the army, both in peace and war. But when Colonel Walter A. Dunne came to Rome, he came here to die, although he was only 55 years of age, and he would not even pray for his own recovery, but "only that the will of God might be done." The last months of his life were passed in the Hospital of the Little Company of Mary, where he was tenderly nursed, and where he edified everybody by his spirit of resignation and patience. When he died on the Feast of Visitation, the community determined to show special honour to his remains, and when his funeral started from the hospital it passed between a double row of the Sisters holding lighted torches in their hands. May he rest in peace.

20. 25B/972 Private George Edwards, (George Edward Orchard), 'B' Company, 2/24th Foot.

20a. *Western Daily Press*, Bristol, 27 March 1879

A Bedminster Man at Rorke's Drift.

It appears from a letter just received by Mr Orchard, of St. Luke's Road, Bedminster, that George Orchard, formerly of Bedminster, and now in the B Company of the 2-24th Regiment, was one of the gallant band who, under Lieutenants Chard and Bromhead, held the post at Rorke's Drift against the Zulus on the night of the 22nd January. Writing to his brother, at Bedminster from Rorke's Drift, on the 29th January, he says:–

"I have no doubt that you will see by the papers before you receive this that we have had some warm work with the Zulus, they have cut up five companies of our first battalion, and one company of ours. We have had about 800 of our two battalions (1st and 2nd 24th Regiment) killed besides Volunteers, Mounted Police, &c. – a terrible slaughter, I can assure you.

We have lost everything except what we stand upright in, the enemy having captured everything, and two big guns from the Royal Artillery, with all our rifles from our men who were killed, and also our camp. All this happened on the 22nd of this month (January). Our company was fighting hard from three o'clock in the afternoon until 6 o'clock the next morning, when we beat them off, losing 14 killed and 11 wounded, and it was the hardest fight since we have been out. We killed about 500 of the savages, our company being only 80 strong and the enemy was about 1,000 or more, so you see we fought them 12 to 1 and then beat them after all. These Zulus are a strong, savage, determined race of people, and we have not enough British troops out here for the war, so it will take a long time before it is over unless we get more troops as the enemy come in such large numbers."

20b. *Somerset Guardian,* 1 July 1932

Helped to Defend Rorke's Drift.
Paulton Veteran's Recollections.

To-day there must be very few survivors of that comparatively small and gallant band of British soldiers who took part in the famous defence of Rorke's Drift, in the Zulu campaign of 1879.

One of them is Mr. George Orchard, who resides at New Pit, Paulton, and is a well-known and highly-respected parishioner.

A native of Bristol, Mr. Orchard enlisted in H. M. Forces in Newport in 1876, and became a private in the 2nd. 24th Foot Regiment (after the South Wales Borderers). He was then 21 years of age.

Shortly after joining up he was sent with his Regiment to the Kaffir War in South Africa (1877–78). He went right through this campaign, and was present when Sandelli the chief of the Kaffirs, was captured, together with several 100 head of cattle, etc.

After this experience he went on to Zululand with his Regiment, under the command of the late Lord Chelmsford. They were sent up country under a forced march, and he has vivid recollections of marching 25 miles in one day – it was Christmas Day – without a "sup or a bite," because the bullock wagons were unable to get up in consequence of the mud and slush and otherwise difficult state of the road track.

Terrific Fighting.

Upon arrival they at once became engaged in heavy fighting with the Zulus, and then came the famous Defence of Rorke's Drift, on the Tugela River, comprising about 14 hours hard fighting, during which Private Orchard's company of the 24th Foot, under the command of Lieut. Bromhead, was badly cut up.

No fewer than six times did the blacks charge the defenders, only to be repulsed each time. The only means of defence available to the little band of Britishers consisted of rice bags, biscuit tins and such like.

During this terrible fighting the 24th Foot lost their colours, and several guns, their band and drums. The company had 13 killed and 17 wounded.

It was during this fighting that Pte. Orchard saw one of the missionaries serving out ammunition to the British troops.

For the Defence of Rorke's Drift no fewer than six V.C.s were awarded.

Gibraltar and India.

At that time Pte. Orchard was only 23 years of age, and he was personally presented with an illuminated address inscribed, "Presented to the Officers, N.C.O.s and Privates of the 24th Foot, Company, for their splendid defence at Rorke's Drift, which saved the Colony of Natal from being over-run by Zulus."

This he later sold to the officers of the 2nd. Batt. South Wales Borderers when they were stationed at Aldershot, and he has reason to believe that it is still hung in the Officers' Mess of that Regt. at Aldershot.

After the Zulu campaign he was sent to Gibraltar where Lord Napier, of Magdala, presented, in the name of Queen Victoria, a silver laurel wreath to be carried on the Queen's new colours of the 2nd. Batt. S.W.B., presented to replace the colours lost at Rorke's Drift.

While at Gibraltar they were ordered out to reinforce Gen. Fred Roberts (afterwards Lord Roberts) who was then in India for the Afghan War, but by the time they reached Bombay they received orders that they were not wanted because Gen. Roberts had succeeded in getting through from Kabul to Kandahar.

During the Zulu campaign Pte. Orchard and another comrade, simultaneously fired at and wounded in the knee the brother of the King of the Zulus, and he was taken prisoner in consequence.

Funeral Escort for a Prince.

Pte. Orchard was present beyond Lant Man's Drift in Zululand when the Prince Imperial was killed, and was one of the escort of his body in the mule wagon down to Ladysmith, Natal.

He returned to England in 1888, and left the service in 1889, after 13 years with the Colours. When the South African War broke out, he re-engaged for 12 months for home service.

Mr. Orchard's elder son, Mr. William Orchard, served in the Great War, while at present his youngest son, Lance-Corpl. Herbert Orchard is serving with the 1st. Somersets in India.

Mr. Orchard also has a son-in-law, Mr. George Coughlan, who was among the first batch to be called up in Paulton at the outbreak of the Great War, and was one of the "Old Contemptibles" who took part in the Mons retreat and was severely wounded.

Mr. Orchard was 76 years of age last November, but nevertheless, he still retains a military bearing, and is comparatively active.

He is of the opinion that there must be very few alive to-day who served at the Rorke's Drift Defence, but if this article should meet the eye of any of the survivors he would be delighted to hear from them.

20c. Extract from an unidentified West Country newspaper, c. October/November 1938

Bristolian survivor of Rorke's Drift relives his battles.
Is he the only one now remaining of the great African epic?

Nearly 59 years ago a Bristolian won a life pension for gallantry at Rorke's Drift. Now after hearing of the death in South Africa, at the age of 90, of

Mr. G. W. Mabin, who fought in the same engagement, he is wondering whether he is the last survivor of this famous battle.

He is 83 year old Mr. George Edward Orchard who was born at Charles Street, St. James's, Bristol in 1855, and who now lives with his wife in a little cottage at New Pit, Paulton, Somerset. He can remember January 22, 1879 – that fatal day when a British force were slaughtered at Isandhlwana and the Zulus descended on Rorke's Drift – as clearly as though it were yesterday.

Mr. Orchard's father, a tailor, apprenticed him originally to a shoemaker in John Street, Bristol, but this man died, so he moved to a boot factory near Stone Bridge. The factory closed down and off he went to South Wales to work for a builder who proved unsuccessful.

"I was only 21", Mr. Orchard told an Evening Post reporter, "and there I was out of work with a week's wages owing me and not a penny in my pocket."

Queen's Shilling.

"So I took the Queen's shilling and enlisted in the 24th Regiment of Foot – now called the South Wales Borderers – at Newport (Mon.) in 1876".

"I remember they sent me to the 2nd Battalion just in time for my Christmas dinner! The Battalion was ordered to South Africa for the Zulu War, and I was one of those who assisted in the capture of Sandilli the Kaffir chief, whose son we kept with us until he was killed at Isandhlwana."

"My Regiment lost their colours, their band and their drums and practically every man present was killed. I was at Rorke's Drift, about 12 miles away, with B. Company which had been left behind to defend the hospital, where there were 30 or 40 wounded and the commissariat."

"There were only about 80 of us, and after their victory at Isandhlwana several Impis of the Zulu army, about 4,000 all told, came down to the drift to attack us."

Saved Natal.

"We fought them for about 12 hours, and six times they nearly got through our entrenchments. However, the fact that we were able to defend that ground saved the whole of Natal from being over-run by Zulus."

"We had about 17 men killed and 10 wounded by the time they withdrew. I remember I myself shot the Zulu chief, who was their second in command. I should have liked to have brought home his paisley shawl as a souvenir, but there was nothing left of it. The Zulus began to withdraw when, apparently, they heard that Lord Chelmsford and his relief column were coming into sight."

"I remember well that when Lord Chelmsford rode in on the morning of the 23rd, I was sitting on a biscuit box drinking a cup of cocoa. For some reason he stopped to speak to me and asked me my opinion about the defence we had put up. There was only one answer I could make to him, and that was; 'It was an act of providence.'"

Six V.C.s.

"Six of my company were given V.C.s for their bravery during this engagement. I was given a pension of 10s. a week for life for my services. Moreover, I was also presented with an illuminated address by the Mayor and Burgesses of Natal, who entertained those of us who survived to a banquet. The address is hanging to-day in the mess of the 2nd Battalion of my Regiment."

Mr. and Mrs. Orchard have 12 children, 10 of whom are still living, they have 19 grandchildren. The family are well known in the Whitehall district of Bristol, since grandson William Orchard has a business in Whitehall Road.

21. 1643 Gunner Abraham Evans, 'N' Battery, 5th Brigade, Royal Artillery

21a. *Free Press of Monmouthshire,* 18 April 1913

Rorke's Drift.

Sir,

After hearing different statements concerning the battle of Rorke's Drift, which I think should be corrected, I beg a short space in your paper to do so, in the interest of Justice to those left alive after their heroic defence.

I, Gunner A. Evans, "N" Battery, 5th Brigade R.A., of which battery half was lost at Isandhlwana, when the terrible disaster occurred to that notable regiment, the 24th Warwickshire's, now the South Wales Borderers, feel it my duty, being one of the number, to correct the statements I read time after time in the papers.

First of all let me say that anyone who would like to criticise this statement is at liberty to do so while I live, so that I may answer any questions they would like to ask me. I beg to state that after the disaster of Isandhlwana I saw the scout from Isandhlwana gallop to Rorke's Drift to warn them that the Zulus were advancing on that place. This scout was minus any arms or clothing but Jersey and pants, and knowing the danger we were in, made all haste to come to us.

This message was first given to Dr. Reynolds, between 2 and 2.30 in the afternoon. Then he at once set the men to work to form a laager from the hospital to the store. Meanwhile Lieut.s Bromhead and Chard were giving orders elsewhere and making preparations for the best resistance possible with so small a number of men, and many of them sick. I may say that under adverse circumstances as these were, this laager and defences was built from 4 to 4.30pm. I was then standing in the doorway of the hospital, and witnessed five Zulus come in front of the doorway, jumping in their mad frenzy, flushed with their late victory.

Just at this moment my newest mates were Adams and Jenkins, of the 24th Regt. What became of these men I can't say. I never saw them after. There were in all 30 casualties, 17 killed, and 13 wounded, out of the 96 men. The number of rifles in action was 85, and every man a man, and when you know that 17,000 rounds of ammunition were fired during the action, I think you will agree with me that all men were heroes of the first order. Yet there is a lot said now that is not true. There were killed at this battle 700 of the bravest tribe in South Africa, within six hundred yards of the hospital, therefore the ammunition was well spent.

No doubt many wonder what I, a R.A. man, was doing at Rorke's Drift. I was left there sick, but not too sick but that I could not help my comrades in arms to defend our position, and could say many things about it. I beg to inform the Editor of the "Daily Sketch," who published the account of the funeral of V.C. Hitch, that Major H.J. Williams is not a survivor of Rorke's

Drift. There was no officer of that name at all. There are several men left alive today, myself included, in the immediate neighbourhood in which I live, one of them a V.C. man. On the 23rd January I witnessed the burial of those men who were killed on the 22nd, in this historic battle, in two large holes, which our native pioneers had dug for that purpose, and which was done on the return of the Column under General Chelmsford from Isandhlwana.

My position at this time was on the parapet, alongside Lt. Chard, and watching them, the Column, coming down to the pontoon which Dr Reynolds and other officers, Lieut.s Bromhead and Chard, thought were Zulus dressed in our men's clothing, and they asked me to mount the sack and look through the field glasses. As soon as I got there I told them I did not want the glasses for I could see it was our men, and I could see a division of grey horses in the middle of the Infantry. I took up my former position alongside Lt. Chard, on the parapet, until Lord Chelmsford came and spoke to Lt. Chard, thanking him for the way we held the position during the night. Shortly after this our brave men followed up to the laager and into the bush, where they found heaps of dead bodies, and I shall never forget the sound of the click as they fixed bayonets, and there took some revenge for Isandhlwana.

Mr Editor, this statement is made by one who was presented to her late Majesty Queen Victoria – with three others, making two from Rorke's Drift, and two who escaped from Isandhlwana. This was in July, 1882.

(signed)
A. Evans,
Spring Gardens, Varteg, Mon.

21b. Extract from an unidentified Welsh newspaper, c. 1914

Rorke's Drift Hero.
Varteg Man's Interesting Career.

To have served your country and have got nothing for it is the fate of many men. Pensions, recognition, honour, only go the way of the few. After years of faithful service Gunner Abraham Evans is spending the evening of his days at his pretty cottage home – Spring Gardens, Varteg, which is situated on the mountain above Pontypool. Evans' career is one full of brave deeds. He has been in three wars and yet has no pension.

The ex-gunner joined the army in the year 1874, when he enlisted in the Royal Field Artillery at Newport, Mon. three years later his first war campaign was entered upon, for he took part in the Kaffir War of 1877 which involved long marches and much bush fighting. Following that came the Zulu War. Evans was an artilleryman and he can thank heaven that he was too ill to proceed with his column to Isandlwana where a camp had been formed. That illness saved his life for even though he was left in hospital at Rorke's Drift he managed to escape alive.

For guarding the hospital many brave men have received the Victoria Cross. Evans was recently seen by our representative to whom he described the terrible onslaught by the Zulus at Rorke's Drift. One day a Natal Carabineer came to Rorke's Drift at the gallop to tell the story of the disaster at Isandlwana and to warn them that the Zulus were moving on towards the drift. Immediately preparations were made for safeguarding the place against the expected attack. Lieut. Bromhead and Dr. Reynolds superintended the formation of a laager. Evans was well enough to help in this work. He also helped to carry out some of the helpless invalids from the hospital, and he took his part later in the twelve hours defence which repulsed the enemy. The news from Isandlwana was that "our fellows" had been "cut up" by the Zulus. The attack on the hospital at Rorke's Drift, Evans described with tear stained face. He did not like talking about the fight. He was all praise for what the others did.

He described how he and his fellow soldiers kept at it with bullet and bayonet until six or seven patients had been got out of the hospital. Dr. Reynolds' bravery he said, was marvellous, Dr. Reynolds was on a sort of verandah, and there under heavy fire, and a cloud of assegai's he kept up a constant attendance on the sick and wounded. The Zulus would make a rush on the little fort every now and then, but the men did not trouble, they just kept on fighting in the knowledge that they were protecting women and children who were in Natal just over the river. The hospital was being set on fire and the flames from it illuminated a picture terrible to behold. When day broke it could be seen that the Zulus had had enough and were clearing away over a hill in the distance.

It was six o'clock in the morning when relief arrived, Colonel Russell and some mounted infantry going to their assistance. Later Lord Chelmsford arrived with the remainder of the 3rd Column. The Zulus came as if to make another attack but soon went off when they saw relief had arrived.

Apart from Rorke's Drift, Evans has many a tale to tell. He was one of the firing party at the burial of the Prince Imperial. No volleys were fired, ammunition was scarce, and all that was done was to snap the trigger. Afterwards the ex-gunner served in the first Boer War and was in the defence of Potchefstroom, which was besieged by the Boers, he was wounded in the back by a bullet which came through an opening into the gun. Evans suffered from enteric fever during an epidemic which caused many deaths. The succession of deaths lead the pipers of the Scots Fusiliers to march round the camp on many evenings at tattoo playing laments.

On their return to England the Battery was ordered to Windsor Park for inspection by the late Queen Victoria. Evans a veteran of three campaigns and a defender of Rorke's Drift was specially brought under the notice of Queen Victoria, who spoke a few words to each.

Evans was just about finished with the army when the first Egyptian War broke out. At once he applied to have his discharge cancelled, and volunteered to go to the front. He served at Tel-el-Kabir.

22. 25B/954 Private Thomas Evans, 'H' Company, 2/24th Foot

22a. *Western Mail*, 29 March 1879

A Rhondda Valley Man at Rorke's Drift.

It appears that among the heroic hundred men who made the memorable defence at Rorke's Drift, under Lieutenants Chard and Bromhead, was a young married man named Thomas Evans, native of Tonypandy, Rhondda Valley. The following is a translation of a Welsh letter sent by him to his wife;– .

Rorke's Drift, Jan. 28, 1879

Dear Wife,

I send you these few lines to inform you that I was not among those unfortunate men belonging to our regiment who were killed on the 22nd of this month. The camp was left in charge of some 850 privates and officers, and when they were out (allan) they were attacked and killed excepting 20. The Zulus crossed into Natal and attacked another station (gorsaf arall); but another company of our regiment poured out (geliwng allan) such fire against them that they failed to force an entrance, and when they saw what number of men among them was being killed they set fire to the hospital and then retreated.

I was in the midst of this fight, and about 100 of us killed about 600 of the enemy with only a loss of 15 men among ourselves. On the following morning, what remained of our regiment came to us, and we are now waiting for others to come and take our place, because we have neither clothes nor anything else. I do not suppose we shall go to the battlefield again because our companies are so cut up that it will be hardly possible to form us into a regiment (catrawd). I shall write again when that is possible, and will give you full particulars –

Your affectionate husband

Thomas Evans.

22b. Extract from Thomas Evans' service and discharge papers
[National Archives, London, WO97/2756]

1st Class Army Reserve: Brecon District

In Confinement for – Assault 7th July 1884

Imprisoned by Civil Power for 21 days with 14 days hard labour – Malicious Damage 8th July 1884 to 11th August 1884

Released – 12th August 1884

Imprisoned by Civil Power for 2 months with hard labour – Assault 13th August to 12th October 1884

Released 13th October 1884

22c. *Abergavenny Chronicle*, 11 July 1884

Brutality in a Police Cell at Tredegar.

At half-past nine on Monday night, a man named Thomas Evans was taken into custody charged with assaulting a police constable in the execution of his duty, and was placed in the cells. At half-past eleven another man, named Marshall, was brought in on a charge of drunkenness. Shortly afterwards shouts of 'Murder' were heard from the cells. Police-constable Fletcher and Inspector Williams soon appeared on the scene. Inspector Williams found Marshall lying on the floor with his head towards the door, and the prisoner Evans standing about four yards away. Marshall's head and face were beaten into a pulp, and when brought into court on Tuesday he presented a shocking appearance, being literally covered with blood. Dr. Brown, who was on the bench, said that the consequences would probably be serious. A warrant was ordered to be issued to apprehend Evans when he emerges from custody.

23. 2/24 582 Corporal John Barker French, 'B' Company, 2/24th Foot

23a. *West London Observer*, 6 July 1895

Kensington
Sudden Death

Mr C. Luxmore Drew, on Saturday, held an inquiry respecting the death of John Barker French, age 54, who died under the following circumstances at his residence, Vine Place, Holland Street, Kensington. – Elizabeth French said the deceased was her father. His health was good. She last spoke to him on Wednesday night. He made no complaint when she called her brother, who slept in the same room, in the morning. He seemed asleep. Later on she found him insensible on the landing, and sent for a doctor. He died without regaining consciousness. – Mr M. Townsend, surgeon of Upper Phillimore Place, stated that the post-mortem examination, showed the cause of death was rupture of a blood vessel in the brain, due to natural causes. – A verdict in accordance with the medical evidence was returned.

24. 25B/81 Sergeant Henry Edward Gallagher, 'B' Company, 2/24th Foot

24a. Extract from an unidentified newspaper, c. 1931

Hero of famous defence dies at Portsdown Hill, Hampshire. Officers attend West Country Funeral.

Members of the South Wales Borderers Regiment, recruited from Bristol and District, will learn with regret of the death of one of the few surviving hero's of the defence of Rorke's Drift, Zululand in 1879. He is Mr. Henry Gallagher, late Regimental Sergeant-Major of the 24th Regiment of Foot, who collapsed and died at his home at Drayton, Hants. It is believed that only two other members of the defence are still living, one of these is Mr. Charles Hitch VC who sent a wreath to the funeral, which took place with semi-military honours, at Christchurch, Portsdown Hill, Hampshire. A bugler sounded the last post and reveille on a silver bugle presented to the Regiment by Queen Victoria. Officers, Warrant-Officers and Sergeants of the 2nd Battalion 24th Regiment attended the funeral as well as family mourners. There were wreaths in the form of the regimental Cap Badge and forming the numerals of the Regiment in Roman figures.

24b. Extract from the reminiscences of Major (Retired) Edward Lane, R.E., grandson of Henry E. Gallagher [by kind permission of Major Edward Lane and Mr Roger Lane]

H.E. Gallagher, my grandfather, gave graphic pictures of the defence of Rorke's Drift and the way in which B Company withstood the attacks so fearlessly. He remembered the initial horror felt at the sight of the first wave of the attack as so many Zulus in battle array came down on them. But as the fighting progressed all fear left him because he was so busy shooting. He was in-charge of the south wall of bags and waggons, and was latter stationed in the mealie-bag redoubt.

All the defenders were in a state of collapse when the fighting was done. He carried the scars of the defence with a permanent blue mark on the right side of his nose, which was a powder burn caused by the back flash each time he fired his rifle.

My mother, his eldest offspring, told me that when they were stationed in Egypt and he was Garrison Sergeant Major, how particular he was in his (turn out). She was responsible that no blemish was visible on his red tunic, blue trousers, belt, and highly-polished boots, before he left their quarters for his daily duties throughout the garrison. I am sure he was the terror of any soldier who appeared to be idle or slovenly – in spite of his short stature.

He retired from the army in 1897. I remember him from about 1919/1920 until his death. During that period I regularly spent two or three weeks annually at his home in Augustine Road. He was very fond of his grandchildren, and we loved him.

He had a great sense of humour and a real Irish sense of fun. When I first got to know him he would tell me stories of his soldiering, especially South Africa and Rorke's Drift in particular. He was proud of his regiment, the 24th, and maintained his soldierly smartness and appearance all his life. He was a great story-teller on any subject true or fictitious. He was very fond of walking, especially on the Portsdown Hill. He would walk many miles on what he called (Campaigning), me asking questions, and him giving the answers – which I fully believed. But sometimes his deliberate exaggerations gave the clue that it was all his (Irish blarney) coming out. He loved his small garden, where he grew most of his vegetables and kept chickens. He died very suddenly in 1931, when strangely, I was stationed with the Royal Engineers in Eire, quite close to Thurles, and from where I kept up correspondence with him.

On the anniversary of the defence of Rorke's Drift each year my grandfather requested to be left alone with his memories.

25. 60B/1123 Corporal James Graham (Daniel Sheehan), 90th Light Infantry

25a. *Aldershot News,* 4 March 1899

Death of Mr Sheehan
A Rorke's Drift Hero.
There is a halo of romance about the men who defended the little river station at Rorke's Drift. This fact has been brought home once more by the death of one of the gallant band of heroes, Mr. Daniel Sheehan, a foreman in the Mobilisation Stores. The deceased was forty-six of age and died on Friday afternoon of pneumonia, at Winchester-street, Farnborough, after ten days' illness. He was a familiar figure in Aldershot and has been an honoured guest at more than one South African celebration. He belonged to the 2nd Scottish Rifles, in which he was a colour sergeant on completing for pension. He was present at Rorke's Drift by an accident, having been sent up in an escort to a convoy after recovery from sickness himself. He was a modest man and it is said that this quality kept his share in the defence quite in the background …

26. Robert John Hall, a civilian meat contractor attached to No. 3 Column

26a. *Times of Natal* (South Africa), 3 February 1879

A letter from a private correspondent.
"… the entire defeat of an enormous force of Zulus by some 130 troops barricaded in the house. R. Hall, who was in the attack at the camp, rode off as hard as he could to Rorke's drift, after seeing the camp taken by the enemy. He joined the soldiers in Rorke's house, and finding the Kafirs there wanting to bolt, fired a shot over their heads, and told them the next would be into them if they would not remain to assist in barricading the place. He made them fill sacks with earth and block up places where an entrance could be effected. He remained until the Zulus were down upon

the place, and made off to Helpmakaar after seeing the soldiers shoot about ten Zulus, and got the people to fortify their position there. I think the reception the Zulus met with at Rorke's Drift is a caution to them against crossing the border. After the fight, the Zulus returned to their own country, after leaving an enormous number killed and wounded. Thirteen soldiers were killed; and it is estimated about 1,000 Zulus fell in this affair; 315 bodies of Zulus were counted all about the house, piled one on the other; as some were killed, others returned to the attack over the dead bodies, and thus added to the pile.

Many wounded must have been too weak to cross the river, and consequently were carried down …"

26b. Hall's account of iSandlwana and Rorke's Drift written in 1906 [Killie Campbell Africana Library, Durban, KwaZulu-Natal, KCM 42358]

Rorke's Drift.
To the Editor of the Natal Witness.

Sir,

I notice in your issue of today an account of the defence of Rorke's Drift, and wondered whether another account, written by one who was there, would be of interest to your readers.

Lieut. Chard is mentioned in your article as having fortified the place etc. but the man who really saved Rorke's Drift was Mr Dalton of the A.S.C.

When Mr Alfred Henderson and myself arrived at Rorke's Drift from Isnadhlwana about 1 or 2 p.m. on that fatal day, Mr Dalton asked us if we couldn't get the native contingent back to build a laager. These natives were emptied by the A.S.C. with their waggons etc. but had just bolted. We got on to our horses, fetched them back and stood over them while the laager was built under the direction of Mr Dalton. Chard and Bromhead were not there. The former was down by the river near the punt and the latter was smoking his pipe above the house.

When the laager was completed, Mr Dalton asked Mr Henderson and myself if we go and reconnoitre over the hill, and we saddles up and went off. At that time all the native contingent had again disappeared, also some natives Mr Henderson had brought with him, mounted boys from Edendale.

We went over the hill and as we were returning we saw some Zulus making a rush for Rorke's Drift House. I remarked, "The Zulus are upon us," and we galloped towards the house.

My horse was the faster of the two, and I got to the house first above the fence, and as I passed within a few yards of the Zulus, the first shots were fired from the hospital and whizzed about my ears.

Mr Henderson went round below the fence and we met outside the wall of the Commissariat shed and the cattle kraal. Here we took shelter and there we stayed and fired away at the Zulus as they came down the hill and squatted themselves in the garden under the peach trees and among the mealies.

I must now tell you that when the Zulus first attacked Rorke's Drift, there were not more than twenty five of them and they kept coming on in batches of twenty five to fifty, and so they continued rolling up, until they set the hospital on fire. At this time Mr. Henderson and I had exhausted all our ammunition and had to move further away to a thorn tree about 500 yards below the house. It was getting dusk, and as we saw no chance of returning to the laager, as the whole place would soon be on fire, we decided to leave, and started to ride to Helpmakaar.

On the way we fell in with a convoy taking ammunition to Rorke's Drift and quietly trekking along in complete ignorance of what had happened there. Mr. Henderson stayed with them the night, and I went off after my cattle at Helpmakaar.

Now, I am not saying anything against the bravery of Lieuts. Chard and Bromhead after the Zulus attacked Rorke's Drift. But I know they did nothing before the attack. Mr. Dalton was the man who saved the place. Captain Dunne was also there, and well I remember his words to Dalton, "Do whatever you think best." Carbineers, Mounted Police, Edendale Mounted Natives, many who had escaped from Isnadhlwana before us, had been there but would not stay, and no laager would have been built had Mr. Henderson and myself not turned up as we did, to make the native contingent return and work at the laager. These natives numbered about 100, and only a few soldiers and A.S.C. men were there, not sufficient to do the work required.

Reading over your account in the "Witness" today, I could not help comparing to myself the ghastly failure of that campaign with the list of unbroken successes achieved by our men in this last native rebellion. All honour to Colonel McKenzie.

As an eye witness I know exactly what happened at Isandlwana and Rorke's Drift, up to the time the hospital was fired, and well can I see the whole thing as it commenced and ended. This I can safely say without fear of contradiction. I was the last white man to leave Isandlwana camp alive. Mr. Henderson, some Natal Police, and Edendale Mounted Natives, were also eye witnesses and we fired several shots at the Zulus who were blocking the way.

When we left the hill where I caught up Mr. Henderson and the Police, the whole of Isandhlwana Nek and hills were covered with the Zulu army. One or two gun carriages were caught just over the Nek, and we watched these being taken back and then we rode on to Rorke's Drift, to end our day working at the laager and eventually being shut out after all.

So ended that day of tragedy, January 22nd 1879. Some other day I will tell you about Isandlwana.

Yours etc.
R.J. HALL
Boschfontein, Brakwal.
October 25th.

27. August Hammar, a Swedish engineer and friend of Pastor Otto Witt who was staying at Rorke's Drift on the morning of 22 January 1879

27a. Extract from a letter written in January 1879 from Hammar to his father, detailing his plan to defend the mission station at Rorke's Drift

… Otto and I have built a fireproof room by lining the ceiling with stone and bricking up windows, so there's only one entrance left. Here we intend to defend our most valuable possessions, since we will be able to defend the little fortress easily with two double-barrelled guns and two revolvers. The

Zulus often burn houses in the night and shoot those who flee, but we are safe from being chased out with fire, and woe to the Zulu who wants to look into the entrance of our little fortress …

27b. Translation from *Nya Dagligt Allehanda* (Sweden), 21 March 1879

Engineer August Hammar, a 22 year old youth from Helsingborg, who travelled to Africa last October, driven by a longing to get to know this continent, has, in connection with the events which the missionary Otto Witt has experienced the last few months over there, been mentioned in the newspapers' stories about said events. However, there has until now been no word regarding where Mr Hammar went following the, for the English, unfortunate battle at Rorke's Drift. It is therefore with pleasure that we now can publish the following information:

Engineer Hammar, who at the outbreak of the war was visiting his friend, reverend Otto Witt, had made daring excursions with W into the hostile territory, where they drew a picture of the burning kaffer-kraal, which was set ablaze by the English, a drawing which, along with another, showing colonel Glyn's crossing of the Buffala river, is included in the English illustrated magazine 'The Graphic.'

When Oscarsberg was attacked by the Zulus, H reported to the commanding officer that he wanted to participate in the defence, but as he could not be issued a rifle, he had mounted a horse, that was given him, and had tried to catch up with W, who had already left. Unable to catch up with W, he turned back to make another attempt to join the defenders. As he approached Oscarsberg, he found it already completely surrounded by Zulus, the battle already raging. He had by then no choice but to continue his ride. The following day he met W, who had been united with his family at a place where there were twelve men who prepared to fight if the Zulus were to attack. No attack materialised, and the entire company managed to escape to Maritzburg, from where they continued to Durban (Port Natal). H was about to join W's family on their travel to the Cape, when he was approached by a newspaper publisher, which wanted information on the war, and also by a surveyor general, who needed his assistance; he therefore stayed in Durban.

28. 2-24/2067 Drummer Patrick Hayes, 'B' Company, 2/24th Foot

28a. *News of the World*, 22 January 1939

Jubilee of Rorke's Drift Epic
When 131 Britons Held Back 5,000 Zulus
("News of the World Special")

Sixty years ago to-day, on Jan. 22, 1879, a band of 131 British soldiers, many of them sick and wounded, held 5000 Zulus at bay during a 16-hour attack on Rorke's Drift.

No fewer than 11 Victoria Crosses were won on that day of epic struggle. One of the few survivors of the noble defence force is Drummer Patrick Hayes, then an Irish lad serving in the 24th South Wales Borderers, and now a grey-haired veteran living in a cosy house in Riverhall-street, Wandsworth-road, London.

He told the "News of the World" a thrilling story of the battle in an interview at his home yesterday.

"My company was left to guard Rorke's Drift while the rest of the battalion went forward nine miles with Lord Chelmsford's column to Isandhlwana, where they camped," he related.

"Lord Chelmsford divided his force, taking the main part of his column on a reconnaissance and leaving the 24th to guard the camp and stores. That provided the opportunity for which the Zulus had been looking, and they attacked the British camp.

Britons Massacred

"The defenders fired back vigorously until the 50 rounds each man carried were exhausted. There was spare ammunition in plenty but it was stored in boxes, the lids of which were screwed down tightly and before it could be served out the enemy rushed camp and massacred the British.

"News of the disaster was brought to Rorke's Drift by a twenty-year-old subaltern destined many years later to play a great part as a military leader. He was Horace Smith-Dorrien, who commanded an Army corps during the retreat from Mons in 1914.

"He warned us to prepare, and, in the short time at our disposal, we worked frantically to fortify the place we held, which was a combination of hospital and store depot.

"A young Royal Engineer officer named Chard directed the barricading of the buildings; our own subaltern, Lieut. Bromhead, posted the men at various points behind the barricade so that we might put up a desperate defence and the medical officer, Dr. Reynolds arranged shelter for the sick and wounded.

"Suddenly the cry went up 'Here they come', and a black yelling mass of frenzied savages could be seen crossing the Buffalo River a short distance away and rushing towards us brandishing rifles and spears. It was a terrifying sight, but the enemy halted as we poured a deadly volley into their midst and followed it up with well-directed independent firing.

"But they soon recovered from their surprise, and came on with a rush, but steady volleys drove them back, and they then started to reply with rifle fire from a distance.

Hand-To-Hand Fight

"Gradually they advanced again and some of them reached the building, which they entered again and again, only to be beaten back by our bullets and bayonets.

"It was a hand-to-hand fight, and it seemed every moment that we would be overwhelmed, but the knowledge of the awful massacre of our comrades earlier in the day impelled us to do our damnedest. It was discipline and leadership against weight of numbers, but 50 to 1 are heavy odds when fighting savages already flushed with victory.

"During a lull in the fighting we saw to our horror that the enemy were lighting firebrands in order to set alight the thatched roofs of our buildings. But that move perhaps proved our salvation, for night was closing in and the glare shed by the burning roofs showed us where the enemy were lurking, enabling us to keep up an effective fire and bayonet all who came too close.

"So the battle dragged on throughout the night. As dawn approached we were at our last gasp, but the enemy were tired also, and after a few more half-hearted rushes at our defences they began to drift away.

Zulus' Red Coats

"Meanwhile Lord Chelmsford had heard the heavy firing at Isandhlwana and had sent back to find out the cause. He was told that the camp was still standing and that men in red coats could be seen walking about. Little did he think that those red coats were being worn by Zulus who had stripped them from the force they had slaughtered.

"When the truth reached Chelmsford at last, he brought his worn-out column back towards the camp, and then pushed forward to Rorke's Drift. On the way the column passed the Zulus, but each side was too exhausted to give battle.

"It was a great and welcome surprise to the head of the column to see our men perched on the blackened rafters of the hospital waving to them now that they knew the peril was over.

"Altogether 11 Victoria Crosses and four D.C.M.s were won that day. Lieuts. Chard and Bromhead were among the V.C.s, and they were not only promoted majors at once, but they received the thanks of both Houses of Parliament.

"After I completed my Colour service I continued to live in barracks as a civilian workman until I was well over 60, so that my experience at Rorke's Drift did not quench my love for army life."

Two other Rorke's Drift survivors Ptes. Lockhart and Dunbar, reside in South Africa, and another Pte. John Thomas, now lives in Canada.

28b. *South Wales Borderers Regimental Journal*, April 1940

Obituary.

No 3949, 25th Brigade., Drummer H. Hayes, formerly of B. Coy., 2nd 24th Regiment, and a survivor of Rorke's Drift, died in London on 4th October at the age of 84, and was buried there on the 8th October.

The Colonel of the Regiment, Lieut.-Colonel F. Bourne, O.B.E., D.C.M., and Mr. Tom Press attended the funeral and the latter laid a wreath on the grave from all ranks of the Regiment.

The East Surrey Regiment kindly supplied a bearer party and a bugler, who sounded the Last Post and Reveille. The widow has presented to the

Regiment Dr. Hayes' Zulu War medal, discharge certificate, and Rorke's Drift bible, which will rest finally in the Regimental Museum. Dr. Hayes joined the Regiment at 14 years of age on the 9th September, 1868, and was discharged to pension on 30th November, 1892, after 24 years, 180 days total service, over 17 years of which was spent abroad.

29. Bob. S. Head, the true name of a soldier of the 2/24th Foot (incorrectly identified as John Williams, VC, in this report, the identity of Bob Head remains unknown)

29a. Extract from an unidentified Irish newspaper, c. November 1932

Mr. John Williams, a hero of Rorke's Drift, and stated to be the oldest surviving holder of the Victoria Cross, died at Cwmbran (Mon.) yesterday, at the age of 75.

John Williams (who enlisted under the assumed name of Bob Head) was one of the eight defenders of Rorke's Drift who were awarded the Victoria Cross. All his officers and comrades are dead.

After the fight he wrote a remarkable letter to his brother, F. Williams, who was at that time employed in Grafton street, and it was printed in the Irish Times in 1879. It is reproduced here in facsimile. The paper cost Williams a shilling, and he used up both sides.

John Williams enlisted in the South Wales Borderers in 1877, and joined the 2nd Battalion. The account of his winning of the Victoria Cross was published in the London Gazette of May 2nd, 1879, and relates how Williams and a comrade made a desperate stand against the Zulus in a hospital, and brought eight patients to safety.

Dear Brother,

I now send you these few lines to inform you of what I daresay you will have seen in the paper before you receive this we under Lieut Chard and Broomhead had a nice night of it at Rookes Drift I call it I never shall forget the same place about as long as I live I daresay the old fool in Command will make a great fuss over our two officers commanding our company in keeping the Zulu Buck back with the private soldier what will he get nothing only he may get praise of the public now I shall if God spares me live and see dear old England again I shall find what I say to be true so now as I had to give a Shilline for this bit of paper you will only be able to know I am ready & willing to lose my life to win back for our sister Battalion 1-/24 Renown so Kindest love to all I am jolly only short of a [a drawing of a pipe] and Bacca

Your loving Brother

Bob S. Head 2/24

30. 25B/1362 Private Frederick Hitch, 'B' Company, 2/24th Foot

30a. *Penny Illustrated News,* 21 June 1879

The Defence of Rorke's Drift
Interesting Narrative by Private Frederick Hitch

Privates Hitch and Waters and Corporal Lyons, who took part in the memorable defence of Rorke's Drift, have reached Netley Hospital, and have furnished the following interesting narratives. That given by Frederick Hitch is as follows:

I am a private in the 2-24th, and left England about 16 months ago, and was engaged in the Cape Colony under Lord Chelmsford. On the threatened Zulu outbreak my regiment was ordered to Natal, and we went up in one of the coast mail steamers. On reaching Durban we stayed there two or three days, the regiment being then 900 strong, with Colonel Degacher in command. We were then ordered to Pietermaritzburg, and we reached there about two months before Christmas. We went to Greytown, and remained there a month, and then proceeded to the front. Our column crossed the Blood River on January 11, and my company was left behind at Rorke's Drift in charge of the stores, Lieutenants Bromhead and Chard being in command.

The first news I had of what had happened at Isandula was when one of the mounted infantry, named Evans, came galloping up to the mission-house, and said that a part of the camp across the river had been destroyed by the Zulus, that two guns had been taken as well as all the ammunition, and that the enemy was advancing in force to attack Rorke's Drift. This was about three o'clock in the afternoon.

I was ordered by Lieutenant Bromhead to mount the roof of the stores to watch for the Zulus. I went up immediately, being the only man up there, and in about five minutes I saw an advance guard of the enemy coming over the brow of a hill on our right front. I at once reported this to Lieutenant Bromhead, but remained where I was, and saw that the Zulus retired in the same direction that they had come. They were apparently awaiting the arrival of the main body.

Every man in Rorke's Drift set to work piling up the mealie bags, and had soon finished. The big mob of the enemy soon came up, extending from the right, and the column appeared to me, as I watched them from the roof of the house, to be about a mile and a half in length. They were then just beyond gunshot, but were perfectly quiet. They then made a right wheel, and the extreme right moved into the caves on the adjoining hill, and as I was about the only man they could see, being on the roof, they took a pot shot at me but missed. I reported the movements to my comrades below, and fired three shots, these being the first that were fired at the Zulus at Rorke's Drift. The enemy made a yell and came at the little front with a rush, and I then got down and took my position with the rest of the company, on the right front, Mr Bromhead being close to me.

The sun was just beginning to set at the time the Zulus came up close to the front, and after they had taken the hospital and were burning it, Lieutenant Bromhead and three privates, with Colour-Sergeant Bourne, kept the position in the right front, in order to keep the enemy from getting a line of fire at the men of the 24th, who were firing to the front from behind a pile of biscuit boxes. I was here for about an hour, being all the time between three cross-fires. I saw one of my comrades – Private Nichols – killed; he was shot through the head, his brains being scattered all about us. He had up to his death been doing good service with his rifle. Another corporal – Sheath, of the Natal Contingent – was shot on my left. I myself kept shooting into a good mob of the enemy, who were very quiet in all they did. About a quarter to seven I was shot from the left, the ball striking me under the right shoulder blade and came out through the shoulder. I knew at the time that the ball had passed right through me. I fell down, and Mr Bromhead said, 'Mate are you hit?' and I said, 'Yes.' I had not had time to form an opinion as to whether the Zulus would take the fort or not. My only wish was – as I believe was that of every other man – to fight as hard as I could, and I did it until I was wounded. I crept to the rear, and, with the assistance of Private Deakin, tied up my wound as well as it could be, tearing off the sleeve of a great-coat for the purpose. I then knocked about as well as I could, serving the others with ammunition until I became exhausted from loss of blood and fell down unconscious. I did not come to before the morning, just at peep of day, and I then found myself in a stable. The Zulus, meanwhile, had retired, but were again advancing to attack us, and they saw the general and his column coming, and again retired. I was sent down to Durban, but did not reach there until the end of April, the journey down being rather rough. I was under medical care at Durban, and was sent home in the Tamar.

30b. *Stroud News and Gloucestershire Advertiser,* 13 June 1879,
reporting the arrival of the troopship *Tamar* at Spithead

Arrival of Sick and Wounded from the Cape.

… Private Hitch, of the 24th Regiment, who comes home dangerously wounded, is one of those who, with four others, when surrounded at Rorke's Drift by the Zulus, held the right front of the position and prevented the enemy from sweeping away the small body of men ensconced behind the barricade of biscuit boxes. Hitch and those who supported him were subjected to a heavy fire from the rear left flank and the front; but they maintained their position until they were incapacitated by reason of their wounds from making further active resistance, and then, after having their wounds dressed, they, with the remaining strength left, continued to serve out ammunition to their comrades during the whole of the time that the gallant resistance lasted. Private Hitch, who still wears his right arm in a sling, was unaware of the honour conferred upon him until his arrival home. On being told he, with much emotion exclaimed 'Have they given me the Cross?' On being assured that Her Majesty had been pleased to confer that distinguished recognition of his services upon him the poor fellow was completely overcome.

Private Waters, another hero of the Rorke's Drift engagement, comes home in the Tamar. He secreted himself in a cupboard in the hospital and shot several Zulus as they came in, but, being at last wounded in the right arm, he covered himself with a black cloak and took refuge in the bush, where he remained all night, at times being passed in dangerous proximity by bands of prowling Zulus. Next morning he got safely into camp to receive the congratulations of his friends. The bullet with which Waters was wounded passed into his shoulder, and made its exit at his elbow, and the missile is now saved and prized by him as a memorable memento of the struggle in which he took part. All agree that the defeat of the Zulus, whose approach in such dense masses against the diminutive garrison is described by eyewitnesses as being really appalling, undoubtedly saved the colony of Natal from utter annihilation. The wounded men arriving home from the affair at Rorke's Drift assert that the Zulus did not throw their assegais, but waited until they had chance of getting within stabbing distance, and then used them with deadly effect …

30c. A private testimonial written by Gonville Bromhead, c. November 1879 [Hitch scrapbook]

I have much pleasure in testifying to the excellent character borne by F. Hitch V.C. whilst serving in the 2/24th Regt. He served under my command in the Kaffir War 1878, and subsequently in the Zulu War and was present with his Company at the Defence of Rorke's Drift. I found him a clean sober & hardworking man, and in the defence of Rorke's Drift he so distinguished himself by his personal gallantry that he was awarded the Victoria Cross which was graciously presented to him by Her Majesty in person.

In this engagement he was severely wounded and rendered unfit for active service as a Soldier.

Gonville Bromhead
Major 2/24th Regt.
Pinetown – Natal
November 1879.

30d. Hand-written letter by Hitch [Hitch scrapbook. A second version of this letter exists at the Royal Welsh Regimental Museum, Brecon, Acc. No. 1996.37]

Frederick Hitch. V.C. Late 2.24th Regt.

As I have been asked many times to give my Illustration of Rorkes Drift I Cannot say it is A Pleasure for me to do so and to think Back on that treable night of the 22 Jan 1879 it Was about 3.30 o clock noon that We heard of that fatal Disaster of Isandhlwana I was Cooking the tea for the company I tryed to get it Done before the zulus attacked the little Post Rorkes Drift Which I managed taken the tea and My rifle and ammunition and four kettles tea I just got in to the fort When Bromhead asked me to try and get on to the top of the house I at once mounted it as soon as I got on the top I Could see that Zulus had got as near to us as they Could Without us seeing them I told Mr Bromhead that they were at the other side of the rise and was extending for attacked Mr Bromhead asked me how many I thought there were I told him that I thought numbered from 4, to, 6000. A. voice from be low is that all we Can mnage that lot very well for a few seconds this were Diffrent opinion I staid on the House watching the Blak mass Extending into there fighting line the same time a number of them creaping a long under the Rocks and took up cover in the caves, and Keep trying to dismount me from the top of the House there Direction was good but there allevation bad a few minutes later one appeared on the Top of the Mountain from the other side he Could see us in the Largher plain Enough to Count us I put myself in a Laying position but my shot fell short of him he than moved steadely to the right and signelled with his arm the main body at once begune to advance I told Mr Bromhead that they would be all round us in a very short time he at once told the Company to take up there post the Enmey making a right wheel, they attacd us in shap of a bullocks horns and in a few minuts was all round us I found as they got close to the Largur I was out of the fighting so I slid down the thatch roof, droping into the Largur fixting my bainet as I run across the largur taking up my Possition on a open space which we had not time to compleat the Deadly work now Commenced.

The Zulus pushing right up to the porch it was not untill the bainet was freely used that they flinched the least bit had the Zulus taken the bainet as freely as they took the bullets we could not have stood more than fifteen minuts – they pushed on right up to us and not only got up to the Largur but got in with us, but they seemed to have a great dread of the bainet which stood to us from beging to end, during that strugle there was a fine big Zulu see me shoot his mait down he sprang forward droping his Rifel and asegis, ceesing hold of the muzle of my Rifel, with his left hand and he right hand hold of the bainet thinking to disarme me he pulled and tryed hard to get the Rifel from me but I had a ferm hold of the small of the butt of my rifel with my left hand

My Cartridges on the Top of the meely bags which enabled me to load my rifel and shot the poor reatch

Wilest holding on to his grasp, for some few moments they droped back into the Garden which served a great proction for them had it not been for the Garden and dead wall they could not haved prolonged the Engagement for thirteen houres as they did, there next object was to get possition of the Hospittal which they did by setting fire to it, The greatest Task was in getting the Sick and Wounded out of the Hospittal, which the zulus had bursted open the doors and killed them in there beds Wilest doing this I noticed it was with great difficalty they were keep back.

They keeping up a heavy fire from front and rear from which we suffered very much it was than about when Mr dalton was shot and Mr Dunn, Mr dolton was very activ up till he was Wounded, we had to fall back to the Second line of Defence and when the Zulus took position of the Hospittal, Bromhead & myself & five others took up the Position on the right of the second line of Defence, which we were exposed to three Cross fires, Bromhead took the center, and was the only one that did not get Wounded, there was four killed and two Wounded myselfe was the last of the six one shot Bromhead & myself had it to our twoselves about an hour & a half, Bromhead using his Rifel & revolver with deadly aime Bromhead keep telling the men not to waist one round, About this time we was pressed very much Bromhead was using his revolver with deadly aime, they seemed determined to move Bromhead & myself, we were so buissey that one had got inside and was in the act of assygien Bromhead not knowing he was I there, I put my rifel on him knowing at the same time it was empty, Instead of him deliving the assygie which no doubt would have been faitle, he dodge down and hoped out of the Largur Again this was just before they tryed to fire the other building they seemed to me as, if they made up there minds to take Rorkes drift with this rush They rushed up madley not with standing the heavy loss they had all ready suffered it was in this struggle that I was shot, they pressed us very hard several of them mounting the Barracade, I knew this one had got his rifel presented at me but at the same time I had got my hands full in front and I was at the present when he shot me through my right Shoulder blaid and passed through my Shoulder which splintered the Shoulder bone very much, as I have had in all 38 pieces of broaken bone taken from my Shoulder I tryed to keep my feet, but Could not, He could have assygide me had not Bromhead shot him with his revolver Bromhead seemed sorry when he saw me down Bleading so Freely, saying Mate I am very sorry to see you down I was not down not more than a few minuets striped in my shirtsleves with my waistbelt on and Fleas straps I put my wounded arm under my waist belt I was able to make another stand Getting Bromheads revolver and with his assistance in loading it I managed very well with it at this time we were fighting by the ade from the burning Hospital, which was much to our advantage, Bromhead at this time was keeping a strict eye on the ammunision and telling the men not to waist one round as we were getting short, I was serving out ammunision myself when I became thurstey and faint I got worse, a Chum tore out the linnin out of Mr dunn's coat and tied it round my Shoulder, I got so thirsty that I could not do much in fact we were all Exhausted and the ammunision was beging to be Counted, Deacken, a Comerade said to me as I was leaning back against the buicust Boxes, Fred when it Comes to the last shill I shoot you I Declyned no they have very near done for me and they Can finish me right out, when it Come to the Last I dont rember not much after that when I came to myself again Lord Chamford had realived us of our task, Bromhead brought his Lordship to me and his Lordship spoak very kindley to me and the Dr. dressed my wound Bromhead was my Principal, visiter and nurse while I was at the Drift.

Finish

30e. *Oxford Times,* 5 June 1880

A Soldier on the Zulu War

Major Evered Poole, late of the 60th Royal Rifles, gave a lecture illustrated by dissolving views in St Aldate's Rectory room on Saturday evening last … Referring to the defence of Rorke's Drift, he said that Hitchcock, who was one of the heroes of that notable incident, had told him that he had, during the night, fired no less than 300 rounds of cartridge and, although he did not notice it till afterwards, the barrel of his rifle got so hot that the skin was taken off his hands. When the Queen pinned the Victoria Cross to his manly breast, he was far more afraid than he had been of the Zulus. A grateful country had bestowed upon this fine specimen of a British hero a pension of one shilling per day for twelve months …

30f. *Newcastle Daily Journal,* 1 September 1880

De Neuville's Great Battle Picture
"The Defence of Rorke's Drift,"
Now on View
Messrs. Mawsom, Swan and Morgan's Fine Art Galleries
21,22, and 23, Grey Street, Newcastle

Private Frederick Hitch, V.C., one of the heroes of 'Rorke's Drift,' is with the picture and gives any information that visitors may require.
Admission: Ten to Five – 1s. Five to Seven – Sixpence.

30g. *Truth,* 18 September 1902

I have been asked to try and recover a Zululand Victoria Cross which was recently stolen from the owner. I do not suppose I can do this, but a warning on the subject may be useful to the collectors who purchase such articles, and to whom the stolen Cross is pretty certain to be offered sooner or later. The man who has been robbed is Mr. Frederick Hitch, and he won the decoration at Rorke's Drift, where he was shot through the shoulder. After leaving the Army, Hitch became a porter at the United Service Institution, and his Victoria Cross was displayed upon his livery, to which it was sewn. The livery was left at the Institution every night. While Hitch was away ill the Cross was cut off his coat, and no trace of the thief was ever found. After placing the matter in the hands of the police the Committee of the United Service Institution announced that they had come to the conclusion that it was a mysterious disappearance which they could not unravel, which Hitch took to imply a suggestion that he had perhaps made away with the Cross himself. Naturally resenting this, he left the Institution, and at the present time this Rorke's Drift hero is driving a cab about the streets of London. The man keenly feels the loss of the decoration, which he had hoped to leave to one of his two sons, both of whom are in the Service; and his fear is that, should the Cross ever turn up, their claim to it may be defeated by the suggestion that he himself sold it. Of course it will turn up sooner or later, and the first honest person who comes across it ought to know these facts.

It seems that the selling price of a Victoria Cross ranges, according to the state of the market, from £90 to £120. Collectors of curios have a good deal to answer for in putting such a temptation in the way of soldiers to sell decorations which they ought to consider 'Beyond price,' I suggested to Hitch that he should bring an action against the United Service Institution to recover this amount, for so far as one can judge from his statement, the Cross was clearly in the custody of the Institution at the time of the theft, and the circumstances of the theft raise a pretty strong presumption of negligence.

30h. *Chums – An Illustrated Paper for Boys*, No. 809, 11 March 1908

Fighting For Empire.
The Story of Private Hitch, V.C.

[For the first time Private Hitch relates his story of the gallant defence of Rorke's Drift, one of the most stirring and heroic fights of the Zulu War of 1879. At the time of Rorke's Drift, Private Hitch was twenty-four years of age, and was serving with the 2nd Battalion of the South Wales Borderers.

"B" Company of his regiment had been left to guard a depot and hospital, which had been established at a Mission Station a few hundred yards from a river crossing known as Rorke's Drift.]

We did not expect any fighting that day, and were occupied in our usual duties, little thinking that a horde of Zulus – the pick of the Zulu Army, in fact – were marching on us, determined to kill every man at our little post.

About one o'clock two men galloped to the Drift, bringing the news that the Zulus had annihilated our force at Isandhlwana, and that they were now marching on to attack our post at Rorke's Drift. Lieutenant Bromhead, who was in charge of the post, and Commissioner Dalton at once held a conference. The position was a difficult one: our little force only consisted of a handful of men, whilst the approaching Zulus, mad with success, must have numbered at least four thousand. And many of them, moreover, were armed. At first it was thought the better part of valour to desert the post, but fortunately this decision was altered. We were to defend the post, and hold it at all costs.

With us were four hundred friendly natives, and these men we at once set to work carrying mealie (corn) bags and boxes of stores, which we placed in position as barricades, making an enclosure or laager of which the mission house, used as a hospital, and some out-buildings formed a part. Just before the barricades had been completed the friendly niggers began to funk it, and as soon as they found out that the Zulus were really coming down upon us in great force they commenced to sneak away. We tried to rally them, but it was of no use. Then their captain went after them with the intention of bringing them back; but he disappeared too. Just to show these black gentleman what we thought of their conduct, some of us, including myself, sent a few shots after them, which brought down dead one of their white non-commissioned officers.

While the men were still barricading the place, Lieutenant Bromhead asked me to climb to the top of a building, which I believe had been used as a church, and keep a look-out for the enemy. Having got to the top of the building I could plainly see the Zulus forming up just over the brow of a hill.

"They are ready to attack, sir," I called out to Lieutenant Bromhead, "and I think there are about four thousand of them."

A little fellow named Morris, who heard me, remarked:

"Oh, if that's all there are, we can manage that lot all right!"

Presently I saw a Zulu, evidently one of their chiefs, who was standing on the summit of a hill, gave the signal by extending his arms, and immediately the whole force commenced to advance on us. They seemed to work on a pivot, the pivot being only about three hundred yards distant, when the final advance began; so that, in order to attack us on all sides at once, the other end of their line had come on at a tremendous pace.

My position on the housetop was a pretty good target for them, but none of their shots hit me. As soon as I saw them on the move, I dropped down into the laager and fixed my bayonet. I was only just in time, which will give you some idea of the rapidity of their movements.

On they came with a rush. With one hand the warriors held their shields, and in the other hand they carried their deadly assegais. A few were armed with rifles, just taken from the poor fellows whom they had annihilated at Isandlwana.

We volleyed into the mass as they advanced, but there was little hesitation. Our bullets accounted for many, but there were hundreds to fill their places. They still came on right up to the barricades, and were only turned by the good cold steel of our bayonets, for which they had far more respect than for bullets.

Then it was load and fire and bayonet just as fast as we could. The niggers would retire and come on again in rushes, each rush being announced by a short war cry. This war cry, by the way, was very useful to us: we knew what to expect. Even when darkness came upon us they continued to use their war shout, which was not altogether wise on their part, because it at once put us on the alert. However, we didn't complain on that score.

Fortunately those of the Zulus who had rifles knew very little about their weapons or how to use them. Their shots appeared to go either much too high or too low. I suppose they did not understand the sighting. Had there been a few marksmen amongst them I fear myself and many more would have gone under at Rorke's Drift.

Soon it was discovered that it was impossible to defend the laager which we had made, so Major Chard gave an order to make a second line of barricades, inside the outer one. This work was carried out under great difficulties and under heavy fire from a cave close by, where a few Zulus had taken cover. Had the four hundred friendly native troops not bolted, the larger laager would have been none too roomy. This second line of barricades proved a great success, as it meant that we had less ground to cover.

There was a certain space of about nine yards where the barricading was uncompleted. It was, of course, the weakest link in the chain, and the Zulus were not long in discovering this fact.

In this position eight of us – Bromhead, Nicholls, Fagan, Cole, Dalton, Schiess, Williams, and myself – made a stand, and it was here, I think, that the hardest work was done.

Though the situation was so uncomfortable, there was no bungling. Each man in a businesslike manner singled out the nigger who was nearest him, and dealt out death if he could. In one of these nasty rushes three Zulus were making for me; they seemed to have specially marked me out. The first fellow I shot; the second man I bayoneted; the third man got right into the laager, but he declined to stand up against me. With a leap he jumped over the barricade, and made off.

A few yards from the barricade lay a wounded Zulu. We knew he was there, and that he had only been wounded, and so wanted watching. At the moment we were far too busy with the more active members to find time to put him right out. Presently I saw him, with rifle in hand, taking aim at one of my comrades. It was too late to stop him; he fired, and poor Nicholls fell dead, shot through the head.

I practised a little ruse upon a Zulu at which I had to smile even at the time. This particular Zulu had got through the barricades into the laager, and was in the act of throwing an assegai at Lieutenant Bromhead, whose attention was directed elsewhere. At that moment my rifle was unloaded, and there was no time to reload. I shouted to the Zulu, and brought my rifle up to my shoulder as if to fire. My Zulu soldier didn't wait. With a duck of the head and a mighty leap he bounded over the barricades and made off in a manner worthy of any eminent acrobat.

In one of the many rushes a nigger, who had missed our bullets, came full tilt at me, and seized my bayonet with both his hands. This was quite a new experience for me. There was no time to lose: I had to settle up with him quickly or not at all. For a few seconds we struggled for possession of the rifle; then I managed to point the barrel at his stomach, and fired whilst he still clutched the bayonet. He was a brave fellow.

Parson Smith, our chaplain, kept us well supplied with ammunition. Now and then he would ask our men not to swear so much. But the men continued to swear, and fight the harder.

We knew that the poor fellows in the hospital were fighting against great odds for their lives, but we could not see what was going on there. Jones, Williams, Hook and their comrades had kept the enemy off for some time, but now the Zulus had set fire to the roof, which was of thatch, and the patients had to be taken away. In order to reach the laager the patients and their defenders had to cross an undefended space, which was swept by the enemy's bullets. One by one the poor fellows scrambled out of the burning building, and ran the gauntlet. We covered them as much we could, but many of them went under.

When the Zulus set fire to the hospital the other company of the battalion, for which we had been so anxiously waiting, appeared in sight. But they didn't march to our rescue. Seeing the hospital on fire, they came to the conclusion that we had all been annihilated, and with drooping spirits we saw our comrades turn back and retire. It was at this time that the Zulus made one of their most desperate charges, and Rorke's Drift was all but lost. Lieutenant Bromhead encouraged the men.

"Don't lose heart," he called out; "Our men will return as soon as they find we are holding out."

The hospital fire became more fierce. This fire turned out to be our salvation, for as darkness came on it lit up the ground on all sides of the laager, and enabled us to see the Zulus whenever they approached the barricades.

The fighting went on desperately. Rush after rush had been repelled. Of the eight who held the unbarricaded position only two of us were left, Lieutenant Bromhead and myself. Nicholls, Fagan, and Cole were killed, whilst Dalton and Williams were wounded. So Bromhead and I went on together for about an hour, and a rough time we had too. More than once the Zulus got inside the laager, but were beaten back or killed.

We were both very busy with Zulus in front when one of the niggers managed to pass us and get inside. I knew he was there. I was just about to shoot down a Zulu in front, when the Zulu inside shot me through the right shoulder, carrying away the scapula.

Turning round quickly, Bromhead at once shot down the man who had wounded me. I got up again, and attempted to use my rifle, but it was no use; my right arm wouldn't work, so I strapped it into my waist belt to keep it out of the way. Then Bromhead gave me his revolver to use, and with this I think I did as much execution as I had done before I was wounded.

Seeing how badly wounded I was, one of my comrades, a man named Deacon, asked me whether he should "put me out" when it came to the finish. He could see that my strength was fast failing, and that if the devils got through I would be quite unable to strike a blow for myself.

"No, I don't think I want any," I said, I had no desire to have my life ended, but it was kind of my friend Deacon to think of me in this way.

It was about ten o'clock. Four hours I had been bleeding from the wound in my back, and I was getting very faint from loss of blood. I knew that I was losing consciousness, the last of my recollection being that Bromhead still held his post. Then I went down where I had been fighting for seven hours. I was told that later on they dragged me inside the inner laager.

It was not till the next morning that I came to, when I found we had just been relieved by a column under Lord Chelmsford. My chum was one of the relieving force. He, good chap, came and changed my shirt, which was saturated with blood, and did what he could for me.

Later on in the day towards evening Lord Chelmsford himself came to me, and, bending down beside me, said:

"Mr. Bromhead has given me an account of your excellent services. I will recommend you for the V.C., and, if you only survive, you may be sure I will do everything that lies in my power for you."

30i. *The People,* 4 October 1908

His Second V.C.
War Office replaces lost decoration

Pte. F. Hitch, a Rorke's Drift hero, who was awarded the Victoria Cross, and lost the precious decoration in 1879, has been promised a new one by the War Office. Hitch was invalided home after Rorke's Drift, and received the cross from the hands of the late Queen Victoria at the Netley Hospital. "Some time after I left the Army," says Hitch, "I entered the service of the United Service Institution. Soon after I went there I put my knee-cap out and had to be taken off to the hospital. I hadn't my coat on at the time, and my cross was sewn on it. As soon as I was conscious I remembered, and sent for my coat. It was too late – the cross had been cut off. Of course, I told the authorities, and they informed Scotland Yard. I told Colonel Holden that I held the Institution responsible for the loss, and in the end matters got so unpleasant that I had to leave.

Kept on Worrying

I kept on worrying them, though, and after a long time, Col Holden offered to replace my V.C. with a dummy one out of the Institution museum. I wasn't going to be put off with that, though. The loss was bad enough, but what was worse was an idea some people had that I had disposed of my V.C. for money. I have never stopped hunting for a clue as to the whereabouts of my own cross, or asking the Army Council to grant me a new one. Lately some of the officers of my old regiment, the 24th Foot, now the 2nd South Wales Borderers, have taken the matter up. I had to sign a paper promising to give the new cross up if ever I found my old one, but I didn't mind doing that. Every Victoria Cross has its owner's name, regimental number, and the name of the engagement for which it was given engraved on the back, so whoever has got my old V.C. can't show it about much."

30j. *London Evening Standard,* 22 December 1908

Situations Wanted

Doorkeeper, Attendant, Commissionaire, or any Position of Trust: Possessor of V.C. for the defence of Rorke's Drift: highest references up to date. Address R.D. 5125, Standard Office, Fleet-st, E.C.

30k. *Daily Telegraph,* 11 July 1910

V.C. Taxi-Driver

The only taxi-driver in London, and possibly in the United Kingdom, possessing the Victoria Cross is Mr Frederick Hitch, of Pond House, Pond-place, Chelsea. Mr. Hitch received the coveted award for an exceptional act of gallantry at the defence of Rorke's Drift on Jan. 22. 1879. He was serving with the 24th Regiment (South Wales Borderers) and, in company with Private William Allen, who also received the V.C., held open the communication between the hospital and the inner defence, enabling the wounded to be carried across when the Zulus set fire to the thatched building. He was very badly hit by a roughly-made bullet, which inflicted a fearful gash in his shoulder, no less than thirty-six pieces of bone being taken away from the wound. When prevented from firing he served out ammunition during the night. He received the Victoria Cross from Queen Victoria at Netley Hospital on being invalided home.

Mr. Hitch was born in 1856 at New Southgate, and previous to the Zulu War had served through the Kaffir War of 1877–8.

30l. *Marylebone Mercury & West London Gazette,* 11 January 1913

Rorke's Drift.
Another Hero Dead.

Believed to be the last but one of the surviving Victoria Cross heroes of Rorke's Drift, Frederick Hitch, a Chiswick taxi driver, passed away late on Monday night.

His friend and neighbour, Mr. H. Wiley, was reading to him when he suddenly collapsed, and died in Mr. Wiley's arms. As one of those who had taken a splendid part in the defence of Rorke's Drift, on January 22 and 23, 1879, Hitch was very well known in Chiswick, as well as in the City of London, and indeed in all parts of the metropolis.

After three years or more of service in Zululand with the gallant 2nd Battalion 24th Regiment, Hitch returned to England, and at the end of his service became commissionaire at several places.

Among other posts he occupied was one at the Royal United Services Institution, in Whitehall. While there he had the Victoria Cross stolen bodily from his coat, and he was almost inconsolable at the loss, but the late King Edward heard of his grief and a little later caused a facsimile to be prepared and presented to the brave soldier.

Some time later he became the owner of several horse cabs in Chiswick, but had to give way before the taxi invasion. But he was not one to sink before trouble, and, recognising that the new machines had come to stay, he took service with the General Motor Cab Company at their Chiswick garage.

It was one of the pleasures of his life that he had been chosen by Lady Butler to sit for her while painting one of her pictures, a copy of which occupied the place of honour in his room at Cranbrook-road.

31. 25B/1373 Private Henry (Alfred) Hook, 'B' Company, 2/24th Foot

31a. *South Wales Weekly Telegram,* 18 April 1879

Monmouth Soldiers at Rorke's Drift.

A letter has been received by Mrs. E. Hook, Drybridge Street, from her son Henry, a private in B Company, 2 24th Regiment, Rorke's Drift. Referring to Rorke's Drift, he says: –

"After the enemy had fled from the general's camp they came across the river here, and attacked our commissary stores, but fortunately we got an hour's warning, and made a fort. By-and-bye down they came in thousands – one black mass – so many we did not know where to fire first, they being so many, and we were about 100 all told. But, thank God, after a night of great fighting, we drove them off, and we saw the general's forces coming over the hill, and that gave us great relief, I can tell you. There were four Monmouth men killed, vis.: – Sergeant Maxfield (Cinderhill Street), Private Hopkins (formerly a servant at Gibraltar House, Monmouth, and later a policeman stationed at Llanarth), Private Charles (Penalt, near Monmouth), and Thomas Bennett (Monnow Street). Sergeant Maxfield was burnt alive in the hospital; the enemy swarmed around and burnt the place before we could save him, and as he was raving mad with fever, he could not save himself. Hopkins and the others were killed in the fight at the general camp. I had a very narrow escape, for I was in the hospital, and when the enemy set fire to it I had to get out of the window and fight my way through them … I am now servant to Major Black (his man having been killed), and a nice gentleman he is, and I like him very much."

31b. *Manchester Evening News*, 6 September 1879

A Dramatic Incident of the Zulu War

Writing from Rorke's Drift on the 8th ultimo, the correspondent of the Daily News says: – "A very dramatic incident occurred here the other day. Private Hook, of the 24th, received from Sir Garnet's hands the Victoria Cross for his share in the defence of Rorke's Drift. He was one of the men who defended the hospital step by step whilst it was in flames, and succeeded in saving all who could be moved of the patients there. As Sir Garnet said to him in presenting the precious token, it can very seldom happen that the general who has to present the prize in Her Majesty's name is able six months after the event to give the reward of valour on the very spot where it was earned, and the fact not a little enhanced the interest of the ceremony. Sir Garnet the same day, after inspecting the famous house and grounds, rode over some five miles of the most intolerably bad of riding countries to look at the graves of Coghill and Melville, where stands now a simple cross on the spot where they died, and where they were found with the colours they had saved.

31c. *County Observer and Monmouthshire Central Advertiser*, 21 May 1881

How He Won his Victoria Cross.

As our Monmouth correspondent states, it is a well-known fact it is always with great difficulty that a soldier who has very active service, and especially if he had so signally distinguished himself as the hero of this notice, can ever be cajoled into talking of an engagement. But after many futile attempts, our correspondent managed to elicit the following interesting facts from Mr. William Hook, V.C., late of the 2-24th Regiment.

The reader is particularly requested to understand that Mr Hook had the statement given below drawn from him in answer to numerous questions, all of which were given reluctantly, and totally without any idea of boasting. Instead of giving the answers as received, we prefer to give them in the form of a narrative;–

"I was in the army three years and hundred and sixty-three days, and I had only had nine months training in England before I was sent out to Zululand on active service; but I should say that I was in the Royal Monmouth Militia for five years previously, being now quite twenty-six years of age. After I had been 'out' three months I joined the Good Templars at Pietermaritzburgh, and kept that pledge as long as I remained in that country. As you are aware, [we saw his letters], in all my letters home I made no allusions to any serious hardships, nor attempted to credit myself with any deeds of bravery, it being my desire not to alarm my parents. One man who was not within eighty miles of Rorke's Drift sent home a fictitious account of the battle; his letter got in the papers, and the colonel saw it; the man, who was a corporal, was tried and reduced for the offence.

I was on guard at the hospital at Rorke's Drift, when the attack upon it was made, and there were nine others with me. Almost the first thing I knew was that I was fighting 'over the soles of my boots in blood,' The hospital was fired by the blacks. How did poor Macksfield of Monmouth die do you ask? Well, [and here a suspicious watery appearance came into the speaker's eyes], I think I only know; he was a sergeant, and was a very smart young fellow when he was last at home, but when he got out there the climate did not agree with him, and he was attacked by dysentery, and a kind of rheumatic fever, which made him quite mad. Poor fellow, in his delirium he tried to get at the enemy, but I tried all I could to keep him back, having one or two narrow shaves of being killed myself in the attempt; however all I could do was useless, he got among the crowd of savages, and soon fell wounded, being killed soon after, – not burnt to death as some suppose. I was able to identify him after because I knew where he fell and he had a blue check shirt on; there wasn't much left to identify – only a small piece of his shirt as large as a lady's handkerchief, and a small part of his body, all the rest was burnt. But, [with a fiery flash of the eye], the man who killed was killed and fell in the fire. But I don't like talking of these things – Yes, in the smoke I did manage to carry seven out of the nine who were with me to a place of safety – the other two were killed. I got off very lucky, only getting a scar on the head, which looks now more than it was even when it was done. Many of us were over two years without knowing what it was to sleep in a bed, and often had to rabble away the mud and water from the ground before we could lie down upon it, using a stone covered with our helmets for a pillow. No, we had no waterproof sheets, or top-coats – I had a mealy sack, with holes cut in it for my arms and head to go through for a top-coat, and I have seen officers, with no other. A lot of our young men could not stand it, and were invalided in the first twelve months; they were too young. Yes, I got the Victoria Cross, and a day or two ago the Zulu War medal. The cross was presented to me not much than 600 yards from the spot where the hospital stood. I was sorely tempted to break the pledge the day I got the cross – even the officers offered me drink, but I firmly refused; I had not even been in the habit of drinking my allowance of rum; I gave that away. I was very ill when I came home, and that is why I left the army."

Mr Hook, V.C., is now living in Monmouth, his native town.

31d. *Strand Magazine,* Vol. 1, January to June 1891

Stories of the Victoria Cross: Told by Those who have Won it. Private Henry Hook.

On January 22nd 1879, Private Henry Hook, with his company, under Lieutenant Bromhead, was stationed at Rorke's Drift, to guard the ford and hospital and stores. He thus tells his gallant story:–

Between three and four in the afternoon, when I was engaged preparing the tea for the sick at the out-of-door cooking place, just at the back of the hospital – for I was hospital cook – two mounted men, looking much exhausted, and their horses worn out, rode up to me. One was in his shirt sleeves, and without a hat, with a revolver strapped round his breast; the other had his coat and hat on. They stopped for a moment and told me that the whole force on the other side of the river had been cut up, and that the

Zulus were coming on in great force. They then rode off. I immediately ran to the camp close by and related what I had heard. We were at once fallen in and set to work to strengthen the post by loopholing the windows of the buildings, and to make breastworks of biscuit boxes and mealie bags. About half an hour later the Zulus were seen coming round a hill, and about 1,200 yards off. We were then told off to our posts. I was placed in one of the corner rooms of the hospital.

About this time Captain Stevens and all his men, except one native and two Europeans, non-commissioned officers, deserted us, and went off to Helpmakaar. We were so enraged that we fired several shots at them, one of which dropped a European non-commissioned officer. From my loophole I saw the Zulus approaching in their thousands. They begun to fire, yelling as they did so, when they were 500 or 600 yards off. They came on boldly, taking advantage of anthills and other cover, and we were soon surrounded. More than half of them had muskets or rifles. I began to fire when they were 600 yards distant. I managed to clip several of them, for I had an excellent rifle, and was a "marksman." I recollect particularly one Zulu. He was about 400 yards off, and was running from one anthill to another. As he was running from cover to cover, I fired at him; my bullet caught him in the body, and he made a complete somersault. Another man was lying below an anthill, about 300 yards off popping his head out now and again to fire. I took careful aim, but my bullet went just over his head. I then lowered my sight, and fired again the next time he showed himself. I saw the bullet strike the ground in a direct line, but about ten yards short. I then took a little fuller sight, aimed at the spot where I knew his head would come out, and, when he showed himself, I fired. I did not then see whether he was struck, but he never showed himself again. The next morning, when the fighting was over, I felt curious to know whether I had hit this man, so I went to the spot where I had last seen him. I found him lying dead, with his skull pierced by my bullet.

The Zulus kept drawing closer and closer, and I went on firing, killing several of them. At last they got close up, and set fire to the hospital. There was only one patient in my room with a broken leg, and he was burnt, and I was driven out by the flames, and was unable to save him. At first I had a comrade but he left after a time, and was killed on his way to the inner entrenchment. When driven out of this room, I retired by a partition door into the next room, where there were several patients. For a few minutes I was the only fighting man there. A wounded man of the 24th came to me from another room with a bullet wound in the arm. I tied it up. Then John Williams came in from another room and made a hole in the partition, through which he helped the sick and wounded men. Whilst he was doing this, the Zulus beat in the door, and tried to enter. I stood at the side, and shot and bayoneted several – I could not tell how many, but there were four or five lying dead at my feet. They threw assegais continually, but only one touched me, and that afflicted a scalp wound which I did not think worth reporting; in fact, I did not feel the wound at the time.

One Zulu seized my rifle, and tried to drag it away. Whilst we were tussling I slipped in a cartridge and pulled the trigger – the muzzle was against his breast, and he fell dead. every now and again a Zulu would make a rush to enter – the door would only let in one man at a time – but I bayoneted or shot every one. When all the patients were out except one, who owing to a broken leg could not move, I also went through the hole, dragging the man after me, in doing which I broke his leg again. I then stopped at the hole to guard it, whilst Williams was making a hole through the partition into the next room.

When the patients had been got into the next room I followed, dragging the man with the broken leg after me. I stopped at the hole to guard it whilst Williams was helping the patients through a window into the other defences. I stuck to my particular charge, and dragged him out and helped him into the inner line of defences. I then took my post behind the parapet where three men had been hit just before. One of these was shot in the thick part of the neck, and was calling on me all night to shift from one side to the other. On this side the blaze of the hospital lighted up the ground in front, enabling us to take aim. The Zulus would every quarter of an hour or so get together and make a rush accompanied by yells. We let them get close, and then fired a volley – sometimes two. This would check them and send them back. Then after a time they would rally and come on again. About 3a.m. day began to break, and the Zulus retreated. A party, of which I was one, then volunteered to go across to the hospital, where there was a water cart, and bring it in to the inner enclosure, where there was no water, and the wounded were crying for it. When the sun rose we found the Zulus had disappeared. We then went out to search for our missing comrades. I saw one man kneeling behind the outer defences with his rifle to his shoulder, and resting on the parapet as if he were taking aim; I touched him on the shoulder, asking him why he didn't come inside, but he fell over, and I saw he was dead. I saw several others of our dead ripped open and otherwise mutilated. Going beyond the outer defences I went, as I have said before, whither I had killed the man at whom I had fired three shots from the hospital. Going on a little further I came across a very tall Zulu, bleeding from a wound in the leg; I was passing him by when he made a yell and clutched the butt of my rifle, dragging himself on to his knees. We had a severe struggle which lasted for several seconds, when finding he could not get the rifle from me, he let go with one hand and caught me round the leg, trying to throw me. Whilst he was doing this I got the rifle from him, and drawing back a yard or two, loaded and blew his brains out. I then was fetched back to the fort, and no one was allowed to go out save with other men. Then several of us went out together, and we brought in several wounded Zulus. By this time it was about eight or nine o'clock, and we saw a body coming towards us; at the same time Lord Chelmsford's column came in sight, and the enemy retired.

Lord Chelmsford, soon after he arrived, called me up to enquire about the defence of the hospital. I was busy preparing tea for sick and wounded, and was in my shirt-sleeves, with my braces down. I wanted to put on my coat before appearing in front of the General, but I was told to come along at once, and I felt rather nervous at leaving in such a state, and thought I had committed some offence. When Lord Chelmsford heard my story he praised me and shook me by the hand. The Cross was presented to me on August 3, at Rorke's Drift, by Sir Garnet Wolseley.

31e. *The Sketch*, 20 April 1898

A Hero of Rorke's Drift.

Sergeant Hook, V.C., the subject of this interview, is an obliging attendant at the British Museum, where, in company with a comrade, he is in charge of the Vestiary attached to the Reading-Room.

Twelve years ago, after serving for five years in the Royal Monmouth Militia, he joined the 1st Royal Fusilier Volunteers, in which he now holds the rank of Sergeant; and it is in the uniform of that corps that he is here depicted. But it was as private in the 2nd Battalion of the "Noble 24th," South Wales Borderers, which in the sanguinary engagements against overwhelming hordes of savage Zulu warriors at Isandhlwana and Rorke's Drift lost in killed alone the appalling total of 21 officers and 587 men, and won eight Victoria Crosses, that Sergeant Hook commenced his military career, and conquered the coveted decoration for signal gallantry in face of the enemy that ornaments his breast.

Born in the pretty village of Churcham, Gloucestershire, the Sergeant is now forty-five years of age. He stands 5 ft. 7 in. in his socks, measures 42 in. round the chest, and is a rather stout but hale and robust man, with a kindly expression of countenance, and a heavy fair moustache. He married just a year ago.

Rorke's Drift, he tells me, was a Missionary Station, consisting of a church and house built of sun-dried bricks. The military had formed a camp there, converting the unpretentious place of worship into a dépôt for stores, and the dwelling into a hospital.

The first news the company in charge received of the massacre at Isandhlwana was when two troopers came tearing into camp on horseback, one with his revolver strapped to his wrist, the other in his shirtsleeves, and, after giving the alarm, rode off to apprise stations further away of the terrible disaster, while the missionary, without a moment's hesitation jumped on his ass and succeeded in making good his escape. Some time afterwards he sent in a bill to the Government for compensation for the loss of his property.

When four thousand Zulus were sighted at half-past four on the afternoon of Jan. 22, 1879, shortly after the two troopers had left the station, advancing at a distance of a thousand yards round the hill to the left of the hospital front, Sergeant Hook was engaged in the peaceful occupation of preparing tea for the forty invalids, a few of whom only were able to defend themselves.

"The Zulus," he says, "once in sight of the station, immediately divided into two columns, advancing at an acute angle, taking advantage of the multitude of huge ant-hills, four or five feet high, and of the dry gullies that had served as water-courses in the rainy season, to shelter themselves. We let them come on until within six hundred yards, when we gave them a volley which brought down a few and drove some back; but the others continued dashing forward, bounding over the ground, leaping six feet in the air, amid deafening shrieks and yells. With long bucklers, pointed at either end, on their left arms, they brandished spears and guns in their right hands, flinging assegais at us in showers, discharging their firearms, apparently indifferent to our fire and to the havoc our bullets played among them.

"They kept on charging, numbers of them coming right abreast of our defences; but we held our ground driving them back over and over again. Each time they withdrew they had a war-dance in the distance, to brace their nerves for another attack, and then came bounding on again in the same mad rush as before.

"During the space of four hours I held my ward with two other men, both of whom were slain. At last I ran short of ammunition, and things became so frightfully hot that I felt I should not be able to stand it much longer. For a space I defended the threshold with my bayonet, husbanding the few cartridges I had left, and at every lull in the enemy's frantic onslaughts I piled corpse upon corpse in the doorway before me, along with anything else I could lay my hands on, until I had formed a solid breastwork reaching my shoulders.

"This massive, hideous barricade afforded me some protection and relief; but the Zulus by now had set fire to the building. Grasping a pick, I rapidly made a small hole in the dry, sun-burnt brick partition, and dragged several sick and wounded men through it into the next ward. In this manner I caved in three walls, and, meeting Lance-Corporal Williams on the way, with his assistance succeeded in bringing eight invalids into the last room, where we managed to get them out of a window, and finally gained the inner defence near the church. When I found myself safe within the inner defence, the perspiration was running off me in a stream, so to say, and my undergarments were wringing wet. Three men had already been killed at the post assigned to me after leaving the hospital. It was a dark but fine night, and the Zulus, taking advantage of the obscurity, constantly came creeping stealthily up to the breastwork protecting us, clutching at the muzzles of our rifles in the hope of being able to wrench them from our grasp in a moment of inattention.

"Presently the hospital flamed up, and to this I attribute our escape. The glare of the burning building revealed the tactics of our savage foes, who every twenty minutes or so would hold a frantic war-dance, as in the afternoon, and then dash on to us in an impetuous charge, causing the very ground to tremble beneath our feet as they came bounding along. As soon as they got within six hundred yards we poured volley after volley into them, bowling them over like rabbits. This kind of thing continued throughout the night.

"In the meanwhile, we had been getting short of water. The water-cart was standing some forty or fifty yards off, close to the hospital. During a lull a few of us rushed out, at the risk of our lives, and succeeded in dragging it within the second defence without incident. Finally, at three o'clock in the morning, after over twelve hours' constant fighting, the Zulus withdrew. Our casualties were then seventeen killed and fifteen wounded.

"Daylight revealed an appalling sight. A few yards away were the smouldering ruins of the hospital, with the charred remains of our slaughtered comrades amid the heap of smoking rubbish. Hard by lay the bodies of other brave fellows, all assegaied and mutilated in a most shocking fashion. Around, for hundreds of yards, the ground was strewn with the ebony corpses of the ferocious savages we had laid low with our rifles during the afternoon and night, along with firearms and assegais presenting steel heads of various forms steeped in gore. Those having crescent-shaped blades were the most terrible among the weapons of this description that we had to fight against. A wound from one of them, when it had been twisted round and withdrawn, proved inevitably mortal, and brought death amid atrocious agony. There was also a quantity of guns.

"I went out with some others to ascertain if, perchance, there were any of our comrades still alive, and to see what we could pick up. I very nearly met my death for my pains. I was proceeding, quite alone, along one of the gullies with which the ground in parts was intersected, when I came upon the body of a Zulu, a great giant of a fellow, stretched on the ground. As I approached him, I noticed blood oozing from his ankle. 'Hum! That looks strange.' I thought. 'You don't often see blood coming from a dead man.' I nevertheless went on. Just as I was passing him, he suddenly stretched out his arm and clutched the stock of my rifle; then, springing to his knees, he made a terrific effort to wrest the arm from me. We had a rare struggle for mastery – he was nearly as tall as myself, even kneeling – but, in the end, I managed to wrench the gun away, and, giving the Zulu a frightful blow in the wind, bowled him over. I then stepped back four or five paces and calmly put a bullet through his head. After that we were only allowed to leave camp in parties of three or four."

When Lord Chelmsford came to the relief of Rorke's Drift early the same morning, Sergeant Hook was the first man sent for to give him an account of how he had managed to move the sick and wounded from the hospital. The Sergeant was presented with the Victoria Cross on Aug. 3, 1879, by Lord Woleseley, at a spot only about eight hundred yards from where the battle was fought.

"For weeks after that fight," says Sergeant Hook, "I was a victim to nightmare. In the middle of my sleep I would jump up in bed, my eyeballs starting from my head, my hair on end, my face and body dripping with perspiration. Imagining myself surrounded by shrieking, savage Zulus on the point of plunging their cruel asseagais into me. It was the shock to the nerves, you know. Even now I at times feel dizzy about the head."

Sergeant Hook thinks the Zulus will make fine fighting material to swell the ranks of our colonial force in Africa later on. He also thinks, and he will not be single in that opinion, that the Government ought to do more for our Victoria Cross men.

31f. *Macmillan's Magazine,* May to October 1898

Private Hook, V.C.

It was half-past three o'clock in the afternoon; the sun from out a cloudless sky poured down his scorching rays, and Rorke's Drift lay baking in the heat of the African summer. Shade there was none, nor was there any breeze to sway the poplars: the grass was shrivelled and brown, the tented camp dazzling in its whiteness; and the bare rocky ledges of Oscarsburg, seeming so near in that transparent atmosphere that one might almost distinguish the flies crawling on them, quivered in the palpitating air.

Private Henry Hook (second battalion of H.M. 24th Foot) with his shirt-sleeves rolled above his elbows, was out in the open making tea for the sick in the hospital. Suddenly he heard the sound of hoofs, and, looking up, saw two horsemen approaching at a furious gallop, like those who ride for their lives. The jaded horses were covered with sweat and foam, and their riders, one of whom was almost in rags, reeled like drunken men in the saddle. The horror of a great catastrophe was written on faces grimy with dust and powder, for they were two out of the handful of survivors from the fatal field of Isandlana, where, an hour before, the first battalion of the 24th had been practically annihilated by the Zulus.

"Stand to your arms, and defend yourselves as best you may; the enemy is at our heels, and will be here directly!"

Such was the dreadful message which one of them delivered, while the other galloped on in order to warn the defenders of Helpmakaar some twelve miles off.

There were but eighty fighting men at Rorke's Drift, and thirty-six invalids in the hospital with a few attendants; of friendly natives there were two hundred, who would probably show their friendliness by running away on the first chance. The commander, Major Spalding, had ridden over to Helpmakaar early in the afternoon; the two chief officers remaining were Lieutenant Gonville Bromhead of the 24th, and Lieutenant Chard, R.E.; an urgent message was at once despatched to the latter who was down by the river seeing to his ponts, as upon him devolved the defence, and, pending his arrival, the camp was struck, and the two wagons loaded with the sick men, ready to be driven off for greater safety to Helpmakaar.

Rorke's Drift is in Natal, but close to Zululand, from which it is separated by the Buffalo River. It takes its name from one Rorke, a border-agent, who built a house for himself, and farmed the land. Afterwards the place was purchased by the Reverend Otto Witt, a clergyman of the Swedish Church, who established here a Zulu mission. The big hill at the back was named Oscarsburg, out of compliment to his Scandinavian Majesty. The farm itself, with its enclosed garden in front, stood upon a terrace some two or three acres in extent. The ground was planted with standard grape-vines, orange, apricot, and other fruit-trees, Cape poplars, large gum-trees, and luxuriant shrubs and bushes, so that one could not see far for vegetation. The dwelling-house, which had been converted into a hospital, was about eighty feet long by sixty broad, and consisted of a ground-floor only. The end walls were built of stone, the side walls of kiln-dried bricks, and the partition walls of bricks dried in the sun. Some of the rooms were entered from the outside; others only communicated with each other; six of them were occupied by patients. Close to the house stood the church, a smaller building, which had been converted into a store, wagon-house, and stable, and, like the house, was thickly thatched with grass. Beyond them was a kraal, or enclosure for cattle. The whole pace was quite unfortified, and open to attack; none knew this better than the handful of men now so suddenly menaced.

On second thoughts it was judged too hazardous to attempt to move the sick to Helpmakaar, as they would be almost certain to fall into the hands of the Zulus. The wagons therefore were unloaded, and helped to eke out the line of defence, which consisted of bags of mealies (or maize) placed in such a way as to connect the hospital, store, and kraal by a complete rampart. The friendly Kaffirs were compelled at the point of the bayonet to bring the bags of mealies from the store and place them in position. The walls were loopholed, doors and windows blocked and ammunition served out, and the water-cart was filled and brought within the enclosure.

A hundred native troopers of Durnford's Horse now rode up, and an officer asked for instructions, Colonel Durnford having been killed. The men were ordered to watch the enemy, hold them in check as long as possible, and, when that became impracticable, to retire on the post, and help in the defence.

In a about an hour, and before much could be done by way of fortifying the camp, the sound of distant firing announced the approach of the Zulus. With the first boom of the guns the two hundred friendly natives ran off to a man, and the troopers of Durnford's Horse, demoralised by the loss of their leader and exhausted with a hard day's fighting, galloped off towards Helpmakaar, to the consternation of the little garrison. The defenders being this diminished in numbers the line of defence was too long for them to hold; a row of biscuit-boxes was therefore hastily thrown across to provide a second rampart behind which they might retire if necessary.

The Zulus advanced at first in three companies, about fifteen hundred men in each, under the command of Cetewayo's brother, crossed the Buffalo River about four miles below Rorke's Drift, climbed some rising ground, and, squatting on the grass, took snuff and considered the situation. They were not long in deciding on their plan of attack, and were soon seen pouring round the Oscarsburg in a dense mass. As they advanced in good order, the column of men opened and threw out horns with the object of surrounding the place. The main body, with yells of savage exultation, charged the hospital at a run, thinking to make short work of the English. Most of those who had guns climbed the heights of the Oscarsburg, whence, secure among the clefts of the rocks, they poured in such a continuous rain of bullets as would have speedily put an end to the unequal contest had their marksmen been skilful.

At the end of the hospital furthest from the store four men were stationed. Privates John Williams and Joseph Williams defended one of the wards in which were four patients, and Privates Hook and Cole defended a small room which formed the back corner of the building next to a ward containing six patients. On the approach of the enemy Cole made his escape by the front of the house, and joined the main body of his comrades behind the barricade, where he was one of the first to fall mortally wounded by a Zulu bullet.

Hook, who was now left by himself, had a Martini-Henry rifle with bayonet attached, and previous to the assault had distributed about his clothing more than a hundred cartridges. He, and the two Williams, kept up a steady fire on the advancing Zulus through loopholes in the walls.

But the work was too rapid for safety, and during an interval in the combat Hook discovered to his consternation that the heat of his gun had jambed a cartridge. The piece was now useless! Seizing his cleaning-rod he rammed it down the barrel with the energy of despair, and succeeded in forcing out the spent cartridge just in the nick of time; however, the rush of Zulus was too strong for one man to cope with, and he had to retreat into the next room, – the ward containing the six patients.

Meanwhile the two Williams had been hard pressed. Fourteen Zulus had fallen under their fire; but in one of the furious assaults, the door of the room they were in (an outer door which had been blocked) was burst open and Joseph Williams with two patients was dragged out and cut to pieces. While this was going on, John Williams made a hole with his pick through the inner wall of the room, and now, with the two other patients crawled into the ward where Henry Hook was. This room therefore contained eight sick men and the two privates. Meanwhile the Zulus, who had advanced against the front of the hospital under cover of the garden, were not idle, though repulsed with great loss, kept up a persistent attack. At last by sheer force of numbers they drove the English to take refuge behind their second rampart, and swarming over the first line of defence, broke into the hospital through the front doors. Some set fire to the thatched roof which soon began to blaze; others rushed towards the ward in which the ten men were entrapped.

"Quick!" said Hook to Williams. "Make a hole with your pick into the next room, while I defend the doorway; it's our only chance!". A slender chance indeed, as Hook knew full well! As he spoke the Zulus were upon him. They advanced with fiendish yells to complete the work of massacre, hurling their assegais, one of which wounded Hook in the forehead.

And now commenced a struggle for life against time, fire, and overwhelming odds. Fortunately Hook kept quite cool, and at each shot a savage fell. Sometimes the foe came on so quickly that the men had no time to fire, and then the bayonet did good service. Seven men lay dead before the fatal doorway, but still the Zulus fearlessly pressed forward over the bodies of their comrades. Seizing the muzzle of the gun, even as its contents were about to be discharged into their naked breasts, they tried to wrest the weapon from Hook's grasp; the barrel grew so heated with constant use that it took the flesh off his blistered hand. Overhead, the blazing roof crackled fiercely as the flames gathered force, and the smoke mingled with the smoke of the gun. The ammunition was fast disappearing, and still Williams worked hard with the pick. The sick men were powerless to help. Was it possible for Hook to hold out?

At last the hole was made, and Williams managed to drag seven of the invalids through; the eighth, who had a broken leg which had not long been set, still remained. Hook seized him by the collar, and made a rush for the opening. As he did so a Zulu bullet lodged in the man's coat, and it was only at the cost of breaking his leg a second time that Hook managed to drag him through.

The room in which they now found themselves had only an outside door, and this had been securely blocked; could they have got through it they would have fallen into the hands of the Zulus. The one thing to be done was to pass from room to room of the burning house, and join the main body of the defenders. While Hook therefore undertook the now easier task of defending the hole instead of the door, Williams wielded the pick, and made a hole through the wall on the further side of the room, by which they all crawled into the next ward. This too had only an outer door which had been blocked, and another hole accordingly to be made before they could pass into the farthest room.

On the opposite side of this room a small window was just discernible through the wreathing clouds of smoke, and by it they must escape, for they could not break through the wall which was an end one, and built, as has been said, of stone. There were two doors to this apartment, and outside the one that led through the inner, the Zulus could be seen brandishing their assegais as they came on to the attack. The sight of them, their horrid yells, the crackling of the blazing roof which threatened every instant to fall, the noise of the guns, the apparent hopelessness of their position, drove out one of the patients, who was somewhat light-headed with fever, mad; making a rush for the door, he was after a fierce struggle seized and hacked to pieces outside. His death gave the others time to clamber through the window and drop to the ground; and the nine men were now so far safe that they were clear of the burning hospital just as the ammunition was exhausted.

They had, however, only exchanged one form of danger for another. Unknown to them, the English had been driven behind the second line of defence, the single row of biscuit-boxes more than a hundred feet from the hospital. The intervening space was thick with the smoke of the guns; it was swept by Zulu bullets from the heights of the Oscarsburg; corpses covered the ground; assegais were flying in all directions; yet only by crossing this field of death could precarious shelter be reached.

Hook managed to hoist the broken-legged man on to his back. He was tall, and, powerless to help himself, hung like a sack, his feet dragging along the ground. The slow progress was frightful. An assegai hurled through the air struck the man, but fortunately stuck harmlessly in his over-coat. Great beads of sweat gathered on Hook's brow; his veins stood out like cords; his breath came in broken grasps; his legs tottered beneath him. One more supreme effort and he neared the barricade; he was seen, recognised and helped inside, both rescuer and rescued unharmed by spear or bullet.

Faint and exhausted as Hook was, he had to turn to immediately, and fight shoulder to shoulder with his sorely pressed comrades for dear life.

Suddenly, there being no twilight in this region, night fell, and the enemy would have made short work of them, had not the flames from the burning hospital, the roof of which had by this time fallen in, lighted up the darkness, and rendered each Zulu warrior as he broke cover an easy target for the guns. The dead lay so thick as to form a kind of rampart round the beleaguered place, yet again and again with the utmost courage the enemy came on, climbing over the bodies of their comrades, swarming over the defences, and seizing the rifles pointed at them. Six times they got inside the first line of defence, and six times were driven back by the bayonet, the little garrison sallying out and harassing their retreat. Before each attack the enemy always performed a war-dance, and then, having worked themselves into a frenzy, rushed fearlessly with devilish yells at the barricades. An attempt was made by them to fire the store-house, and one fellow was shot as he was in the act of applying a lighted torch to the roof.

Thus the fight raged without ceasing for eleven hours. Marvellous to say, the defenders had lost only seventeen men. While between three and four hundred Zulus had fallen. Suddenly, about three o'clock, the attack ceased, and the enemy retired in apparent discouragement. This short respite was made the most of by strengthening the defences. Two or three men climbed on to the roof of the store-house, and began to strip it off to prevent its being fired; but they had not made much progress, when they happened to catch sight of the Zulus stealthily returning to the attack. They at once gave the alarm, and the wearied soldiers, standing to their arms, prepared to renew the desperate struggle.

To remain on the roof was but to furnish a target for the enemy's guns; the men therefore descended one by one, and the last to leave, before he followed his comrades, cast a comprehensive glance around. In that clear atmosphere, as has been said, one can see a long distance, and the sight that met his eyes made his heart beat fast, and his cheek flush with excitement. "Hurrah!" he shouted joyfully, "hurrah! The army of Lord Chelmsford is in sight!" And sure enough, over the low hills eastward, though still some miles distant, the English soldiers could be plainly seen advancing. The little garrison cheered lustily and turned again to the struggle with new hope. But it was soon seen that the Zulus also had got hold of the intelligence, and after some hesitation, they finally withdrew. Rorke's Drift was safe.

Messengers from Isandlana the day before had brought word to the Commander-in-Chief that an attack in force had been made on the camp, and he had returned in hot haste to find that the force left there had been practically annihilated. From thence he marched to Rorke's Drift full of the gloomiest forebodings with regard to its fate, – forebodings confirmed apparently by the column of smoke rising from the burning hospital. If Rorke's Drift had fallen, so probably had Helpmakaar, leaving Natal, and indeed South Africa, at the mercy of the Zulus. His army was exhausted by four and twenty hours' forced march; it was destitute of provisions, and almost entirely of ammunition. Lord Chelmsford was therefore distracted with anxiety, knowing that he stood in the greatest jeopardy.

And now through their field-glasses the officers saw some one on the roof of the store waving the English flag. Was it only a ruse of the enemy? Colonel (now Sir Baker) Russell, and a troop of mounted infantry dashed forward in advance, and crossed the Buffalo River warily, straining their eyes and ears for some sign which might allay their apprehensions. Then, as they came within hail, a ringing British cheer resolved all doubts. Soon the rest of the troops came up, and as the General rode round the smoking ruins and battered defences, saw the heaps of dead Zulus, and heard the thrilling story of the siege, he heartily thanked the brave handful of defenders, and enthusiastically acknowledged that it was the most gallant action he had ever heard of.

Later on the same morning Private Hook was again busily engaged, this time in making coffee for his thirsty comrades. He was in his shirt and trousers, his braces hanging down behind; and, as he had had no opportunity to wash, his face and hands were still black with smoke and powder. Suddenly he received a peremptory order to appear before the General, and as there was no time to make himself respectable, he obeyed with a quaking heart, and was ushered into the presence of the Commander-in-Chief and the assembled officers.

Lord Chelmsford began to question him with regard to the defence of the hospital, but he was so overcome with confusion that it was with difficulty he could stammer forth a few words in reply. However, the whole story had been already told by the grateful broken-legged man and the other patients. The Commander-in-Chief shook hands with him, and highly complimented him upon his bravery; and this so added to his confusion that he hardly knew whether he stood on his head or his heels. Nor did the matter end here; he was recommended for the Victoria Cross together with his comrade Private John Williams (1). And so it came to pass that six months later, on August 3rd, 1879, before the assembled officers and in the presence of his fellow-soldiers, Hook was thanked for his share of the gallant defence of the hospital; and on the very scene of the exploit, – a rare occurrence – Sir Garnet Wolseley (as he then was) with his own hands pinned to his breast the bit of ribbon from which hung the most coveted of medals, bearing the simple inscription, *Private Henry Hook, January 22nd and 23rd, 1879.*

A.E. Bonser.

(1) Private John Williams received the Cross afterwards at Gibraltar.

31g. Extract from *V.C.*, c. 1904

How V.C.'s Are Won
Private Hook at Rorke's Drift

I was coming out of the British Museum Reading Room when I met him first – a short, broad-shouldered, kindly-looking man in a uniform something between that of a recruiting sergeant and an undertaker's mute. He was handing me back my umbrella in return for a check, when one of the two medals shining on the breast of his dark uniform caught my eye.

"Halloa!" I exclaimed, and my excitement and interest must have been very boyishly in evidence, for the old man smiled at me as I spoke. "Isn't that the Cross you're wearing?"

"Yes, sir."

"And the Zulu medal beside it – Why? you must be Sergeant Hook?"

He smiled again – a pleasant, tired smile. "I'm all that's left of him, sir."

What a difference! This man who handed me my umbrella and called me "sir" was the same who, with blazing rafters overhead and all Hell loose in front, stood fighting single-handed in defence of the wounded and dying on that long-ago day in the little hospital of Rorke's Drift. The story of the fight is well known. I will give Mr. Hook's account of it as near as may be in his own words:–

"I was placed in one of the corner rooms of the hospital, the Zulus kept drawing closer and closer, and I went on firing, killing several of them. At last they got close up, and set fire to the hospital. There was only one patient in my room. He had a broken leg and was burnt, poor fellow for while I was shooting the flames became so fierce that I could not save him. At first I had a comrade but he left after a time, and was killed on his way to the inner entrenchments.

"When driven out of this room, I retired by a partition door into the next room, where there were several patients. For a few minutes I was the only fighting man there. A man of the 24th came to me from another room with a bullet wound in the arm. I tied it up. Then John Williams came and made a hole in the partition, through which he helped the sick and wounded men. Whilst he was doing this, the Zulus beat in the door, and tried to enter. I stood at the side and shot and bayoneted several – I could not tell how many, but there were five or six lying at my feet. They threw assegais continually, but only one touched me, and that afflicted a scalp wound which I did not think worth while reporting. In fact, I did not feel the wound at the time. One Zulu seized my rifle and tried to drag it away. Whilst we were tussling I slipped a cartridge in and pulled the trigger – the muzzle was against his breast, and he fell dead. Every now and then a Zulu would make a rush to enter – the door would only let one man in at a time – but I bayoneted or shot every one. When all the patients were out except one – who owing to a broken leg could not move – I went too, dragging him after me, in doing which I again broke his leg. I then stopped at the hole to guard it whilst Williams was making a hole through the partition into the next room. I stuck to my particular charge, and dragged him out and into the inner line of defence. I then took my post behind the parapet."

J.H.K.A.

31h. *Royal Magazine*, February 1905, Hook's account of Rorke's Drift, edited and transcribed by Mr Walter Wood

Survivors' Tales of Great Events.
How they held Rorke's Drift.
From the Narrative of Sergeant Henry Hook, V.C.

"… Everything was perfectly quiet at Rorke's Drift," he told me, "after the column had left and every officer and man was going about his business as usual. Not a soul suspected that only a dozen miles away the very men that we had said, 'Good-bye!' and 'Good luck!' to were either dead or standing back-to-back in a last fierce hand-to-hand fight with the Zulus. Our garrison consisted of the B Company of the 2nd Battalion of the 24th, under Lieutenant Bromhead, and 'details,' which brought the total number of us up to 139. Besides these, we had about 300 men of the Natal Native Contingent; but they didn't count, as they bolted in a body when the fight began. We were all knocking about, and I was making tea for the sick, as I was hospital cook at the time.

"Suddenly there was a commotion in the camp, and we saw two men galloping towards us from the other side of the river, which was Zululand. Lieutenant Chard, of the Engineers, one of the finest officers in the world, was protecting the ponts over the river, and, as senior officer, was in command of the drift. The ponts, floating bridges, were very simple affairs, one of them being supported on big barrels, and the other on boats. Lieutenant Bromhead was in the camp itself. The horsemen shouted, and were brought across the river, and then we knew what had happened to our comrades.

"They had been butchered to a man.

"That was awful enough news – but worse was to follow, for we were told that Zulus were coming straight on from Isandlwana to attack us. One of the horsemen was Lieutenant Adendorff, and the other was a Natal carabineer. The lieutenant stayed behind with us, and the carabineer, who was in his shirt sleeves, dashed on to Helpmakaar, twelve miles away, to take the news to two companies of the 24th there. At the same time, a note was received by Lieutenant Bromhead from the 3rd Column – that which had left the drift, and part of which had been cut up – to say that the enemy was coming on, and that the post was to be held at all costs.

"For some little time we were all stunned, then everything changed from perfect quietness to intense excitement and energy. There was a general feeling that the only safe thing was to retire and try to join the troops at Helpmakaar. The horsemen had said that the Zulus would be up in two or three minutes; but luckily for us, they did not show themselves for more than an hour.

"Lieutenant Chard rushed up from the river, about a quarter of a mile away, and saw Lieutenant Bromhead. Orders were given to strike the camp and make ready to go, and we actually loaded up two waggons. Then Mr. Dalton, of the Commissariat Department, came up, and said that if we left the drift every man was certain to be killed. He had formerly been a sergeant-major in a Line regiment, and was one of the bravest men that ever lived. Lieutenants Chard and Bromhead held a consultation, short and earnest; and orders were given that we were to get the hospital and storehouse ready for defence, and that we were never to say 'die' or 'surrender.'

"Not a minute was lost. Lieutenant Bromhead superintended the loopholing and barricading of the hospital and storehouse and the making of a connection of the defences between the two buildings with walls of mealie-bags and waggons. The mealie-bags were good big heavy things, weighing about two hundred pounds each, and during the fight many of them were burst open by assegais and bullets, and the mealies (Indian corn) were thickly spread about the ground. The biscuit-boxes contained ordinary army biscuit. They were big, square wooden boxes, weighing about a hundredweight each. The meat boxes, too, were very heavy, as they contained tinned meat. They were smaller than the biscuit-boxes.

"While these precautions were being made, Lieutenant Chard went down to the river and brought in the pont guard of a sergeant and half-a-dozen men, with the waggons and gear.

"The two young officers saw that every soldier was at his post. Then we were ready for the Zulus when they cared to come.

"They were not long. Just before half-past four we heard firing behind the conical hill at the back of the drift, called Oscarberg Hill, and suddenly about five or six hundred Zulus swept around, coming for us at a run.

"Instantly the native – Kaffirs who had been very useful in making the barricade of waggons, mealie-bags, and biscuit-boxes around the camp

– bolted towards Helpmakaar, and, what was worse, their officer and a European sergeant went with them. To see them deserting like that was too much for some of us, and we fired after them. The Sergeant was struck and killed.

"Half-a-dozen of us were stationed in the hospital, with orders to hold it and guard the sick. The ends of the building were of stone, the side walls of ordinary bricks, and the inside walls, or partitions, of sunburnt bricks of mud.

"These shoddy inside bricks proved our salvation, as you will see. It was a queer little one-storeyed building, which it is almost impossible to describe; but we were pinned like rats in a hole, because all the doorways except one had been barricaded with mealie-bags, and we had done the same with the windows. The interior was divided by means of partition-walls, into which were fitted some very slight doors. The patients' beds were simple, rough affairs of boards, raised only about half a foot above the floor. To talk of 'hospital' and 'ward' conveys the idea of a big building; but, as a matter of fact, this hospital was a mere little shed or bungalow, divided up into rooms so small that you could hardly swing a bayonet in them.

"The half-dozen of us who had been told off to defend the hospital were put in corners where we could shoot best through loopholes which we had made with picks. I was a good shot, being a 'marksman,' and was able to clip more than one Zulu at a good distance before we came to the hot fighting at close quarters. In the hospital there were about nine men who could move; but altogether there were about thirty. Most of these, however, could help to defend themselves.

"As soon as our Kaffirs bolted, it was seen that the fort as we had first made it was too big to be held, so Lieutenant Chard instantly reduced the space by having a row of biscuit-boxes drawn across the middle, about four feet high. This was our inner entrenchment, and proved very valuable.

"The Zulus came on at a wild rush, and although many of them were shot down, they got within about fifty yards of our south wall of mealie-bags, biscuit-boxes and waggons. They were caught between two fires – that from the hospital and that from the storehouse – and were checked; but they gained the shelter of the depôt cookhouse and ovens and gave us many heavy volleys.

"During the fight they took advantage of every bit of cover there was – anthills, a tract of bush that we had not had time to clear away, a garden or sort of orchard which was near us, and a ledge of rock and some caves which were only about a hundred yards away. They neglected nothing and, while they went on firing, large bodies kept hurling themselves against our slender breastworks.

"But it was the hospital they assaulted most fiercely. I had charge, with a man that we called 'Old King Cole,' of a small room with only one patient in it; and two men named Joseph Williams and John Williams had charge of another. There were two men named R. Jones and W. Jones in a different part of the hospital. One was an old soldier, the other a young one. Cole kept with me for some time after the fight began, then he said he was not going to stay. He went outside and was instantly killed by the Zulus; so that I was left alone with the patient – a native whose leg was broken, and who kept crying out: 'Take my bandage off so that I can come!' But it was impossible to do anything except fight, and I blazed away as hard as I could.

"By this time I was the only defender of my room. Poor 'Old King Cole' was lying dead outside, and the helpless patient was crying and groaning near me. The Zulus were swarming around us, and there was an extraordinary rattle as the bullets struck the biscuit-boxes, and queer thuds as they plumped into the bags of mealies. Then there was a whiz and rip of the assegais, the spears with which the Zulus did such terrible work during the war, and of which I had had experience during the Kaffir Campaign of 1877–78. We had plenty of ammunition, but we were told to save it, and so we took careful aim at every shot, and hardly a cartridge was wasted. One of my comrades, Private Dunbar, shot no fewer than nine Zulus one of them being a Chief.

"From the very first the enemy tried to rush the hospital, and at last, although they failed to take it, they managed to set fire to the thick grass which formed the roof. This put us in a terrible plight, because it meant that we were either to be massacred or burned alive, or get out of the building. To get out seemed impossible; for if we left the hospital by the only door which had been left open, the others having been blocked up, we should instantly fall into the midst of the Zulus. Besides, there were the helpless sick and wounded, and we could not leave them. My own little room communicated with another by means of a frail door like a bedroom door. Fire and dense choking smoke forced me to get out and go into the other. It was impossible to take the native patient with me. And I had to leave him to an awful fate. But his death was, at any rate, a merciful one. I heard the Zulus asking him questions; and he tried to tear off his bandages and escape.

"In the room where I now was there were nine sick men, and I alone to look after them for some time, still firing away, with the hospital burning. Suddenly, in the thick smoke, I saw John Williams, who had rushed in through a doorway communicating with another room, and above the din of battle and the cries of the wounded I heard him shout: 'The Zulus are swarming all over the place! They've dragged Joseph Williams out and killed him!'

"John Williams had held the other room, with Private William Horrigan, for more than an hour, until they had not a cartridge left. The Zulus then burst in and dragged out Joseph Williams and two of the patients, and assegaied them. It was only because they were so busy with this slaughter that John Williams and two of the patients were able to knock a hole in the partition and get into the room where I was posted. Horrigan was killed.

"What were we to do? we were pinned like rats in a hole. Already the Zulus were fiercely trying to burst in through the doorway. The only way of escape was the wall itself – by making a hole big enough for a man to crawl through into an adjoining room, and so on until we got to our inmost entrenchment outside. Williams worked desperately at the wall with the navvy's pick, which I had been using to make some of the loopholes with.

"All this time the Zulus were trying to get into the room. Their assegais kept whizzing towards us, and one struck me in front of the helmet. We were wearing the white tropical helmets then. But the helmet tilted back under the blow, and made the spear lose its power, so that I escaped with a scalp wound, which did not trouble me much then, although it has often caused me illness since.

"Only one man at a time could get in at the door. A big Zulu sprang forward and seized my rifle; but I tore it free and, slipping a cartridge in, I shot him point-blank. Time after time the Zulus gripped the muzzle and tried to tear the rifle from my grasp, and time after time I wrenched it back, because I had a better grip than they had.

"All this time Williams was getting the sick through the hole into the next room – all except one, a soldier of the 24th named Conley, who could not move because of a broken leg. Watching for my chance, I dashed from the doorway, and grabbing Conley I pulled him after me through the hole. His leg got broken again, but there was no help for it. As soon as we left the room the Zulus burst in with furious cries of disappointment and rage.

"Now there was a repetition of the work of holding the doorway, except that I had to stand by a hole, instead of a door, while Williams picked away at the far wall to make an opening for escape into the next room. There was more desperate and almost hopeless fighting, as it seemed; but most of the poor fellows were got through the hole. Again I had to drag Conley through, a terrific task, because he was a very heavy man.

"We were now all in a little room that gave upon the inner line of defence which had been made. We – Williams and R. Jones and W. Jones and myself – were the last men to leave the hospital, after most of the sick and wounded had been carried through the small window and away from the burning building; but it was impossible to save a few of them, and they were butchered.

"Privates William Jones and Robert Jones during all this time were doing magnificent work in another ward which faced the hill. They kept at it with bullet and bayonet until six out of the seven patients in that ward had been removed. They would have got the seventh – Sergeant Maxfield – out safely, but he was delirious with fever, and, although they managed to dress him, he refused to move. Robert Jones made a last rush to try and get him away like the rest; but when he got back into the room he saw Maxfield was being stabbed by the Zulus as he lay on his bed. Corporal Allen and Private Hitch helped enormously in keeping up communication with the hospital. They were both badly wounded, but when they could not fight any longer, they served out ammunition to their comrades throughout the night.

"As we got the sick and wounded out they were taken to a verandah in front of the storehouse, and Dr. Reynolds under heavy fire from clouds of assegais, did everything he could for them. All this time, of course, the storehouse was being valiantly defended by the rest of the garrison.

"When we got into the inner fort, I took my post at a place where two men had been shot. While I was there another man was shot in the neck, I think by a bullet which came through the space between two biscuit-boxes that were not quite close together. This was about six o'clock in the evening, nearly two hours after the opening shot of the battle had been fired.

"We were glad enough to be in the shelter of the little inside fort," continued Hook.

"Every now and then the Zulus would make a rush for it and get in. We had to charge them out. By this time it was dark, and the hospital was all in flames, but this gave us a splendid light to fight by. I believe it was this light that saved us. We could see them coming, and they could not rush us and take us by surprise from any point. They could not get us, and so they went away and had ten or fifteen minutes of a war-dance. This roused them up again, and their excitement was so intense that the ground fairly seemed to shake.

"Then, when they were goaded to the highest pitch, they would hurl themselves at us again. We could sometimes, by the light of the flames, keep them well in sight, so well that we could take steady aim and fire cooly. When we could do this they never advanced as far as the barricade, because we shot them down as they ran in on us. But every now and then one or two managed to crawl in and climb over the top of the sacks. They were bayoneted off.

"I need hardly say that we were using Martinis, and fine rifles they were too. But we did so much firing that they became hot, and the brass of the cartridges softened, the result being that the barrels got very foul and the cartridge-chamber jammed. My own rifle was jammed several times, and I had to work away with the ramrod till I cleared it. We used the old three-sided bayonet, and the long, thin blade we called the 'lung' bayonet. They were very fine weapons too; but some were very poor in quality, and either twisted or bent badly. Several were like that after the fight; but some terrible thrusts were given, and I saw dead Zulus who had been pinned to the ground by the bayonet going through them.

"All this time the sick and wounded were crying for water. We had the water-cart full of water, but it was just by the deserted hospital, and we could not hope to get at it until the day broke, when the Zulus might begin to lose heart and to stop in their mad rushes. But we could not bear the cries any longer, and three or four of us jumped over the boxes and ran and fetched some water in.

"The long night passed and the day broke. Then we looked around us to see what had happened, and there was not a living soul who was not thankful to find that the Zulus had had enough of it and were disappearing over the hill to the south-west. Orders were given to patrol the ground, collect the arms of the dead blacks, and make our position as strong as possible in case of fresh attacks.

"One of the first things I did was to go up to the man who was still looking over our breastwork, with his rifle presented to the spot where so many of the Zulus had been. I went up to him, and saw that he did not move, and that he looked very quiet.

"I went nearer and said: 'Hello, what are you doing here?'

"He made no answer, and did not stir. I went still closer, and something in his appearance made me tilt his helmet back, as you sometimes tilt back a hat when you want to look closely into a face. As I did so I saw a bullet-mark in his forehead, and knew that he was dead.

"I went away, and was walking up the dry bed of a little stream near the drift, with my own rifle in my right hand and a bunch of assegais over my left shoulder. Suddenly I came across an unarmed Zulu, lying on the ground, apparently dead, but bleeding from the leg. Thinking it strange that a dead man should bleed, I hesitated, and wondered whether I should go on, as other Zulus might be lurking about. But I resumed my task. Just as I was passing, the supposed dead man he seized the butt of my rifle and tried to drag it away. The bunch of assegais rattled to the earth.

"The Zulu suddenly released his grasp of the rifle with one hand, and with the other fiercely endeavoured to drag me down. The fight was short and sharp; but it ended by the Zulu being struck in the chest with the butt and knocked to the ground.

"The rest was quickly over.

"After that we were not allowed to go on with our task except in twos and threes.

"When we had done this work we went back to the inner line of defence, sad enough, even the most cheerful of us. But we had no time to dwell on the awful scenes about us. We did not know how soon another assault might be made, but we did know that if the Zulus kept on attacking us it was only a question of time before we were cut to pieces, as our comrades a dozen miles away had been destroyed.

"The roof of the hospital had fallen in by this time, and only the storehouse was standing. We were ordered to put ropes through the loopholes of the walls of the hospital, and pull them down. This we did, and the walls, which had already been weakened by our picks, partially collapsed. Then we tore away the thatch from the storehouse, so that the Zulus could not, even if they wished, set fire to it, as they had fired the hospital. With the ruins of the walls we strengthened our little fort, and again waited for the Zulus – if they cared to come. But they had finished their attack.

"We looked about us everywhere for signs of relief, but saw nothing and our hearts sank. Then came an awful time of suspense. Two of our men had been on the roof of the storehouse signalling with flags when the Zulus meant to attack us. This gave us time to make ready for them. The signallers were still able to stand above the ground, so that they could be seen at a good distance. We saw their flags going wildly. What was it? Everybody was mad with anxiety to know whether it could be friends to relieve us, or more Zulus to destroy us. We watched the flags flapping, and then learnt that signals were being made in reply. We knew we were safe and that friends were marching up to us.

"We broke into roar after roar of cheering, waving red coats and white helmets, and we cheered again and again when, at about six o'clock in the morning, Colonel Russell rode up with some mounted infantry. We saw them come in, and at the same time we saw that the Zulus had once more got ready to sweep around the mountain to attack us. But it was too late, and on seeing that we were reinforced, they turned silently away, and only their dead and a few wounded were left with us.

"Lord Chelmsford and what was left of the 3rd Column came up to Rorke's Drift soon after. There was no time to sit down and mope, and there were sick and wounded as well as the rest to look after. So when the Commander-in-Chief arrived I was back at my cooking in my shirt sleeves, making tea for the sick.

"A Sergeant ran up and said:

" 'Lieutenant Bromhead wants you.'

" 'Wait till I put my coat on,' I said.

" 'Come as you are – straight away,' he ordered, and so, in my shirtsleeves, and with my braces hanging about me, I went into the midst of the officers, and Lord Chelmsford asked me all about the defence of the hospital, as I was the last to leave the building. An officer took our names, and wrote down what we had done. He was the first officer to be killed in the last South African war – Major-General Penn-Symons, at Dundee.

"When the relief had come up the men of the column were sent out to bury the Zulus. There were 351 dead blacks counted, and these were put into two big holes in front of the hospital. The column made the Kaffirs who were with them dig the trenches; but although they dug the holes, they positively refused to bury the bodies. There were only a few badly wounded left, as the Zulus had carried off their wounded as they retired. A great many dead were found in a mealie-field not far from the hospital.

"As for our own comrades, we, who had fought side by side with them, buried them. This was done the day after the fight, not far from the place where they fell, and at the foot of the hill. Soon afterwards the little cemetery was walled in and a monument was put in the middle. The lettering was cut on it by a very clever bandsman named Mellsop, who used bits of broken bayonets as chisels. He drew a capital picture of the fight. Those who had been killed in action were buried on one side of the cemetery, and those who died of disease on the other side. A curious thing was that a civilian named Byrne, who had taken part in the defence and was killed, was buried outside the cemetery wall. I don't know why, except that he was not a regular soldier.

"I was at Rorke's Drift for six months after the fight, but we were moved about a quarter of a mile away from the storehouse and hospital. On August 3rd, at Rorke's Drift, where I was the only recipient of the Victoria Cross, the others having left, I was decorated with the cross by Lord Wolseley, at a special parade. It was curious, but until then I had scarcely ever thought about the V.C. – in fact we did not know or trouble much about it, although we had a V.C. man in the regiment – Griffiths they called him. He was killed, with the rest, at Isandhlwana."

31i. Extract from *The Bronze Cross,* by F. Gordon Roe, London, 1945

Rorke's Drift
A V.C.'s Own Story

… For their splendid work in the defence, Chard and Bromhead, Reynolds and Dalton, Allen, Hitch, Hook, the two Joneses, Williams and Schiess, all receive the Victoria Cross.

Of Hitch, who incidentally had fired the opening shot of the action at Rorke's Drift, it is noted in O'Moore Creagh and Humphris's *The V.C. and D.S.O.* that he was in after years the sufferer by a particularly mean theft. His Cross was stolen from his coat, but by King Edward VII's order was replaced by another. As for Pte. (later Sergeant) Hook, he eventually became an attendant at the British Museum, where, incidentally, my Father met and talked with him. He claimed to be "the only man" of the Rorke's Drift survivors "who got the V.C. on the spot where it had been won." A representative of the since defunct *Daily Graphic* mentioned this in an account of Hook's own story, in the V.C.'s obituary published on March 14th, 1905.

"'Lord Wolseley gave it to me,' he said, 'on August 3rd, within seven or eight hundred yards of the hospital …'"

"'The Zulus attacked it, as you know,' continued the V.C., 'and we watched 'em coming nearer and nearer. I was a marksman of my troop, and I dropped some of them. One of them, sheltering himself behind an anthill, I had three shots at. I remember,' said Private Hook reflectively, 'that I went out the next day to see whether I'd hit him the third time. He was lying behind the anthill with a hole in his skull. I'd clipped him …'"

"'Well, at last they got close up and set fire to the hospital, and we defended it. We had to get through one partition of the hospital after another, as I daresay you know. They were only poor brick partitions, and we had to break holes through two of them.'"

"'I didn't know. I suppose the attacking Zulus drove you from room to room?'"

"'That's it. In the second room there were several patients; and for a few minutes I was the only fighting man there. A man of the 24th came to me from another room with a wound in his arm. I tied it up. Then John

Williams came in from another room and made a hole in the partition, and we got the sick through that. While he was doing it the Zulus smashed the door open and tried to get in. So I stood at the side of it, and shot at them and bayoneted them as they tried to get in. But they could only get in one at a time, and I killed them as they came in. One Zulu got hold of my rifle and tried to drag it away. But I slipped in a cartridge – the muzzle was against his breast – and so he fell dead. When all the sick were out [i.e., of that part of the hospital], but one who couldn't move, having a broken leg, I went through the hole too, dragging him after me. I broke his leg again doing that. Then I stood at the other side of that hole, as before, while Williams made another hole into the next room. And so on.'"

"'Yes,' said the *Daily Graphic*."

"'And so at last Williams and I got them all through,* one hole after another, and then through a window into the outer defences. And there we stopped with the rest during the Zulu attack. They kept making rushes every quarter of an hour or so. But the blaze of the hospital gave us light to take aim by.'"

"'Yes?'"

"'And so,' concluded Sergeant Hook – for he was then a Sergeant in the 1st V.B., Royal Fusiliers – 'that's the way it happened …'"

From the thunder and flame of Rorke's Drift to the echoing peace of the British Museum: a fitting pendant.

* As reported, Hook was speaking in general terms. It is stated in the obituary that he "was reluctant to dwell upon his part in the affair" and had to be "pressed for particulars," and consequently this interview cannot be regarded in the light of a considered statement. Actually, some of the sick were killed in or outside the hospital.

31j. *Natal Witness*, 15 March 1905

Obituary.

Sergt. Hook, V.C.

Gloucester, March 14

Sergeant Hook, V.C., is dead.

32. 2077 Gunner Arthur Howard, 'N' Battery, 5th Brigade, Royal Artillery

32a. *Lloyd's Weekly Newspaper*, 30 March 1879

The following letter is from Gunner Howard, servant to Colonel Harness, to his family in England. A telegram published in the Cape papers, dated Pietermaritzburg, January 29, states that Howard "had a narrow escape, but got away from the hospital and sat in the bush all night, exposed to the fire from both sides:" –

"Helpmakaar, Feb. 7, 1879.

Just a line to let you know that I am still in the land of the living. I dare say before you get this you will have heard of the massacre. They killed just half of our battery, and nearly all the 1st-24th regiment. The awful black devils watched the General out of camp, and then, as soon as his column had got clear away, they came down – about 1,500 of them – like bees out of a hive, and there was awful slaughter. They took everything belonging to officers and men – all but what they stood upright in – burnt the huts, and scattered the provisions all about the place. There was a deal of money in camp – my Governor lost a bit, but, as it was Government money to pay the battery with, he will get back again.

I was not in the camp, for I had the diarrhoea and was left behind at a place they call Rorke's Drift, where there was a temporary hospital. One company of the 24th, 90 strong, was left to protect it. Well, the same day as the other affair happened about which I have just told you, 4,000 or so of them paid us a visit at the hospital. But we had about three hours' notice, and plenty of sacks of oats, with which we threw up a temporary fortification round this old place. When the Zulus arrived, about five in the evening, they did not find it quite as comfortable as they thought, for they expected that they would have nothing to do but assegai us at their pleasure, and possess the place, but we had knocked holes through the house to fire through. So what with the sacks and the holes through the house, we had very good cover. Boxes of ammunition were placed beside us. Forty men were in hospital, and nearly all able to fight when it came to the pinch. I had a rifle belonging to a sergeant who was too ill to use it. The Zulus made short work of him.

When waiting for the approach of the enemy we would see them half a mile before they got to us. When I beheld the swarm I said to myself, 'All up now,' but I was wrong, and we all agreed to fight till only two were left, and these were to shoot themselves. Well, we all got behind our ramparts, and when the Zulus were about 400 yards off, like a wall coming on, we fired the first volley. The rifles being Martini-Henry's, our firing was very quick, and, when struck by the bullets, the niggers would give a spring in the air and fall flat down. The enemy advanced to within 300 yards, and then it did not seem healthy to come any nearer, so we continued to fire at them till it got dark. Then, as the roof of the hospital was of thatch, they crept up and set it on fire. When the flames burst out it was all the better for us, for we could see the niggers and their movements, though they could not see us. Didn't we give it to them then, anyhow!

They sheered off, all but a few who hung about us all night; but as soon as it was light we finished off all we could see, and I can tell you that when I saw the general's column coming to our relief I was glad. The general said we were a brave little garrison, and that this showed what a few men could do if they only had the pluck. I had a letter and a paper, and was glad to see that you got the clock. I shall not be able to write very often."

32b. *The Times*, 11 February 1930

A Survivor Of Rorke's Drift

The death is announced in a Reuter telegram from Sydney, of Mr. Howard, a survivor of Rorke's Drift. Mr. Howard who was 74, arrived in Australia in 1908. As recently as Friday he complained of an assegai wound received in the fight. In addition to Neuville's famous painting of the defence of Rorke's Drift, the Sydney Art Gallery has a picture showing Mr. Howard assisting and carrying a wounded man from the blazing hospital …

32c. *Daily Mirror*, 14 February 1930. [The Mr Howard mentioned was in fact Howard English, a successful businessman and horse owner, who died in Sydney, Australia in 1930. English, real name Robert Howard Hewitt was born in England in 1859.]

Told He Was 'Dead'
Rorke's Drift Survivor and a Newspaper Report
Picture Mystery

Mr. Arthur Howard, a hero of Rorke's Drift, has just learned that his own death has been reported.

It was announced in the newspapers several days ago that he had died in Sydney, Australia, after complaining of an old assegai received in the historic Drift fight.

Mr Howard expressed great surprise to a Daily Mirror representative when he was informed of the report. Although he is now seventy-eight years of age and blind, he is an active and alert man, and takes a keen interest in present day affairs.

"I cannot understand how there can be any mistake," he said. "I have been living in Kent now for forty years, and I have certainly never been to Australia.

"As you can see for yourself, I am quite alive and able to tell you about the battle. I was at Ulundi, too, where we beat the Zulu armies in forty minutes.

"My relatives tell me that the photograph in the papers is of me all right.

"I never received a wound of any sort from an assegai, or from anything for that matter, though I was in the hospital with fever when the Zulus burned it during the battle.

Picture of Rescue
"I Never Carried Anyone to Safety at Famous Battle," says Mr. Howard

"At Rorke's Drift, 4,000 Zulus attacked eighty-six men, eighty of them South Wales Borderers under the command of Lieutenants Chard and Bromhead. Half of the men were in a small farmhouse which had been turned into a hospital.

"How Sydney Art Gallery can have a picture of me leaving the burning hospital carrying another man over my shoulder is more than I can understand. It certainly cannot be a picture of me. It was as much as I could do to leave the building myself, without carrying anyone else.

"There were only eighty-six of us all told, and I don't think it is at all probable that there was another Arthur Howard among us, though of course it is possible. I knew most of the men, and I never met anyone of my own name.

"I think the Australian report must be incorrect in the name."

33. Trooper Sidney Robert Hunter, Natal Mounted Police

33a. A letter written by Sidney Hunter's father to the Master, Supreme Court, Pietermaritzburg: [Pietermaritzburg Archives Repository, Pietermaritzburg, NAB, MSCE 5/84]

Union Street
Barnet Herts
England
June 29th 1880

Sir,

I have received a letter from Sergt. Maclaren of the Natal M. P. to inform me that the Balance due to me in the Estate of my late son, Sidney Hunter …

… my wife who is now on her Death Bed has never fully recovered from the shock of the sad news of his death …

Yours Respectfully

R. Hunter
Union Street
Barnet Herts
England

P.S. I am truly a great sufferer from that Cruel & uncalled for Zulu War

33b. *Barnet Press,* 17 May 1879

News from Rorke's Drift

The following letters will convey to many of our readers in Barnet direct information of a fact concerning which they can have had but little doubt for some time past, namely that the name 'Hutter' or 'Hunter' given in the published lists of soldiers killed at Rorke's Drift was no other than that of the son of our deservedly respected fellow-townsman Sergeant Hunter:–

Panmure, East London, Cape of Good Hope,
1st April, 1879.

My dear Sir, I am afraid that I must be the bearer of evil tidings to you, which, unless you have already heard them, will be a great grief to you. Your son, Sidney Hunter, was a great friend of ours, and spent many happy evenings in my house at Seymour. He went to the Transkeian front, and on the 31st May, 1878, got his discharge from the F.A.M. Police. He then went up to Natal, to the war there, and joined the Natal Rifles. Damp and exposure laid him up in hospital with rheumatic fever, and his last letter to us was written from the hospital in Pietermaritzburg. He must, after this, have got better and crossed the Tugela, for he was at Rorke's Drift on the sad day of the Isandhana disaster. You will have read the narrative of the gallant stand made by the little band of heroes at Rorke's Drift, on the night of the 22nd January. The enclosed note from one of his old comrades of the F.A.M. Police will tell you all the rest. I deeply sympathise with you, for I loved Hunter as a brother.

Very faithfully yours,
W.S. Caldicott
Wesleyan Minister

Mr. R. Hunter, Union Street, Barnet, Hertford
Rorke's Drift, Natal
January 29th, 1879

My dear Sir, You have, perhaps, heard of our disaster in Zululand, and our retirement to this place; it was held by 89 men of the 24th against 3000 Zulus, who were defeated with a loss of about 400, and retired; the first man I saw when we arrived was poor Hunter, of No. 9 Troop late F.A.M. Police. He was in the Natal Mounted Police; being in hospital here with rheumatics he was left behind; the enemy burnt the hospital; Hunter came out, shot three Zulus with a revolver, and was assegaied in three places in the chest, but not mutilated. I saw him buried as decently as possible. My object in writing is to ask if you know his parents' address and communicate with them. £3 was found in his pockets; his horse equipments, etc., are in possession of Major Dartnell, commandant of the Natal Mounted Police. If anything more you should wish to know, write and I will attend to it.

Yours etc.,
William Hicks,
Lieut. And Quartermaster, 1-3 N.N. Contingent,
Care of Commandant Lonsdale, Natal.

34. 25B/295 Private David Jenkins, 'G' Company, 1/24th Foot

34a. *Brecon County Times,* 29 March 1879

The Battles of Isandula & Rorke's Drift.
Thrilling and heart-touching narratives from Brecon men.

Another letter has been received from Zululand, written by David Jenkins, a son of Mr. Thomas Jenkins, Tanners' Arms, Devynnock, who was present at the bloody massacre at Isandula. The letter will be of great interest to his friends, in the neighbourhood of Devynnock, where the writer is well-known. It is a follows: –

Zululand
January 28, 1879

Dear Father, – Just a few lines to let you know that I am one of the ten that escaped out of the five companies. The remainder were cut to pieces – in fact, cut in bits – with these savages. About 15,000 of them came on the camp when the column was out. All in camp were killed – 493 of our regiment and about 300 of different corps. Oh! I never saw such a sight. Please to pray to God to continue to save my life. There are only 240 men remaining in our regiment. So no more. Dear father, please go personally or write a letter to Isaac Lewis, Pendre, Brecon, and tell him that his son-in-law Sergeant Chambers, is killed; his son Thomas is alive, but is still in hospital with the fever. He had a very narrow escape. He crept on his hands and knees and came from the hospital to the fort through all the firing. Please give my love to all, and write soon. –

Your affectionate son.

D. Jenkins.

P.S. I think we will go down to the colony to get re-fitted, as we have lost everything.

No.295 David Jenkins
G Company, 1-24th Regiment
Pietermaritzburg, Natal.

34b. *Brecon County Times*, 26 April 1879

Another letter from a Breconshire hero who fought at Rorke's Drift.

Mr Thomas Jenkins, of the Farmer's Arms, Defynnock, forwards us the following letter written by Private David Jenkins (his son) to another brother.

Helpmakaar, March 11th, 1879

Dear brother, – I wrote a letter to you about Christmas last, when stationed at Greytown; whether you received it I cannot say. I can assure you, dear brother, that there are hundreds of letters and papers lost and mislaid. We have lost two English mails, the runners or mail bag carriers being captured by the enemy. They were killed, and the bags and contents destroyed. I received a paper from you on the 9th instant, dated the 2nd November, 1878. I have written four letters, two in November from King Williamstown, two from here to my father, and one to Cousin Thomas, but I have not received any answer to either of them.

I dare say you have read in the papers of the great massacre at Isandula Camp on the 22nd of January last. We lost five companies, band and drummers, and the staff, consisting of 541 men, about 181 of the 2-24th, some volunteers, waggon drivers, and some of the Natal mounted police – making a total of about 975. When the enemy attacked the camp the column was out skirmishing some twenty miles from camp; about 30,000 Zulus attacked us. We were under the command of Colonel Durnford, R.E.; he took the command from Colonel Pulleine. He sent one company out skirmishing, and they were seen no more. Our men fought splendidly; they fired until all their ammunition was spent. They then charged with fixed bayonets, but were soon overcome, the enemy being so strong. They all died the death of brave and gallant soldiers. The Zulus cut a great many of them in pieces, the same as a butcher does his meat. They hung the drummer boys upon hooks, opened them, and cut them up the same as you would an animal. Our men killed about 7,000 of the Zulus.

I was that day at a place called Rorke's Drift, some twelve miles from the other camp. About 5,000 of them attacked us on the same day. We had two hours' notice of their coming. We converted mealie and oat sacks in a kind of fort. There were only 96 of us able to fight in this place. However, the hand of God being with us, and these sacks forming a wall, so as we could kill them as they were trying to rush in. We were able to hold our position until nine a.m. on the 23rd, when the column came to our assistance. We killed 900 of the Zulus, and least 13 on our side and 10 wounded. There were only six of our regiment at this place; we happened to be there on escort. Out of the 551 of our regiment that were engaged on the 22nd January only ten are alive – a narrow escape. I thought every minute that the black savages would cut me in pieces. It was an awful sight to see the dead men lying in heaps all over the camp. I think we are coming home soon, as we cannot go to the front any more. We have lost everything. Thank God for my life. I hope I shall be spared to see you once more, when I can explain things to you. We are in a fort this last six weeks, sleeping with our clothes on, and lying out like cattle, with our ammunition by our side, ready at any minute, as we do not know when they may attack us. So no more.

Please give my kind love to all at home, and all old friends. Hoping this will find you quite well and happy, as I am. Please write soon.

Remaining your affectionate brother

David Jenkins

P.S. There is a rumour of the colonial people presenting us, for the gallant defence of Rorke's Drift, with a colonial medal.

34c. *Brecon County Times*, 22 August 1912

Breconshire Worthy Dead.
Rorke's Drift Hero.

On Wednesday night, the 14th inst, the death took place of one of Swansea's best known figures in the person of Mr David Jenkins, of 52 Brynmelin road, who passed away after a painful illness of about nine months, which eventually developed into a state of paralysis.

The deceased, who was 66 years of age, was the eldest son of one of the oldest and most highly respected of the inhabitants of Devynock, who formerly kept the Tanner's Arms, and who previously had resided for many years at the Angel Hotel, Brecon. He was one of the heroes of Rorke's Drift, when 80 Welsh Borderers held the hospital, where many of their comrades lay wounded, against thousands of Zulus. For 36 hours the small force held out against great odds until relief came, which found the brave and heroic band literally surrounded by the dead bodies of their enemies.

When he took part in the historic defence, deceased was serving in the 1st Battalion of the 24th Regiment (now the S.W. Borderers) and he held a medal and clasp for the Zulu War.

Many interesting letters which he sent home at that time to his parents giving accounts of this stirring and arduous campaign, and which were afterwards published in the "Brecon County Times."

Deceased was one of the foremost members of the Swansea United Service Brigade and was best known on account of his having posed for Lady Butler's famous picture "The Roll Call" which commemorated the scene after the heroic defence of Rorke's Drift.

Some years ago, Lady Butler sent Mr Jenkins a letter of appreciation for his sitting for the painting. When the late King visited Swansea deceased was singled out at the dockside by General Butler and introduced to his Majesty, who shook the hero heartily by the hand and expressed his pleasure at the introduction. For many years he had been employed at the Swansea Corporation yard as a storekeeper, which post he afterwards relinquished for one under Messrs Bacon. He leaves a family of a widow and 7 sons, for whom much sympathy is felt, as well as with his aged father, brother and sisters. The funeral took place at Cwmgelly cemetery on Thursday.

35. 25B/1061 Private John Samuel Jobbins, 'B' Company, 2/24th Foot

35a. *Monmouthshire Merlin and South Wales Advertiser,* 28 March 1879

The Zulu War.
Letter From A Pontypool Man.
Rorke's Drift, Natal, South Africa.
February 6th, 1879.

Dear Father and Mother, –

I now have the pleasure to pen you a few lines, hoping they will find you quite well, as they leave me at present. Since I wrote to you last we have had a deal of hard work and terrible fighting. But before you receive this letter I expect you have heard something about it by the newspapers. But I will tell you a little about it what I have seen myself.

On the 22nd January, about four o'clock in the morning, the General left camp with about half the division in search of the Kaffirs. They threw out a few thousand men as a decoy for our troops to follow, which they did do, instead of following the main body of the Kaffir army. When our men got about 16 miles out of the camp they could see large numbers of the enemy approaching the camp which they had just left.

But our wise commanders did not think it necessary to turn back to protect the camp until it was too late; they still kept marching on after the other few men in front. Well, there were about 20,000 Zulus attacked the camp (but, mind, I was on detachment about 12 miles away with our company, in charge of the commissary stores). There was left in camp five companies of the 1-24th, one company G of ours on picquet, and a lot more men of ours on guard, and on the staff, officers, servants, and cooks, five little band boys, and our new bandmaster just come to the regiment, and there was a lot of volunteers left in camp, and two guns of the Royal Artillery. The guns opened fire on them, but it was no use; as fast as the fire mowed them down their place was filled up again by more of them. All our men that fell, and especially the little boys, were cut to pieces by the Zulus; they are not satisfied with killing us, but they mutilate the body afterwards.

These names I mention are known very well by me and you. Poor Alfred Farr, Charlie Long, George Morrison, Harry Smith, (who used to live at Sow-hill), Dick Treverton, and Will Reece, they have all been killed. There were about 16 white men escaped from the camp out of about 900 men; all the others, officers and men, were all killed.

There were two officers who escaped on horseback with the colours of the 1-24th; they got down to the river called the Buffalo, when they were both knocked over, the colours were found a few days after in the river at the side of the two poor officers. All that did escape were on horseback.

At night the General received a messenger from the camp to say it was taken, and all the ammunition, two guns, about 1,000 rifles, and thousands of pounds in cash. Well, the General says to the men, we must take the camp at the point of a bayonet, and they first had to shell the camp with the six guns which the General had out with him. When the men got to camp they could see the Zulus retiring, and the men had to sleep that night amongst the dead, and some terrible sights there was; but there was, say, about 10 black men killed to each white man.

Before it was daylight the next morning what was left of our poor soldiers had to retire upon the stores, where I was, with about 120 men our company and volunteers. The day before four men on horseback arrived at the stores who escaped from the camp, and told us what had happened; this was about three o'clock in the afternoon of the 22nd January. We at once let our tents fall to the ground and got inside the stores, and made a small fort with sacks filled with grain. Just as we had finished our little fort, we could see thousands of niggers coming down on our little body of men. At the end of the fort was a large house which had been turned into a hospital, the owners of which were Swedes, who fled as soon as the Zulus were in sight. There was a lot of sick men in the hospital at the time. One poor Sergeant Maxfield was insane, and he was burnt alive, or killed, and then burnt; well, we fought hard from about 3.30 p.m. till the following morning when they retired; but they killed about 12 of our men, but we killed at least 450 of them. They were charging over the sacks, but we repulsed them. All that night a minister was praying in the fort that they would go away. God helped us and gave us the victory; in the morning we could see in the distance a large body of men approaching; we did not at first recognise them, but after a bit we could see the welcome red coats retiring on us from the other unfortunate camp; then we all gave hearty cheer, as we felt safe when we was all together. Nothing important has happened since the 22nd, but we have ever since been making the fort stronger, and we sleep in our clothes every night on the look out. One of the poor fellows who was wounded is a Corporal Lyons, him who used to go about with Jim Sullivan, but he is expected to get over it. Poor M. Morgan is here very bad with the fever, but he seems to be getting over it. The General has sent to England for 10,000 more troops; we shall advance no further till they come out here. I send my kind love to brothers and sisters and Mrs. Sullivan, and all friends, thanking God I am well, and hope you are all the same.

Your affectionate Son,

J. Jobbins.

No. 1,061. J. Jobbins, B. Company 2-24th Regiment, Natal, South Africa.

Good bye, and bless you all.

(The writer of the above is a son of Mr. Jobbins, the post boy, at the Crown Hotel, Pontypool.)

35b. *Free Press of Monmouthshire,* 14 September 1934

Survivor of Rorke's Drift lying ill at Pontnewynedd, after visit to military tattoo, his thoughts in the past.

A grand old man of Pontnewynedd is lying seriously ill at his home in Machine-meadow. He is Pte John Jobbins, one of the few remaining survivors of the Rorke's Drift episode. Mr. Jobbins, who is 79 years old, visited the Tattoo in July by invitation, he was not well at the time and was thankful to return home to the bosom of his family. His health gradually became worse until today his condition gives cause for anxiety, but the old indomitable spirit still persists. He is today fighting a battle of failing health and his many friends and admirers sincerely hope that he will again emerge with colours flying.

The old warrior has received many distinguished visitors during his present indisposition including Lt. Col Gwynne Thomas of Newport, "I have asked God to spare me a little longer" said the gallant old soldier to a Free Press reporter this week. "I can do no more." The hand that steadied a rifle at Rorke's Drift was withered by age and a little uncertain but he was still able to go to the 'salute.' The eye that had 'sighted' the same rifle lacked its lustre, although an occasional glint was observable as he pictured the scene of 1879 when a small section of the South Wales Borderers faced the Zulu Hordes.

When informed by his son of the identity of his visitor, Pte Jobbins, as he lay on his bed with his beloved clay pipe within reach, was particularly distressed that his visitor should see his new Rorke's Drift medal (his old one being lost). Reminding his son to be careful of a loose portion of the yellow and black ribbon belonging to the medal.

Scenes Recalled

The old warrior's thoughts were in the past and he pictured the whole scene. The few solitary men, the mealie bags as a barricade; the old farmhouse in the pitch black of night and the Zulus circling the whole.

"'A' company came off duty in the afternoon and I suggested going down to the river to wash our clothes and have a bath while our clothes were drying," said Pte Jobbins. "We hadn't been there long when I knew something was wrong and we rushed back. We worked hard putting barricades of mealie bags. We saw a horseman riding towards us, he fell over a barricade riddled with an assegai. They were at us all night, had they come in a mass we should have had them with our rifles but they separated and attacked us from behind as well. They set fire to the house, I helped rescue several of our men and to get them to the old barn. Had they set that alight it would have been all over for us. We didn't say anything about what we did as it was all part of the job. It was now dark and we couldn't see them." And so the old soldier wandered on. Pte Jobbins raised his hand to the salute as the reporter left him.

Old Warrior's better half.

Mrs. Jobbins spoke with pride of her husband. "He is loyal," said the old lady. Mrs. Jobbins and her husband have their 8 children near them, she told the reporter her husband worked during a long and active life. He was one time a fireman in the colliery. He was working at Treharris and was naturally desirous of procuring work nearer home. Mrs. Jobbins decided to interview a certain Eastern Valley colliery director for the purpose of obtaining work locally for her husband, she said, if she was successful it was arranged beforehand that she should wave a white handerkerchief to Mr. Jobbins as the train passed along.

The old lady waved her handkerchief gracefully to show the reporter how she had signalled her husband. She said her husband possessed many treasured testimonials from appreciated employers. She is praying that her husband may be spared a little longer.

35c. *Western Mail,* 25 September 1934

Hero of Rorke's Drift.
Death of Mr. John Jobbins, Pontnewynydd.

Mr. John Jobbins, of Machine Meadow, Pontnewynydd, who has died aged 79, was one of the very few remaining survivors of the epic stand at Rorke's Drift, one of the most memorable defensive operations in the annals of the British Army, by a company of the South Wales Borderers (the old 24th Foot Regiment).

Jobbins was in the small band of about 100 who took part in the heroic defence of the camp, which was attacked by Zulu hordes in the absence of the main column.

Among his colleagues was the late Sergt. John Williams (Fielding), of Cwmbran, who gained the V.C.

Jobbins and a companion had gone to the river for a bathe after coming off duty, and suddenly became aware something was wrong on seeing a horseman racing towards them.

They rushed back to help in the hurried erection of the barricade of mealy bags. Jobbins during the all-night siege helped rescue several men from the farmhouse which was set ablaze by the enemy.

At Catterick, in July, Mr. Jobbins saw the Rorke's Drift episode re-enacted at a military tattoo.

Jobbins, who after his Army career was connected with the mines, and at one period was a colliery foreman, is survived by a widow and eight children – four boys and four girls.

CHAPTER 2

'Finished up at Jim's': The Zulu View of Rorke's Drift

BY IAN KNIGHT

In 1882, the traveller and writer Bertram Mitford undertook a tour of Zululand 'with the object of making the round of the battlefields in succession – which, till then, had not been done by anybody – mixing with the people, observing their character as well as manners and customs, and gathering their opinion on the subject of the recent campaign'.[1] Mitford would prove an interested and perceptive observer, and his account of his adventures offers a rare insight into the condition of the Zulu country in the immediate aftermath of the Anglo-Zulu War. It also encapsulates many of the difficulties and frustrations faced by modern historians who try to glean from sources such as Mitford any sort of Zulu perspective of the fighting. During his travels, for example, Mitford made a point of visiting Prince Dabulamanzi kaMpande in his eZulwini homestead near Eshowe.[2] Typically, Mitford has left us a good physical description of the prince and a realistic appreciation of his military reputation. His opinion of Dabulamanzi's personality, however, had clearly been prejudiced by the prevailing resentment reserved among white traders and officials for Africans who were not intimidated by European culture:

> Before leaving Eshowe I paid a visit to Dabulamanzi, whose principal kraal is about six miles off. This worthy, whose name came greatly to prominence before the war, is one of Cetywayo's half-brothers. Why he should have been made so

much of it is difficult to understand, seeing that he is not an induna in any sense, and whatever lustre may be reflected on him is solely due to his relationship with royalty, except that everyone, having got hold of the name of one man of rank, was determined to make the most thereof. Accordingly, in Natal, Dabulamanzi was forthwith constituted commander-in-chief of the Zulu army, and its leader in every battle, quite irrespective of such trivialities as time and place.

... creeping through the low doorway [I] stood in the presence of the doughty 'Divider of Water'.[3] My lord looked decidedly cool and comfortable, squatting on a mat, without a rag of clothing but his mutya, and the inevitable head-ring encircling his shaven poll. Two of his sons, boys of about ten or eleven, stopped in their play to stare at the umlungu (white man) as I entered. One side of the hut was piled up with trunks; and heaps of rugs, topboots, brass candlesticks, lanterns, and other odds and ends were lying about, the whole suggestive of Isandhlwana loot.

Dabulamanzi is a fine looking man of about thirty-five, stoutly built and large-limbed like most of his royal brethren. He is light in colour even for a Zulu, and has a high, intellectual forehead, clear eyes, and handsome, regular features, with jet-black beard and moustache. But although a handsome face, it is not altogether a prepossessing one, for it wears a settled expression of cunning which would cause you to have little doubt as to the deservedness of public opinion about him if you had heard it, and if you had not, readiness of belief when you should come to do so. That opinion I have heard expressed by those who knew the man, in two words, 'a blackguard'. With missionary and trader alike he is in disrepute, and many are the tales of sharp practice, if not downright rascality, which were told me about him; nor is he popular among his countrymen.

We shook hands, and sitting down opposite the chief, I produced a substantial piece of tobacco, which was promptly transferred to his side of the field. Then he told Andries to bring in my gun – which, in accordance with Zulu etiquette, I had left outside – as he wanted to look at it. He examined it with the air of a connoisseur (the fellow has the reputation of being a good shot), bringing it to his shoulder, trying the hammers, handling the weapon as if he could not bring himself to part with it.[4]

After an attempt to barter with Dabulamanzi for personal souvenirs, Mitford turned the conversation to the war. Here, however, his account is bitterly disappointing for modern historians. Granted a rare opportunity to obtain command insights from the senior Zulu officer at Rorke's Drift, Mitford merely noted that,

> We talked a good deal about the war and subsequent events, but I elicited nothing new in the way of information or incident from Dabulamanzi, who, like many other Zulus of rank, was reticent in matters political to a degree bordering on suspicious – and after a couple of hours indaba (talk) I left him.[5]

Mitford's account of this interview in many ways typifies the record of contemporary Zulu comment on Rorke's Drift. Where a Zulu voice has survived, it is usually by chance, recorded at the whim of a rare passing European, and it is often anecdotal, and almost always incomplete. This is true, of course, of all the battles of the 1879 war, but particularly so of Rorke's Drift. If a remarkable number of accounts have survived from among the tiny garrison who defended the position at Rorke's Drift, only a handful still exist from the many more who were on the other side of the barricade.

There were a number of reasons for this, and the first is simply demographic. The number of men who survived the attack on Rorke's Drift was small compared to the size of the Zulu army as a whole – perhaps 3,000 men at most. Although the four amabutho who took part in the attack – the uThulwana and its associated regiments, the iNdlondlo and the iNdluyengwe, together with the uDloko – were badly demoralised by their failure on that occasion, they continued to fight throughout the remainder of the war. At the battle of Khambula (29 March 1879) they had formed the 'chest' of the attacking army and had charged close to the main British redoubt, suffering heavy casualties as a result. At Ulundi (4 July) they had been committed late in the battle, but had still been exposed to Gatling and artillery fire. Thus many individuals survived Rorke's Drift only to be killed later in the war, and the upheaval which followed the post-war settlement of the country thinned their ranks still further. In 1883, when the British restored King Cetshwayo to his throne, the king had attempted to reassemble what remained of his old regiments. Many individual Zulu no longer recognised his authority, and mustered instead in the service of regional chiefs opposed to Cetshwayo. Nevertheless, allegiance to the amabutho system remained strong among precisely those regiments like the uThulwana – middle-aged and conservative – who had been associated with the king since his youth. Large number of uThulwana had assembled at the reconstituted oNdini in response to the king's call in June 1883; they were still there on 3 July when inkosi Zibhebhu launched a devastating attack upon the royal homestead. King Cetshwayo was forced to flee, and over fifty of the most important men of the kingdom died in the ensuing rout. Some of the uThulwana attempted to stand among the huts of oNdini itself, but were surrounded and killed. Thus, at the very time that white penetration of Zululand increased, the numbers of Zulu who had experienced the events at Rorke's Drift dwindled. Moreover, the men who had attacked Rorke's Drift were mostly in their mid-forties at the time of the battle in 1879; those who survived the ensuing violence were in their sixties by 1900, and most had passed over to join their ancestors by the 1920s.

All of this was in stark contrast to the much larger army of essentially young men who had carried the camp at iSandlwana – some 20,000 of them. Although thousands of these, too, would be killed resisting the British invasion and during the subsequent civil war, thousands more were still alive and vigorous at the turn of the century, and indeed many hundreds survived into the 1930s. For these reasons alone, surviving Zulu accounts of iSandlwana, while small compared to the numbers involved, are plentiful compared to those of Rorke's Drift. There were more veterans of iSandlwana alive for much longer, and some indeed lived to see the birth of modern media interest in the war, which arguably began on the fiftieth anniversary in 1929.

Yet there were psychological reasons, too, why the Zulu preferred to talk about iSandlwana rather than Rorke's Drift. iSandlwana had had an enormous impact on the population of Zululand as a whole; with so many young men taking part, there were few homesteads which did not include at least one veteran of the battle. The importance of the victory was immediately apparent to the nation as a whole; so, however, was the terrible price which had been paid. For most Zulu, the attack on Rorke's Drift was a minor mopping-up operation which had gone badly, tarnishing a great strategic success, and it seemed all the more absurd because it had not been authorised by the king, nor had it been fought to secure any clear objective. In stark contrast to the heroic status accorded the British participants in the battle, the Zulu survivors were mocked and derided by the nation as a whole for their folly. It is scarcely surprising, therefore, that their voice has been largely forgotten.

Even the names of very few participants in the attack have survived, and, as Mitford had wryly noted, only Prince Dabulamanzi achieved any celebrity among his enemies at the time. Even so, Mitford's description is typical of the missed opportunities which characterise white interaction with the Prince. Although Dabulamanzi's surrender to British troops during the closing stages of the war was widely reported, and his role in the post-war movement to restore King Cetshwayo to Zululand was conspicuous – actions which provided ample opportunities to elicit his views on the battle – and he was well known to white traders in the Eshowe district, very few accounts were elicited from him. Perhaps the most telling of those which have survived was given by King Cetshwayo himself, who received the prince's report of Rorke's Drift shortly after the battle occurred. Like unsuccessful commanders the world over, the prince sought to temper the news of his defeat by stressing his successes: 'Of the Rorke's Drift fight, Cetywayo received most imperfect news. Dabulamanzi reported that he had successfully stormed and taken "the house"; he attacked, and then retired, but admitted he had suffered heavily.'[6] According to optimistic reports in the press, the king was so disappointed with the news that he had promptly ordered Dabulamanzi to be executed:

> The Induna on horseback was Vumandaba. He called the force back, and forbade it in the King's name to cross the river. Dabulamanzi refused to go back, and led some of his men over to attack the house at Rorke's Drift. He is now a prisoner, with his hands bound, at the King's Kraal for disobedience to orders. The men whom he took over were the Udhloko and part of the Tulwane Regiment.[7]

A report in the Natal press added:

> In our last, we mentioned a report which we believe to be well founded, that Cetywayo had put Matshana to death for disobedience of orders – attacking the

camp instead of the General and his forces, whom he was ordered to stop. He is also said to have put to death the chief indunas who attacked Rorke's Drift, saying it was bad enough to take the army so far away as the camp, leaving him open to the General's army; but it was still worse, after the heavy losses at Isandhlwana, to go on to Natal, and lose more men there.

Other reasons are assigned for these indunas being put to death: one, the disobedience of the King's orders that the river was on no account to be crossed; another, that he had forbidden the enemy to be attacked except in the open. The Rorke's Drift Post was not a properly fortified place, but the rapidity with which defences were thrown up, and the slaughter the Zulus there suffered, fully justifies Cetywayo's aversion to encounter English forces unless in the open, where the Zulu tactics could be employed.[8]

While the king was undoubtedly angry, there is no evidence that he ever contemplated such drastic action. In fact, Prince Dabulamanzi retired to his personal homestead near Eshowe, where he took a leading role organising the siege of the British garrison there. He was wounded in the thigh during the action at kwaGingindlovu on 2 April, but survived and was present at the final battle at Ulundi on 4 July.

It is clear that the British press quickly formed an opinion of Dabulamanzi. He was described variously as a great hunter and a magnificent shot (one newspaper suggesting that he was perhaps the best in South Africa); and as a clever, unscrupulous, bad-tempered man – feared by the Zulus.[9] Others went as far as tagging him as a 'foxy rascal', and as a mischief maker of a most treacherous disposition.[10] It was claimed that Dabulamanzi had told Cetshwayo not to surrender, whilst he himself plotted to cross over to the British at the earliest opportunity. Indeed various unfounded reports circulated that Dabulamanzi had been caught and killed by a Zulu impi loyal to the king, whilst attempting to flee.

In truth Dabulamanzi, and a small party of his followers (possibly as few as fifteen), surrendered to Colonel Walker at Fort Pearson on 12 July. His arrival in the British camp caused considerable excitement:

When asked by the officer who was bringing him in if he thought the war was over, Dabulamanzi remarked,

> 'Oh yes, you have beaten us; you had the best guns, but we have the best men'; then after thinking for a few moments, he turned and said 'but we'll fight again in two or three years' time.' An officer of Lonsdale's horse who had been treating the warrior to champagne, asked him if he would give him some small keepsake, meaning a snuff-box or some trifle of that kind. It was some time before he could be made to understand what was wanted, but at length he produced a bag of sovereigns, and gravely extracting one, presented it, saying with pride that he got them all at Isandula.[11]

Given food and an old coat, he remained a 'prisoner' amongst the British for some time, before being sent down to Port Durnford under the safe custody of Mr Robertson, a local missionary. Dr Doyle Glanville of the Army Medical Department recalled Dabulamanzi's propensity for free gin and his apparent freedom to move around the camp at leisure: 'He is about thirty-five years of age, has a fine commanding presence, and a bright, good-natured, intelligent face. He rides about our camp mounted on a Cape pony, wearing a pea jacket and an old silver-laced Yeomanry forage cap.'[12] Another correspondent, writing for one of the Cape papers added,

> He came in with a few followers, and for some days remained in the camp at Fort Durnford as happy as possible, very proud in the possession of a wideawake hat and an Ulster, and chatting with anyone who could talk to him. He never tried to escape and was never fired at, and consequently never wounded. He was, however, allowed to go back to his own kraal.[13]

Dabulamanzi was the subject of one final interview, probably conducted in 1885,[14] by Walter Stafford, who, as a captain in the 1/1st Regiment, NNC, had himself survived iSandlwana. Stafford, however, elicited little more information about Rorke's Drift than had Mitford:

> A few years after the war another man and myself had a store about 15 miles out of Vryheid. I heard that Dabulamanzi was at a kraal nearby visiting. I rode over to see him, when I got to the kraal I told one of the men to tell him that a white man who escaped at Isandhlwana wanted to see him. He sent back word saying that I was lying – that no white men had escaped. I went into the hut and Kuleka

> him. I said 'Listen to me and I will convince you.' After I had spoken for some time he handed me a pot of beer and said 'puza'. I asked him if it had been his intention to invade Natal. He said 'No' that Cetywayo told him that the flooded rivers were a bigger King than what he was. I then said 'Then why did your men shout out, both at Isandhlwana and at Rorke's Drift – Nina manga – which means you are kidding yourselves, tomorrow night we will sleep with your wives and sisters in Umgungumhlovu (Maritzburg)'. He said that was only bravado – 'But had Rorke's Drift fallen I should certainly have taken my army into Natal.' If that had happened all the Natal natives and the Cape natives would have joined him as a matter of policy to save their own skins. It is too awful to contemplate what the result would have been (Hell upon Earth).[15]

This last comment should perhaps be taken to reflect deep-seated colonial fears rather than as a true statement of intent. Even had Rorke's Drift fallen, Dabulamanzi's troops would have been exhausted by their exertions on 22 January, and, unsupported by the rest of the army, were in no position to launch a major incursion into Natal. Moreover, as many of the African groups in Natal had a long-standing antagonism towards the Zulu Royal House, and had supplied troops for auxiliary units such as the NNC, it seems unlikely that they could so easily have changed sides. A fear of a widespread rising among African groups was a common cause of settler disquiet, however.

Whether or not Prince Dabulamanzi might one day have had more to say of Rorke's Drift, the desperate nature of post-war Zulu politics robbed him of the chance. An ardent supporter of the exiled king, he was marked down in European eyes as a troublemaker, and in September 1886 he was arrested together with his son Mzingeli by Boers in the newly formed Vryheid district on a trumped-up charge of stock theft. While en route to Vryheid, escorted by Wilhelm Joubert and Paul van der Berg, (known to the Zulus as Peula), Dabulamanzi and his son suddenly broke away. Both were mounted, and they galloped as far as a homestead on the Nondweni river belonging to a headman known to the prince. This homestead lay in territory recently annexed by the British, and believing himself to be safe from his pursuers, Dabulamanzi entered the huts. The Boers caught up with him, however, and van der Berg dismounted and threatened to shoot the prince in the hut if he didn't surrender. Dabulamanzi protested that he was on British territory, and demanded that if the Boers took him anywhere, it be to the headquarters of Lt. Col. Cardew, the British Sub-Commissioner at Nquthu. What happened next was related the following morning (23 September) by Mzingeli:

> The Boers replied, 'All right, come out, we will take you to the Colonel.' My father said, 'Will you swear that you will do me no harm if I come out?' to which Peula replied, 'I swear.' My father then came out and after we had proceeded a short way towards the Colonel's office Peula, who had handed his rifle to Wilhelm, caught hold of my father and attempted to tie him up with reims, saying, 'Now I will take you to Vryheid.' My father resisted, saying, 'No, if you take me anywhere you must take me to the Colonel as I am.' Peula and my father then struggled together, my father seizing hold of Peula's bandolier. After a bit they separated, my father having possession of the bandolier and Peula of my father's knobkerrie. I was prevented from assisting my father by the other Boer who threatened to shoot me. Peula said, 'Give me back my bandolier.' My father replied, 'Return to me my knobkerrie'. My father threw the bandolier to Peula who then seized the gun from Wilhelm and said he would shoot my father if he wouldn't go to Vryheid. My father replied, 'You won't shoot me on Government ground.' Peula said he would and after some more words he shot my father who was standing within two or three yards of him, through the body, the bullet entering his stomach below the left side and coming out above the right hip. My father ran away, and as he was doing so Peula shot at him again twice, the first shot struck him above the left hip, the second passed through his right elbow and left wrist. Peula then fired two shots at me as I was riding away on which the horse bucked me off and I sprained my knee. My father, after receiving the second shot, fell close to me; he had only run about 200 yards. After this I saw the Boers seize our horses and ride away, and presently the people from the nearby kraal came up and carried us to their huts. It was dark by the time we arrived at the kraal. My father was then in a very weak state. This morning about sunrise he died. His last words were, 'I don't know why they killed me on Government ground.'[16]

It was a squalid end to a man whose name, in 1879, had been the terror of Natal.

It was left to ordinary Zulu to offer more detailed accounts of the fighting. Many, like Mehlokazulu kaSihayo, a junior commander in the iNgobamakhosi ibutho, had fought at iSandlwana rather than Rorke's Drift and knew the story of the latter second-hand:

> The men who fought at Rorke's Drift took no part at Isandhlwana; they were the men of the Undi regiment, who formed a portion of the left wing. When the camp at Isandhlwana had been taken, these men came up fresh and pursued the fugitives right over the Fugitives' Drift into Natal. There was a long line of stragglers, as we supposed, making for Jim's house. The other reserve regiments, intending to cut them off, crossed the Buffalo at the point where the Bashee flows into it, and came round crossing the road near the kraal of Inswarele. These reserves complained that they had had no opportunity of taking part in the battle of Isandhlwana, and therefore they went on to Rorke's Drift, and fought there. These were men with rings. I only followed the fugitives a little way, I did not go as far as the Buffalo. We who had fought at Isandhlwana were as tired as the Englishmen, and many more of the English forces would have escaped if the reserve regiments had not come up.[17]

Mehlokazulu said of the Zulu losses at Rorke's Drift that they numbered 'about 300'. He seems to have shared the prevailing Zulu view that the attack was ill-conceived. Asked whether Prince Dabulamanzi was a good general, he replied, 'no; he is too hasty.'[18]

One man who had apparently fought at Rorke's Drift, a warrior named 'Umtyololo', was interviewed shortly after being found wounded by the British on 23 January. He confirmed Mehlokazulu's impression of how the attack had developed:

> A few [survivors of Isandlwana] were met and killed by the Undi, but that Corps, believing that the Camp was already plundered, decided to make the best of their way to Rorke's Drift, and plunder it, never dreaming that any opposition could be offered by the few men they knew to be there. The loss of the Zulus must have been exceedingly heavy …
>
> … and the loss of the Undi at Rorkes drift cannot be less than 500. They killed all their own wounded who were unable to get away. Much astonishment was

expressed by the Zulus at the behaviour of our soldiers – firstly regarding their death dealing powers considering their numbers, secondly because they did not run away before the enormously numerical superiority of the enemy.[19]

An unidentified 'Zulu Deserter', also questioned by the British, offered much the same story:

When at last we carried the camp our regiments became mixed up; a portion pursued the fugitives down the Buffalo, and the remainder plundered the camp, while the Undi and Udhloko regiments made the best of their way to Rorke's Drift to plunder the post there, in which they failed, and lost very heavily, after fighting all the afternoon and night.[20]

Sofikasho Zungu, who fought with the iNgobamakhosi at iSandlwana, saw something of the pursuit, and recalled details of the fight that were typical of those told by returning survivors:

I saw quite a lot of white men escape on horseback soon after we attacked, they rode off on horseback to Jim's place at Rorke's Drift. Jim was a storekeeper. These men who rode away were dressed in black, they were cowards to leave their brothers behind.

I know that that night there was a big fight at Jim's place. Two regiments who were too late to fight at Isandhlawana, the Mbhoza and the Lulorga[21] attacked at Jim's place at night. I know that the Mbhoza threw lighted grass attached to Mkontos into the roof of a building there and set it alight but the soldiers fought bravely and the Zulus never got in to kill them.[22]

Those accounts of the battle which have survived from Zulu participants offer little in the way of tactical detail, but instead conjure up what must have been the overwhelming impression of those who took part – that of a desperate and confused struggle fought out at close-quarters and mostly in the dark. Perhaps the most graphic description was given by Muziwento ('Umsweanto'), a 'Zulu boy' who was interviewed in 1883. Muziwento's family lived close to iSandlwana, and at the start of the war had moved away from the danger posed by the advancing British troops. Muziwento's father had fought at iSandlwana and later at Ulundi. Muziwento himself heard the story of Rorke's Drift from Munyu, a friend of his father who had fought with the uThulwana. This account, recorded in idiomatic style, focused on the brutal fighting at the very doors of the mission buildings and commented wryly on the way in which both sides, coming close to exhaustion after dark, expressed their defiance in war chants and cheers. It describes, too, the bitter response of the nation as a whole to the battle:

> Presently they [the uThulwana] said, 'O! Let us go and have a fight at Jim's!' The white men had by this time made their preparations; they were quite ready. The Zulus arrived at Jim's house. They fought, they yelled, they shouted, 'It dies at the entrance! It dies in the doorway!' … They stabbed the sacks; they dug with their assegais. They were struck; they died. They set fire to the house. It was no longer fighting; they were exchanging salutations merely.
>
> The uThulwana regiment was finished up at Jim's – shocking cowards they were too. Our people laughed at them, some said, 'You! You're no men! You're just women, seeing you ran away for no reason at all, like the wind!' Others jeered and said, 'You marched off. You went to dig little bits with your assegais out of the house of Jim, that had never done you any harm!'[23]

A similar sense of a perspective limited by the frantic nature of fighting in a confined space is evoked in a description by Col. H.C. Lugg of a chance encounter which befell his father, Henry, who had fought in the battle as a trooper in the Natal Mounted Police:

> Rorke's Drift was to have an interesting sequel some twenty-three years later, when in 1902, Henry was carrying out inspections of war graves at this spot and at Isandlwana, where by chance he met an old warrior bearing a number of obvious war scars. A bullet had seared his scalp, another his left shoulder and two through the calf of his leg, all received at Rorke's Drift. Being anxious to hear the old man's version of the affair, Henry got him to tell his story, being careful not to disclose his own participation in the affair. And what a story! Told as it could only be by an old Zulu in language rich in allegory and metaphor.
>
> Soon the old scene came back to life as the old fellow recounted the sounds of rifle fire, the shouts of the Zulu war cry, 'Usuthu!, Usuthu!, Inkomo ka baba,'

as they rushed to the attack, determined to prove their worth as worthy sons of a worthy sire, for this is what the cry implied;[24] the crackling of flames from the burning building, the groans of the wounded, and the din of battle generally. How often, in turn, I have been privileged to hear such stories, and told in just such a way!

One of the stories Henry used to recall was of a Zulu, who during the height of the fight, availed himself of the semi-darkness to creep into the kitchen to light his smoking horn or gudu from the glowing embers, and was promptly shot by Henry.[25] When the old man had come to the end of his story, Henry casually asked him who the man was who had met his death in the kitchen. Greatly taken aback, he exclaimed, 'Kanti nawe wawukhena? Wafa uMngumle! Sizinja ngaphansi kwezinyao zenu.'

'And were you there also? And so perished Mngamule. We were merely dogs under your feet.'[26]

During his expedition of 1882, Bertram Mitford also met a number of ordinary veterans of the battle. Like Lugg, he recorded little in detail of what they told him, perhaps feeling that Zulu accounts of Rorke's Drift could not easily be conveyed in writing. Exploring the battlefield of Hlobane one day,

> … a snort from my pony caused me to look up. Within a few yards, leaning against a rock, stood a couple of stalwart savages calmly looking at me. I saw that one of them carried an assegai with a blade like a small claymore, and, seeing, coveted and resolved to have it if possible. I climbed to where they stood; the warriors greeted me as usual, 'Inkos!', and of course were anxious to know all about me. The one with the assegai was a fine, tall fellow, with a cheery countenance and hearty manner, and we speedily became friends; the other, dark, taciturn, and unprepossessing, I didn't much like the look of. But he of the assegai did his companion's share of the indaba and his own too. He belonged to the Udhloko regiment, and had been present at the attack on Rorke's Drift, which battle he proceeded to fight over again for my enlightenment with an effusiveness and pantomime accompaniment thoroughly Zulu; going into fits of laughter over it, as though one of the toughest struggles on record were the greatest joke in the world. At a judicious moment I produced some 'gwai',[27] which was received with acclamation, even my saturnine friend's dark countenance expanding into a grin.

> Then taking up the assegai I began to examine it, suggesting that we should make an exchange, and throwing out all sorts of inducements. Not a bit of it; the jovial warrior would about as soon think of parting with his head-ring – or his head. He had fought with that very weapon at 'kwaJim' (Rorke's Drift) &c. &c; no, he couldn't give it away on any account. It was a splendid specimen of a spear, but on no terms could I obtain it.[28]

It was one of Mitford's informants, nonetheless – part of a group of three, two members of the oNdini amabutho, and one of the iNgobamakhosi, with whom he discussed the war in a roadside encounter near Mthonjaneni – who offered the most perceptive observation on the battle:

> '... at Rorke's Drift – there were no big guns there, and the English could have stood here (making my hand into a hollow) while the Zulus were everywhere; how is it that you didn't make a better fight of it?'
>
> 'The soldiers were behind a schaans (breastwork), and,' added the narrator significantly, showing all his ivories, 'they were in a corner'.[29]

One thing that the Zulu were agreed upon was that the attack on Rorke's Drift had been hugely costly. Although the Zulu seldom offered figures for their losses, the most authoritative reports at the time suggested that they might have been as high as 600 men – at least 15 per cent of those who took part.[30] As one of Bishop Schreuder's informants suggested, the combined effect of exhaustion and these devastating losses left the attackers utterly spent:

> The detachment of the Zulu army seen by Glyn's column on its way, the 23rd January, back to Rorke's Drift, was part of the Undi corps and Utako retreating from the unsuccessful attack on the commissariat stores at Rorke's Drift. Amongst the horsemen was Udabulamanzi, who says that they were so tired and glad that Glyn's column did not attack them, for if attacked they would have bolted everyone.[31]

As one Cajana kaMatendeka put it,

> The Tulwana regiment then crossed and attacked the camp at Rorke's house, without success; they were beaten off, they say, with very heavy loss. Masipula's chief son, and a number of his brothers, Untabatu ka Maxoza, and his brother Uncuncwana, Umgamuli kaUmbaugulana[32] were killed and many other headmen. The dead are not to be counted there are so many. The whole Zulu nation is weeping and mourning.[33]

Captain Norman MacLeod, the British political agent operating on the Swazi border, reported simply that, 'they say themselves that the Tulwana Regiment (the King's Own), which attacked Bromhead, is gone. They say there is no Tulwana now.'[34]

Cornelius Vijn, a trader who had entered Zululand before the war and was detained throughout under the king's protection, saw at first-hand the suffering caused by the loss of so many family heads in the fighting of 22 January, particularly at Rorke's Drift:

> About 2 P.M., while I lay in the hut, talking with one of the men of Ziwedu (Cetshwayo's brother), who had been sent by the king to learn about me, whether I was alive, and how it went with me, our attention was drawn to a troop of people, who came back from their gardens crying and wailing. As they approached, I recognised them as persons belonging to the kraal in which I was staying. When they came into or close to the kraal, they kept on wailing in front of the kraals, rolling themselves on the ground and never quieting down; nay, in the night they wailed so as to cut through the heart of anyone. And this wailing went on, day and night, for a fortnight; the effect of it was very depressing; I wished I could not hear it.
>
> The reason of this was that the headman of the Kraal, Msundusi, a trusty person and the husband of four wives, had fallen at Isandlwana.[35]

'Job' Telezi, a Zulu who converted to Christianity in 1883, and who seemed to have lived something of a charmed life, later recalled his own family tragedy:

> Well, I must not cry for that which cannot be undone, but my heart is sore for my children, who have all been killed in the wars and disturbances. One was

> killed at the battle of Isandhlwana; his brother brought him home, but I could not get the bullet out, and he died. My heart was too sore at the time to mind his death much for I was crying for my two eldest boys, both of whom had fallen at the fight at Rorke's Drift. I know not where their bones are laid. Shall I ever see my children again?[36]

The heavy losses of 22–23 January – including those from the simultaneous actions in the northern and southern parts of the country – had a deeply unsettling effect on the Zulu. It was obvious that iSandlwana had been an extraordinary victory, an act of concerted defiance which would alter the course of the war. Yet the brutal cost of that victory was equally obvious, and left the king and his councillors full of foreboding. Moreover, there was no such ambiguity about the lessons of Rorke's Drift; although it had been a minor affair, the Zulu had proved utterly ineffectual in the face of determined troops protected by even the most rudimentary barricade. 'The Zulus say', noted Schreuder, 'that the affair at Isan'lwana commenced with a victory and ended with a fight … a defeat.'[37] When a new phase of fighting began in March, a warrior named Mgelija Ngema of the uVe ibutho recalled that King Cetshwayo's instructions were quite specific on the matter of attacking British strongholds: 'Cetewayo actually said you are not to go into the hole of a wild beast or else you will get clawed, wait until the soldiers come out of their laager and then fall on them.'[38]

Tragically, for the young men who made up the bulk of the army, and who had not run the gauntlet at Rorke's Drift, this advice proved difficult to follow, and the lesson had to be learned again at Khambula, and finally at Ulundi – ultimately with devastating consequences.

APPENDIX I

'Have they given me the Cross?': Honours and Awards

Official letter from Colonel, the Hon. Frederick A. Stanley, then Secretary of State for War [National Archives, London, WO32/7710]

Lt. Gen. Lord Chelmsford KCB

My Lord,

I have received with great satisfaction your despatch of the 8th Feb. last, and its Enclosure from Lt Chard R.E. containing a narrative of the heroic defence of the Post at Rorke's Drift on the night of the 22d Jan. last.

Having laid these documents before The Queen, I have received Her Majesty's Commands to express to you Her admiration of the gallantry of all who took part in that brilliant defence. The fertility of resource displayed in improvising defences and the cool & determined courage by which they were guarded and maintained have been especially remarked by Her Majesty and will worthily take a prominent place in the annals of the British Army.

I have conferred with H.R.H. the FM C in C as to the recognition which those officers, N.C.O's Privates & others who are officially mentioned should receive, and I shall lose no time in making the necessary recommendations to Her Majesty on the subject

I have &c

Fred Stanley

London Gazette, various dates, 1879

War Office, May 2, 1879.
The Queen has been graciously pleased to signify Her intention to confer the decoration of the Victoria Cross on the undermentioned Officers and Soldiers of Her Majesty's Army, whose claims have been submitted for Her Majesty's approval, for their gallant conduct in the defence of Rorke's Drift, on the occasion of the attack by the Zulus, as recorded against their names, viz: –

Royal Engineers – Lieutenant (now Captain and Brevet Major) J. R. M. Chard
2nd Battalion, 24th Regiment – Lieutenant (now Captain and Brevet Major) G. Bromhead – For their gallant conduct at the defence of Rorke's Drift, on the occasion of the attack by the Zulus, on January 22nd and 23rd, 1879.
The Lieutenant-General commanding the troops reports that, had it not been for the fine example and excellent behaviour of these two Officers, under the most trying circumstances, the defence of Rorke's Drift post would not have been conducted with that intelligence and tenacity which so essentially characterised it.

The Lieutenant-General adds that its success must, in a great degree, be attributable to the two young Officers who exercised the Chief Command on the occasion in question.

2nd Battalion, 24th Regiment – Private John Williams – Private John Williams was posted, with Private Joseph Williams and Private William Horrigan, 1st Battalion, 24th Regiment, in a distant room of the hospital, which they held for more than an hour, so long as they had a round of ammunition left: as communication was for the time cut off, the Zulus were enabled to advance and burst open the door; they dragged out Private Joseph Williams and two of the patients, and assegaied them. Whilst the Zulus were occupied with the slaughter of these men a lull took place, during which Private John Williams, who, with two patients, were the only men now left alive in this ward, succeeded in knocking a hole in the partition, and in taking the two patients into the next ward, where he found Private Hook.

2nd Battalion, 24th Regiment – Private Henry Hook – These two men together, one man working whilst the other fought and held the enemy at bay with his bayonet, broke through three more partitions, and were thus enabled to bring eight patients through a small window into the inner line of defence.

2nd Battalion, 24th Regiment – Private William Jones and Private Robert Jones – In another ward, facing the hill, Private William Jones and Private Robert Jones defended the post to the last, until six out of the seven patients it contained had been removed. The seventh, Sergeant Maxfield, 2nd Battalion, 24th Regiment, was delirious from fever. Although they had previously dressed him, they were unable to induce him to move. When Private Robert Jones returned to endeavour to carry him away, he found him being stabbed by the Zulus as he lay on his bed.

2nd Battalion, 24th Regiment – Corporal William Allen and Private Frederick Hitch – It was chiefly due to the courageous conduct of these men that communication with the hospital was kept up at all. Holding together at all costs a most dangerous post, raked in reverse by the enemy's fire from the hill, they were both severely wounded, but their determined conduct enabled the patients to be withdrawn from the hospital, and when incapacitated by their wounds from fighting, they continued, as soon as their wounds had been dressed, to serve out ammunition to their comrades during the night.

War Office, June 17, 1879.

Army, Medical Department – Surgeon-Major James Henry Reynolds – For his conspicuous bravery, during the attack at Rorke's Drift, on the 22nd and 23rd January, 1879, which he exhibited in his constant attention to the wounded under fire, and in his voluntarily conveying ammunition from the store to the defenders of the Hospital, whereby he exposed himself to a cross-fire from the enemy both in going and returning.

War Office, November 17, 1879.
Commissariat and Transport Department – Acting-Assistant (now Sub-Assistant) Commissary James Langley Dalton – For his conspicuous gallantry during the attack on Rorke's Drift Post by the Zulus on the night of the 22nd of January, 1879, when he actively superintended the work of defence, and was among the foremost of those who received the first attack at the corner of the hospital, where the deadliness of his fire did great execution, and the mad rush of the Zulus received its first check, and where by his cool courage he saved the life of a man of the Army Hospital Corps by shooting the Zulu, who, having seized the muzzle of the man's rifle, was in the act of assegaing him.

This Officer, to whose energy much of the defence of the place was due, was severely wounded during the contest, but still continued to give the same example of cool courage.

War Office, November 29, 1879.
Natal Native Contingent – Corporal Schiess ... – For conspicuous gallantry in the defence of Rorke's Drift Post on the night of the 22nd January, 1879, when, in spite of his having been wounded in the foot a few days previously, he greatly distinguished himself when the Garrison were repulsing, with the bayonet, a series of desperate assaults by the Zulus, and displayed great activity and devoted gallantry throughout the defence. On one occasion when the Garrison had retired to the inner line of defence, and the Zulus occupied the wall of mealie bags which had been abandoned, he crept along the wall, without an order, to dislodge a Zulu who was shooting better than usual and succeeded in killing him, and two others, before he, the Corporal, returned to the inner defence.

Register of the Distinguished Conduct Medal
[National Archives, London, WO146/1]

"Most Humbly submitted to Your Majesty by His Royal Highness the Field Marshall Commanding in Chief ..."

28th July 1879: Color Serjeant Frank Bourne, 2nd Battalion 24th Foot (with £10.00 Annuity)
29th July 1879: 2nd Corporal Attwood, Army Service Corps (with £5.00 Gratuity)
31st October 1879: Private William Roy of the 1st Battalion 24th Foot (without Annuity)
15th January 1880: 2nd Corporal McMahon, Army Hospital Corps (Submission cancelled – 29th January 1880)
11th February 1880: Gunner John Cantwell, Royal Artillery (without Annuity)

The Times, c. March 1879

… Although Majors Chard and Bromhead have not been gazetted to the Victoria Cross, there is no doubt that they will shortly receive that much coveted decoration, and that the men specially mentioned in the despatch will be similarly rewarded. It is probable that the medal for distinguished service in the field will be given to the whole of the garrison of Rorke's Drift, and that B Company, 2d Battalion, 24th Foot will be permitted to wear on its appointments the words 'Rorke's Drift' in commemoration of the gallant stand it made on the 22nd January 1879. This will be a lasting honour to the company and the regiment.

It is satisfactory to note that the non-combatant officers have also received a step in rank. Surgeon-Major Reynolds and Messrs. Dalton and Dunne have richly deserved their promotions …

Extract from an unidentified Natal newspaper,
possibly the *Times of Natal*, c. 1879

Recognition of the Rorke's Drift Action

A correspondent writes us: –

"I am desirous of getting up a subscription for the men who defended Rorke's Drift, not to exceed a sovereign – less if you like. Of course we cannot give the soldiers money, though I dare say we can, for all that, manage to please them."

We quite fall in with our correspondent's view, and would be very glad indeed to bring home to the gallant fellows who so nobly defended their outpost, the thorough appreciation the colonists entertain of their gallant conduct. We shall be glad to head a subscription list and receive contributions.

Natal Mercury, 29 May 1879

The Rorke's Drift Defence.

We have received the following from Mr. Jameson: –

To the Editor of the Natal Mercury.

Durban, May 27,1879.

Sir,– The little brochure containing the account of the Rorke's Drift defence, the M.S. of which I hold, has been received with so much favour in its former limited private circulation, that I am induced to believe very many people will be glad to purchase copies if procurable. I have, therefore, placed it in the hands of the printer for republication, with the intention of handing the entire proceeds of the sale to our Mayor, towards forming the nucleus of a fund to purchase some colonial testimonial, to be presented to the survivors of the night of the 22nd January; feeling confident that not only would it be graceful thus to recognise their services, but that it is widely felt by colonists in all districts to be a duty we owe to those who so gallantly and successfully saved our colony from the horrors of an invasion by a horde of savages, flushed with victory and eager for fresh plunder.

Particulars I send for your advertising columns, – I am, &c.

R. JAMESON.

Times of Natal, 21 April 1879

General Orders No. 84, dated 13th April 1879

1. The Lieut-General Commanding sanctions the free issue of a pair of trousers and a flannel shirt to each soldier employed recently in the construction of field works at Rorke's Drift, in such cases where the commanding officer certifies to these articles having been rendered unserviceable through the labour entailed.

London Evening Standard, 6 June 1879

… Chard and Bromhead have been awarded the Victoria Cross, and have been deservedly promoted for their gallant defence of Rorke's Drift. Nor have the brave men who served under them been forgotten. An order has just been issued to the effect that, in consideration of the gallantry displayed by the non-commissioned officers and men present on that memorable occasion, a pair of new trousers and a flannel shirt are to be allotted to each of them to compensate for the damage to their clothing. As the brave fellows probably fought in their shirt sleeves, it would follow that there was no necessity to present each of them with a new coat; but a few days' extra pay in the pockets of those brave trousers would make them all the more acceptable.

Hansard HC, Vol. 246, 16 June 1879

Mr. Stacpoole asked the Secretary of State for War, If an order was issued by his or any other authority, that in consideration of the gallantry displayed by the non-commissioned officers and privates at Rorke's Drift, the issue of one flannel shirt and one pair of trousers to each man, in compensation for damage done to their clothing, is sanctioned?

Colonel Stanley: "Sir, so far as I can understand, such an order was issued by the General Officer commanding the troops for the issue to the men of a flannel shirt and one pair of trousers, in compensation for damage done to the clothing. Whether regard was had to it as a reward for gallantry or not I cannot say."

Oakham Advertiser, Uppingham Times and County of Rutland Echo, 12 March 1881

A committee, with Mrs. Forster, of Eccles, Lancashire, as hon. sec., was formed shortly after the news was received of the battle of Rorke's Drift with the object of raising a small fund for the purposes of presenting each of the surviving defenders – now about 100 in number – with a souvenir of the event. It was arranged to give each officer and soldier a Bible, and these are now being despatched. Those for the officers are handsomely bound, and those for the men are very neat. Each book is lettered in gold on the outside, 'Souvenir of Rorke's Drift, January 22–3, 1879.'

Extracts from *Sir Garnet Wolseley's South African Journal, 1879–80*, edited by A. Preston, London, 1973

Wednesday, 16th July 1879

… I presented Major Chard R.E. with his Victoria X: a more uninteresting or more stupid-looking fellow I never saw. Wood tells me he is a most useless officer, fit for nothing. I hear in this camp also that the man who worked hardest in defence of Roorke's Drift Post was the Commissariat officer who has not been rewarded at all. The only one who behaved badly was the Doctor, & reports say that he is a coward. Bromhead of the 24th Regt. who was the 2nd in Command of the post is a very stupid fellow also …

Sunday 3rd August

… I gave away a Victoria X this morning to a private of the 24th Regt. named Hook …

Thursday 21st August

… The Revd. Mr. Smith who was at the defence of Roorke's Drift is reported to have corrected the men for cursing whilst the fight was at its height. 'Don't swear men, don't swear, but shoot them boys, shoot them.' …

Thursday 11th September

… The troops paraded at 9 a.m. I gave away two Victoria Crosses, one to Major Bromhead 24th & the other to Private Jones 24th Regt. – I have now given away these decorations to both officers who took part in the defence of Roorke's Drift, and two duller, more stupid, more uninteresting even or less like Gentlemen it has not been my luck to meet for a long time …

Extract from Queen Victoria's private journal, 11 August 1879 [The Royal Archives, Windsor, RA VIC/MAIN/QVJ (W) (Princess Beatrice's copies), by kind permission of Her Majesty Queen Elizabeth II]

All the wounded were going on well. Young Private Hitch of the 24th, was very severely wounded in the shoulder, affecting the use of the right arm, which he cannot raise to his head, though he can move his fingers now. He behaved most gallantly at Rorke's Drift, defending the Hospital & serving out ammunition to the men, long after he was wounded, till he fell senseless from exhaustion. He is a tall good looking young man, with a very determined expression, but very modest, & bears a high character. One man, had 6 bullet wounds. When I had visited all the Wards, just before leaving, young Hitch was brought to the door, for me to give him the V.C. which I told him I did for his great bravery. He could not say a word, & I hear afterwards fainted. All the others who could leave their wards, came down in their hospital dress, & were drawn up in 3 sides of a square, in order to witness this great distinction, the greatest a soldier can receive.

The Times, 10 December 1879

… Her Majesty decorated, yesterday, at Windsor Castle, several officers and soldiers who had been selected to receive honours in recognition of their services during the recent South African campaign …

… Lance Sergeant William Allen of the 2d. Battalion 24th Regiment, takes the Victoria Cross for bravery at the defence of Rorke's Drift, where he was wounded in the left shoulder, on the night of the 22d of January, in this year, while serving under the command of Lieutenants Chard and Bromhead; and Corporal Roy, who was engaged in the same memorable action, has the distinguished conduct medal for having, while a patient himself in the hospital, broken through the wall and removed, under fire, six of the sick to the laager …

The Times, 9 March 1880

Court Circular.
Windsor Castle, March 8.
The Queen decorated Gunner John Cantwell, of the Royal Artillery, in the corridor at Windsor Castle to day, with the distinguished service medal for gallantry displayed by him at the defence of the hospital at Rorke's Drift …

APPENDIX II

'To a dead soldier I heard a man say as he was lifting him – "Come on, old comrade, I'm main sorry to put you out of sight, but ye had a soldier's death"': Casualty Lists

Extract from John R.M. Chard's official report on the defence of Rorke's Drift [National Archives, London, WO32/7737]

The following is a list of the killed

Sergt.	Maxfield	2/24	Regt.
Pte	Scanlon	"	"
"	Hayden	"	"
"	Adams	"	"
"	Cole	"	"
"	Fagan	"	"
"	Chick	"	"
1398 Pte	Williams	2/24	Regt.
Pte	Nicolls	1/24	"
"	Horrigan	1/24	"
"	Jenkins	1/24	"

Mr Byrne	Commt Dept.
Trooper Hunter	N.M. Police
" Anderson	N.N.C.
1 Pte (Native)	"

Total 15
12 wounded * of whom two have since died
viz, Sergt. Williams, 2/24th. Regt
Private Beckett, 1/24th. "

Making a total killed of 17

* List already forwarded by Medical Officer

Official casualty returns [National Archives, London, WO32/7711]

Compiled from Returns received from various sources from 22nd Jany. to 24th February 1879

Rorke's Drift, 22nd Jany. as reported by the P.M.O.

1/24th Regt.	
Pte. J. Waters	Severely wounded – Gunshot thro' arm & shoulder
Pte. Beckett	Dangerously wounded – Assegai penetrating abdomen
Pte. Desmond	Slightly wounded – Gunshot thro' fleshy part of thumb
2/24th Regt.	
Sergt. T. Williams	Dangerously wounded – Gunshot left side of chest fracturing ribs. Bullet not lodged
Corpl. Lyons	Dangerously wounded: Gunshot neck, fracturing spine of vertebrae, ball lodged
Corpl. Allen	Severely wounded: Gunshot thro' shoulder & arm

Pte. Hitch	Dangerously wounded: Gunshot thro' shoulder joint
Pte. Jones	Slightly wounded: Assegai contusion of abdomen
Pte. Tasker	Slightly wounded: Gunshot splinter of ball breaking skin of forehead
Native Contingent	
Corpl. Scammell	Dangerously wounded: Gunshot, ball passing in at upper part of R. Shoulder & making exit at L. Shoulder
Pte. Scheiss	Slightly wounded: Gunshot contusion of ankle
Commissariat Dept.	
Storekeeper Dalton	Severely wounded: Gunshot thro' fleshy part of shoulder & making exit behind

[signed]
J North Crealock Lieut. Colonel
Asst. Mily. Secretary

Notes

1 Bertram Mitford, *Through the Zulu Country: Its Battlefields and Its People*, London, 1883.

2 The British had destroyed the original eZulwini homestead in April 1879, at the end of the Eshowe campaign.

3 The meaning of Dabulamanzi, so named by his father, King Mpande, to commemorate his passage across the river Thukela in 1840 – an act which secured Boer support for Mpande's ultimately successful campaign to win the Zulu throne.

4 Mitford, *Through the Zulu Country*.

5 Ibid.

6 Quoted in C. de B. Webb and J.B. Wright (eds), *A Zulu King Speaks: Statements Made by Cetshwayo kaMpande on the History and Customs of his People*, Pietermaritzburg and Durban, 1978.

7 Vumandaba kaNthali, as reported in the *Edinburgh Daily Review*, 19 April 1879.

8 An unidentified Natal newspaper, possibly the *Natal Witness*, c. 1879.

9 *South London Press*, 16 August 1879.

10 *Morning Post*, 29 September 1879.

11 'From a correspondent in Natal', *Truth*, 16 October 1879.

12 *The Graphic*, 11 October 1879.

13 *Birmingham Daily Post*, 29 August 1879.

14 Stafford refers to the town of Vryheid. If his memory is correct, this would place the interview some time between the end of 1884, when construction of Vryheid began, and September 1886, when the prince was murdered.

15 Captain Walter H. Stafford, late of the Natal Native Contingent, in his own recollections of the battle of iSandlwana, c. 1939, Killie Campbell Africana Library, Durban, KwaZulu-Natal, South Africa.

16 Cardew's report, BPP C.4980. Reproduced in C.T. Binns, *Dinuzulu: The Death of the House of Shaka*, London, 1968.

17 Account by Mehlokazulu kaSihayo, war supplement to the *Natal Mercury*, 1879. Also see Charles Norris-Newman, *In Zululand with the British Throughout the War of 1879*, London, 1880.

18 Ibid.

19 'Statement made by natives regarding the action of the 22nd January at the Sandhlwana Hill', compiled by W. Drummond. 'Umtoyolo' was described as 'A Zulu well known to Mr. Longcast, Interpreter to the Lt. General. Found wounded at Rorke's Drift on the 23rd January'. National Archives, London, WO32/7711.

20 Reported in the *Natal Witness*, 24 February 1879, and reprinted in F.E. Colenso and E. Durnford, *A History of the Zulu War and its Origin*, London, 1880.

21 Mbhoza and uDloko. Mbhoza was another name for the uThulwana.

22 Bowden Papers, Natal Museum, Pietermaritzburg, reproduced in Ian Knight (ed.), 'Kill Me in the Shadows: The Bowden Collection of Anglo-Zulu War Oral History', *Soldiers of the Queen*, No. 74, 1993.

23 G.H. Swinney, *A Zulu Boy's Recollections of the Zulu War and of Cetshwayo's Return*, London, 1884.

24 Inkomo ka baba my father's cow.

25 The smoking horn, igudu, was used for smoking cannabis, which was regarded by the Zulu as a stimulant.

26 H.C. Lugg, *A Natal Family Looks Back*, Durban, 1970.

27 Tobacco.

28 Mitford, *Through the Zulu Country*.

29 Ibid.

30 See, for example, Chard's revised estimate of their losses, and the assessment by Henrique Shepstone, letter to T. Shepstone, Shepstone Papers, Pietermaritzburg Archives Repository, Pietermaritzburg.

31 J.C. Schreuder, letter to W. Littleton, Ntunjambili (Kranskop) mission, 2 March 1879. British Parliamentary Papers, BPP C.2318.

32 It is interesting to speculate whether this is the same Mngamule referred to in the Lugg account.

33 'Statement of Ucadjana, son of Matendeka, belonging to Seketwayo's people, made to me, H.C. Shepstone, Secretary of Native Affairs, Transvaal', BBP C.2260.

34 Norman MacLeod, 'Extract from a private letter addressed the Honourable W. Littleton, Private Secretary to His Excellency the High Commissioner, Derby, February 8, 1879', BPP C.2308.

35 Cornelius Vijn, *Cetshwayo's Dutchman, Being the Private Journal of a White Trader in Zululand during the British Invasion*, London, 1880, entry for 25 January 1879. It is worth noting that while many senior men in command positions were killed at iSandlwana, and that elements of the uThulwana broke away from the reserve to join the attack, the bulk of the casualties were nevertheless suffered by the younger, unmarried amabutho who stormed the camp. Almost all of the men who died at Rorke's Drift, in contrast, were abamnumzana – married homestead-heads.

36 In 'Why I Am Called "Job"', in Frances Awdry (ed.), *The Gospel Missionary for 1891*, London, 1891.

37 Schreuder, letter to Littleton.

38 Knight, 'Kill Me in the Shadows'.

Bibliography

Official Records

South Africa

Brenthurst Library, Johannesburg

Killie Campbell Africana Library, Campbell Collections, University of KwaZulu-Natal, Durban

Local History Museum, Durban

Natal Museum, Pietermaritzburg

National Archives Repository, Pretoria

Pietermaritzburg Archives Repository, Pietermaritzburg

Western Cape Provincial Archives and Records Service, Cape Town

United Kingdom

NATIONAL ARCHIVES, LONDON

WO32 Series: War Office Correspondence: Reports and Diary of Operations from South Africa, 1877–78–79

WO97 Series: Soldiers' Service and Discharge Papers, 1855–1913

WO98/4: The Register of the Victoria Cross, 1864–1900

WO103/13: Queen's Submission Book for the Distinguished Conduct Medal

WO138/3: Confidential Report on the Services of Surgeon Lt. Colonel J.H. Reynolds, V.C., Army Medical Staff

ROYAL ARCHIVES, WINDSOR. BY KIND PERMISSION OF HER MAJESTY QUEEN ELIZABETH II

Handwritten account of the defence of Rorke's Drift by Capt and Bvt. Major J.R.M. Chard, V.C., R.E., dated 21 February 1880

RA VIC/034/64: Letter from Captain Liddell of HMS *Tamar* re. the Services of Pte. J. Connolly, 2/24th

RA VIC/MAIN/QVJ (W): Queen Victoria's Private Journal: 11 August 1879 (Princess Beatrice's copies)

Newspapers and Periodicals

Australia

Catholic Press

India

Bombay Gazette; *Civil and Military Gazette*; *Madras Weekly Mail*; *Madras Weekly News*

Ireland

Tralee Chronicle; *Weekly Irish Times*

South Africa

Eastern Province Herald; *Natal Mercury*; *Natal Witness*; *Times of Natal*; *Natal Colonist*

Sweden

Nya Dagligt Allehanda

United Kingdom

Abergavenny Chronicle; *Aldershot News*; *Alnwick Mercury*; *Barnet Press*; *Batley Reporter and Guardian*; *Birmingham Daily Post*; *Brecon County Times*; *Bristol Mercury and Daily Post*; *Cardiff Times*; *Carnarvon and Denbigh Herald*; *County Observer and Monmouthshire Central Advertiser*; *Daily Mail*; *Daily Mirror*; *Daily Telegraph*; *Dorking and Leatherhead County Post*; *Eastern Counties Times and*

Recorder; *Epsom District Times*; *Free Press of Monmouthshire*; *The Graphic*; *Herald of Wales, Swansea Herald and Monmouthshire Recorder*; *Illustrated Lloyd's Weekly Newspaper*; *Illustrated London News*; *London Evening Standard*; *London Evening Telegraph*; *London Gazette*; *Manchester Evening News*; *Marylebone Mercury*; *Monmouthshire Beacon*; *Monmouthshire Merlin*; *Morning Post*; *Newcastle Daily Journal*; *News of the World*; *Northern Mail*; *Oakham Advertiser*; *Oxford Times*; *Penny Illustrated News*; *The People*; *Preston Pilot*; *Sketch*; *Somerset Guardian*; *South London Press*; *South Wales Weekly Telegram*; *Stroud News and Gloucestershire Advertiser*; *Sunday Express*; *The Times*; *Truth*; *Warwick Gazette*; *Wellington Gazette*; *West London Observer*; *West Sussex Gazette*; *Western Daily Press*; *Western Mail*; *Western Morning News*

United States of America

New York Tribune

Contemporary Journals, Magazines and Miscellaneous Publications

General

Chums; *The Farmer*; *The Listener*; *Macmillan's Magazine*; *The Mission Field: A Monthly Record of the Proceedings of the Society for the Propagation of the Gospel, 1871–1881*; *The Month: Catholic Review*; *Punch*; *Royal Magazine*; *Strand Magazine*; *V.C. Magazine*; *Windsor Magazine*

Medical

The Lancet; *Medical Press and Circular*; *British Medical Journal*

Military

Army Medical Department Annual Reports; *Army Medical Services Magazine*; *Army Service Corps Journal*; *Journal of the Army Medical Corps*; *Royal Engineers Journal*; *South Wales Borderers Regimental Journal*

Published Sources

Ashwood, R., *For Queen and Country: The Zulu War Diary of Lt Wilfred Heaton 24th Regiment of Foot*, Darlington, 2005.

Awdry, E. (ed.), *The Gospel Missionary for 1891*, London, 1891.

Baynham Jones A., and Stevenson, L., *Rorke's Drift By Those Who Were There*, Brighton, 2003

Bennett, I.H.W., *Eyewitness in Zululand*, London, 1989.

Blair Brown, D., *Surgical Experiences in the Zulu and Transvaal Wars*, London, 1882.

Child, D. (ed.), *The Zulu War Journal of Col. H. Harford*, Pietermaritzburg, 1978.

Emery, F., *The Red Soldier*, London, 1977.

Gordon-Roe, E., *The Bronze Cross*, London, 1945.

Hallam Parr, Sir H., *A Sketch of the Kafir and Zulu Wars*, London, 1880.

——, *Recollections and Correspondence*, London, 1917.

Hamilton-Browne, G., *A Lost Legionary in South Africa*, London, 1879.

Holme, N., *The Silver Wreath: Being the 24th Regiment at Isandlwana and Rorke's Drift, 1879*, London, 1979.

——, *The Noble 24th*, London, 1999.

Johnson, B.C., *Rorke's Drift and the British Museum: The Life of Henry Hook V.C.*, London, 1986.

Knight, I. (ed.), *There Will Be An Awful Row At Home About This*, Shoreham by Sea, 1987.

——, *By the Orders of the Great White Queen*, London, 1992.

——, *Zulu: The Battles of Isandlwana and Rorke's Drift*, London, 1992.

——, *Nothing Remains But to Fight*, London, 1993.

——, *The Anatomy of the Zulu Army*, London, 1995.

——, *Rorke's Drift 1879*, London, 1996.

Laband, J., *Fight Us in the Open*, Pietermaritzburg, 1991.

——, *Kingdom in Crisis*, Pietermaritzburg, 1992.

Laband, J., and Matthews, J., *Isandlwana*, Pietermaritzburg, 1991.

Lane, R. *The Quiet Sergeant, Henry Edward Gallagher: A Rorke's Drift Man*, London, 2003.

Lock, R., and Quantrill, P. (compliers), *The Red Book: Natal Press Reports, Anglo Zulu War 1879*, Pinetown, 2000.

—— (compilers), *The 1879 Zulu War through the Eyes of the* Illustrated London News, Durban, 2003.

Lloyd, W.G., *John Williams, V.C.*, Cwmbran, 1993.

Lugg, H.C., *A Natal Family Looks Back*, Durban, 1970.

Lummis, W.C., *Padre George Smith of Rorke's Drift*, Norwich, 1978.

Mitford, B., *Through the Zulu Country: Its Battlefields and Its People*, London, 1883.

Norris-Newman, C.L., *In Zululand with the British throughout the War of 1879*, London, 1880 (reprinted 1988).

Parry, D.H., *The V.C.: Its Heroes and Their Valour*, London, 1913.

Paton, G., Glennie, F., and Symons, W.P., *Historical Records of the 24th Regiment*, London, 1892.

Preston, A. (ed.), *The South African Journal of Sir Garnet Wolseley, 1879–80*, London, 1973.

Rattray, D., *Soldier Artist in Zululand, William Whitelock Lloyd and the Anglo-Zulu War of 1879*, Rorke's Drift, 2007.

Stevenson, L., *The Rorke's Drift Doctor, James Henry Reynolds, V.C., and the Defence of Rorke's Drift*, Brighton, 2001.

Thornton, N., *Rorke's Drift: A New Perspective*, London, 2016.

Vijn, C., *Cetshwayo's Dutchman, Being the Private Journal of a White Trader in Zululand during the British Invasion*, London, 1880.

War Office, Rothwell, J.S. (compiler), *Narrative of Field Operations Corrected with the Zulu War of 1879*, London, 1881 (reprinted 1907 and 1989).

Wheatley, K., *Legacy: Heroes of Rorke's Drift*, Eccles, 2005–10.

Whitton, F.E., *Rorke's Drift*, unknown, 1979 (reprinted from *Blackwood's Magazine*).

Index

Entries in **bold** signify the main entry/account for an individual.